Centering Woman

Centering

Woman

Gender Discourses in Caribbean Slave Society

Hilary McD Beckles

Ian Randle Publishers, *Kingston*

Markus Wiener Publishers, *Princeton*

James Currey Publishers, *Oxford*

First published in Jamaica 1999 by
Ian Randle Publishers
206 Old Hope Road
Kingston 6

ISBN 976-8123-79-6 cloth
ISBN 976-8123-78-8 paper

A catalogue record for this book is available from
the National Library of Jamaica.

Published in the United States of America by
Markus Wiener Publishers Inc.
231 Nassau Street, Princeton, NJ 08540

Library of Congress Cataloging-in-Publication Data

Beckles, Hilary, 1955-
Centering woman : gender discourses in Caribbean slave society /
Hilary McD. Beckles.
p. cm.
Includes bibliographical references.
ISBN 1-55876-204-3 (hc : alk. Paper). —ISBN 1-55876-205-1 (pb : alk. Paper)
1. Women slaves—Caribbean Area—Social conditions. 2. Women—Caribbean Area—History—17th century. 3. Women—Caribbean Area—History—18th century. 4. Women—Caribbean Area—History—19th century.
5. Slavery—Caribbean Area—History.
I. Title. II Title: Gender discourses in Caribbean slave society.
HT1071.B44 1998
305.42'09729—dc21 98-43652
CIP

Published in the United Kingdom by
James Currey Ltd
73 Botley Road
Oxford OX2 OBS

British Library Cataloguing in Publication Data
Beckles, Hilary McD.
Centering woman : gender discourses in Caribbean slave society
1. Women – Caribbean Area – Social conditions 2. Women – Caribbean Area – History 3. Women slaves – Caribbean Area – History 4. Slavery – Caribbean Area – History 5. Caribbean Area – History – To 1810 6. Caribbean Area – History – 1810-1945
I. Title
305.4.2'09729'0903

ISBN 0-85255-772-8

for

Nanny of the Maroons, Nanny Grigg, Sarah Ann Gill,
Amy Garvey, Harriet Tubman, Rosa Park, Winnie Mandela,
Angela Davis, Lucille Mair, Dame Nita Barrow,
Lorna Goodison, Elsa Goveia, Ella Fitzgerald,
Edna Manley, Jacqueline Creft, Cormeta Frase . . .
and those to come

Table of Contents

List of Tables

Preface

A decade ago, it seemed to me that the critical work being done on the Caribbean in history and the social sciences by radical feminists had effectively weakened the conceptual and methodological integrity of the structures that constitute the masculinist canon of nationalist historiography. The objectives of their criticisms were theoretically and politically compelling. For sure, they had captured the imagination of a significant section of the younger generation of researchers who were encouraged to agree that nationalist discourse of an earlier time, though it had shattered the legitimacy of imperialist scholarship, was insufficient with respect to the search for an historiography of everyday life.

Feminist historians, however, were not directly engaged in an elaborate project to rewrite texts, but made important advances with respect to the historiography of slavery. They effectively indicated new paths to the future and articulated modes and patterns of thinking that served as strategic devices in producing alternative histories of women and gender relations. Recognising the considerable productive potential and conceptual sophistication of feminist criticism, and committed, for several private and public reasons, to the discursive enrichment of Caribbean historiography, I sought ways, tentatively and sometimes recklessly, to promote the rewriting of those history narratives that seemed to me oppressively backward within the context of my heightened political consciousness.

Since the moment of that departure I have written several papers on women and gender history with respect to the slavery period, most of which were presented at conferences and some published in edited collections on the subject. The chapters that constitute this book have origins within these circumstances, and were written, therefore, in a piecemeal fashion. All of them addressed serious historical issues that held my gaze over the decade. They all speak to a deep concern to penetrate and comprehend the complex networks of relations and culture that constitute gender domination. I have sought to analyse aspects of the gender order as it determined and defined the everyday worlds of women in slave society, and to explore the effectiveness of feminine agency with respect to the search for ontological autonomy, social justice, ethical community relations, material betterment, economic power, and social security.

Furthermore, I have tried to imagine how women, in discernible ethnic guises and ideological representations, negotiated terms of living as personalised projects. This meant in effect an engagement with the nature of linkages between all categories of women, and an exploration of how and why they considered and contested the very concepts of 'woman' and 'feminine'. Some white women denied, or denigrated, the 'womanness' of black and coloured women, and spoke of their 'manliness' as a negation of their 'femininity'. Each chapter deals distinctly but not discretely, with different aspects of these 'denials' and tortured relations between women whose 'official' identities were socially constructed, refashioned, and politicised by legislated patriarchal power. They also set out the infrastructures and trajectories of women's subscriptive and subversive missions in relation to the established gender order.

Understanding how gender is socially determined, understood, and lived, serves to illuminate why and how some women subscribed to institutional cultures designed by patriarchy, and why and how others launch discreet missions of self empowerment and overt, collective liberation. Throughout the text I have used the method of narrative biography to argue that these positions were not fixed, neither were they ideological polarities, but fluid interactions that yielded varied results overtime but no distinct pattern. Together, however, these narratives of women's choices and postures focus attention on the central theme of their location at the centre of the male-managed colonial world that sought simultaneously to institutionalise their "otherness" through objectified forms of discourse.

Women's missions against 'otherisation' took several forms, from 'death-wish' subversion to over-subscription. I have used the immediacy of their language, script, and 'social' choices in detailing the political natures of their sites at the centre. Debates that utilise the disciplines of economics, sociology, political science, anthropology, and literary criticism, highlight the centrality of women and gender in the construction and evolution of slave relations and society. I have acknowledged the organisations of knowledges about slavery that emerge from these disciplinary methods.

This is a book, then, that could not have been conceived and written with a prior coherence. While its parts fell into place — image by image — over the decade, I realised simultaneously the enormous debt of gratitude I owe to many people who could not have known what their reactions to my submissions would prompt. I wish to acknowledge the generosity of Lucille Mair, Verene Shepherd, Evelyn O'Callaghan, Pat Mohammed, Rhoda Reddock, Eudine Barriteau, Vaneisa Baksh, Christine Barrow, Barbara Bush, Alan Cobley, Rex Nettleford, Robin Blackburn, Barry Gaspar, Barry Higman, James Walvin, John Mayo, and Howard Johnson. Frank Cass Publishers, Manchester University Press, The Press: University of the West Indies, Ian Randle Publishers, and History Workshop, have kindly agreed to my use of material that formerly appeared in essays published by them. I thank my wife, Mary and family, who supported my request for space to carry out this exercise; also my secretaries, Grace Franklin, Camileta Neblett, and Michelle Grandison, who prepared the manuscript.

Special thanks go to the cooperative, efficient staffs at these institutions: in Great Britain, Birmingham Public Library, Lincolnshire Records Office, Bodleian Library of Oxford University, Bristol Records Office, British Library, Brynmor Jones Library at the University of Hull, Guildhall Library, Historical Manuscript Commission, Public Records Office, Lambeth Palace Library, Royal Commonwealth Society, Senate House Library at London University, and the Commonwealth Institute; in the West Indies, the Barbados Department of Archives, Campus Libraries of Cave Hill and Mona at the University of the West Indies, Institute of Jamaica, Jamaica Archives at Spanish Town; in the U.S.A., New York Public Library, Library of Congress; in Canada, York University Library, University of Toronto Library; in Africa, CORDESRIA, University of Dakar, Senegal, Library at University of Dar-es-Salaam, and the Library at the University of Cairo.

While remaining unsatisfied with this project by a strong sensation that more could be said than is done, I would not wish any of these fine people and institutions to share responsibility for the shortfalls perceived or recognised.

Cave Hill Campus
UWI, Barbados

Introduction

Historicising 'Woman' and Slavery

The historiographical departure from 'History' to 'Women's History' in the Caribbean segment of the North Atlantic slave mode of production cannot be described as a mass movement. Throughout the methodologically turbulent 1960s and 1970s excess conceptual inertia shaped and limited the culture of criticism and therefore theoretical enquiry. This was so in spite of a pervasive ideological practice by some nationalist scholars to discredit academically, elements of what was considered the politicised texts of a fractured and retreating colonial tenure.[1]

The radical character of the anti-colonial discourse in the Caribbean, strengthened and supported by ideological imperatives of black redemption and worker empowerment, had the effect of the essential maleness of the targeted colonial historiography. Some feminist historians were swept along by the compelling tide of the new, hegemonic male representation of the nationalist project. While their participation in the discourse was guided by consideration of intellectual decolonisation and nation-building, they applied brakes to the advancing theoretical critique of patriarchy in order to facilitate the suppression of political dissonance. The result of this political posture has been a paucity of texts within the emergent literature that examine specifically women's history, and therefore the existence of an undeveloped theoretical terrain that has inhibited movement towards a rigorous feminist critique.[2]

The pioneering work on women's history by Lucille Mair has had the effect of confirming the basic correctness of this development. For Mair, post-Columbian plantation slavery was the scene of the punishment – the crime having taken place at an earlier time. She called for an examination of women's experiences within the 'living country' of slavery in order to set out the circumstances and moments under which gender identities and ideologies were constructed and represented as relations of power. Furthermore, she insisted that the discursive practice enters, in a pathological sort of way, the social lives of different 'types' of women in order to assess the space that separated them as well as the experiences that held them together.[3]

Subsequent work by Kamau Brathwaite, Verena Martinez-Alier, Arlette Gautier, and more recently by Barbara Bush, Marietta Morriessey, Barry Higman, Hilary Beckles, and Bernard Moitt has significantly advanced the study of women's history in many directions across imperial divisions of the slave mode of production.[4] These contributions were made in a manner that avoided conceptual conflict and hostility; theoretical criticisms have not featured in what seemed to be rather low-pitched academic engagements. It is entirely possible that this state of affairs is indicative of Caribbean historians' cautious appreciation of the directions of post-structuralist theorists especially as Michel Foucault and Jacques Derrida have been read as negating the primacy of human agency in anti-establishment struggles. Certainly, there is no developed discussion of gender as conceptual representation within the texts and subtexts of Gautier, Bush and Higman, neither is there a discourse on the manner in which gender relations, in the context of slavery, operated through the instrument of language. Also, the post-structuralist assertion that the term 'woman' is but a social construct that has no basis in nature has struck no central nerve, an insensitivity which says a great deal about the theoretical state of this recent historiography.

If the movement from 'History' to 'Women's History' was at best a minor historiographical current, though potentially transformative in its intellectual implication, then it is also correct to suggest that the advance from 'Women's History' to 'Gender History' and feminist criticism is still at the stage of gathering the troops, or perhaps in a state of uncertainty with respect to the academic and discursive politics of the project. Historians of slavery have tended to use the term 'gender' in reference to the complex social organisation through which the relations between males and females are understood and expressed. That is, it indicates the power of language in the interpretative framework that offers distinct social meanings which are understood to have a basis in bio-sexual differences. These social meanings are considered as cultural products. They are socially constructed, internalised through communicative systems, and depend for their legitimacy upon hegemonic power. Gender, therefore, as an analytical tool, requires academic specification, and ought not to be used interchangeably with 'sex' which is arguably rooted in nature rather than politics and culture.

Evidence of the tension within the historiography of slavery, then, can be found at two junctures; one, where feminist scholars who adopt methodologies from post-modernist theorists meet with historians of women; two, between empiricist and marxist scholars who continue to debate the validity of sex and gender as useful categories. 'Gender history', meanwhile, is received by sceptics as the privileged domain of literary critics, cultural anthro- pologists, and theoretical sociologists – all of whom they claim share a com- mon measure of conceptual suspicions, if not contempt, for what is termed the 'objective canons of historiography'. For this group of reluctants, however, it would be useful to suggest a visit to Linda Gordon's perceptive assertion that there 'may be no objective canons of historiography, but these are degrees of accuracy' since it is 'wrong to conclude that because there may be no objective truths . . . there are no objective lies'.[5]

Implicit in the research of Mair, Gautier, Morrissey, and Brathwaite, however, are the signposts for the crossing from 'women's history' to 'gender history'; in Beckles' work there is the suggestion that the time is ripe for a 'kind' of crossing. In outlining a framework for detailed historical investigation of the slavery period Mair projected categories for analysis that are typically those used in women's history; these are 'experience', 'identity','relations' to the means of production, and exchange and consumption. Here she states in very moving language, that 'in Caribbean slave societies the black woman produced, the brown woman served, and the white woman consumed' – a typology which calls for an investigation of real life experiences across the social boundaries of race, class and colour.[6]

In addition, Mair signals the need for a more rigorous and conceptually informed gender analysis when she asserts that the textual representations of these three categories of 'woman' tell us very little about them as living beings, but much more about the purposes that such representations were invented and designed to serve. In discussing the socio-sexual manipulation and exploitation of all women by superordinately empowered slave-owning white men, she highlights the common terrain where womanhood and maternity were targeted and preyed upon by patriarchal authority and interest. There is, however, no specific discussion of the range of representations that are present or absent within the texts; neither is there a discourse on how subjects are constructed, and of gender as that which gives social meaning to sexual differences. 'Woman', then, as social concept, whether described culturally as white, brown, or black, is not seen through a post-structural lens; hence we are not told how gender operated under specific social and economic conditions. This is also true for the work of Brathwaite, Beckles, Bush and Gautier, which is tilted in the direction of the social, political, and labour experiences of women, both enslaved and free.

The tendency, then, has been for historians of Caribbean slavery to subject women's experiences to investigations with respect to caste, class, race, colour and material relations, rather than to explore how such representations and discourses are internally organised by patriarchal mobilisations of gender ideologies. The result of this historiographical practice makes for a fascinating social history that identifies, even if in a limited way, the material and social conditions of women's oppression. In addition, by virtue of locating the terms and conditions of oppression in the area of socio-material denial and marginalisation, this literature suggests the ways in which women can and did seek ways of empowerment in order to resist and escape from that which oppressed them.

To date, the primary focus of research – and this is reflected in the structure of the historiography – is the black woman with the brown (coloured!) woman running a competitive second, and the white woman trailing behind at a distance. The texts on black women's enslavement by Gautier, Beckles, Bush, and Morrissey addressed directly, but with significant variation in empirical detail and conceptual concerns, aspects of brown women's experiences and identity, but do not explore systematically the lives of white creole and European women.[7] A number of essays by both Beckles and Bush have outlined the paradoxical but privileged nature of white women's experiences with suggestions for discussions about the shaping of their social identities.[8]

By way of contrast, and this is very critical to a close conceptual reading of the historiography, a major subject of imperial and national(ist) historians has been the study of white male slaveowners. In these texts the slave-based colonial economy is seen as an expression of an elite merchant-planter accumulationalist vision within the rise of hegemonic Atlantic capitalism – non-propertied white males being pressed into their service as labourers, bureaucrats, and military defenders of the enterprise. This historiography focuses primarily on the entrepreneurship and politics of ruling class white males who are represented as having succeeded in fashioning with slave systems a modern, economic order from the chaos and backwardness of a precapitalist, indigenous primitivism.

Caribbean colonisation and slavery for the European, says Brathwaite, was essentially 'a male enterprise'. 'It was not a joint enterprise', nor a 'family enterprise' he insists, but a 'family-stunted and male-oriented enterprise with the wife replaced by housekeeper or mistress.'[9] The white woman, therefore, whether as wife, mother and sister to male slave-owners, or a slaveowner in her own right, is represented by Brathwaite as supportive rather than innovative and autonomous in the material and ideological reproduction of the colonial project.

These historiographic positions can be accounted for in three principal ways. First, they are endemic to an earlier proslavery imperial scholarship that conceptually subsumed the white woman to patriarchal hegemony in the projection and assessment of colonial culture. Second, historians and social anthropologists, inspired by considerations of systemic decolonisation and nation-building, targeted the black woman's history in search of general explanations for social and cultural processes identified as endemic to the legacies of slavery. In this literature, the black woman is represented as 'culture carriers' and 'morality bearers' of a disenfranchised people seeking cohesion and upliftment. These alleged problems include matters such as the perceived instability and problematic matrifocality of the black family, and its perceived inability to rise to the challenges of postcolonial community development. Third, emerging from these two representations is the notion that the ideological formation of the modern Caribbean is in some way best explained in terms of a central paradigm that juxtaposes the white male and the black female as binary signifiers. This paradigm, however, says little about the social logic and systems of representation within the slave mode of production which, it must be emphasised, was constructed as a show piece expression of Renaissance rationality within the colonial sphere.

Emerging from these historiographic patterns and trends are significant conceptual issues that require further discussion. These are: the dangers involved in not clearly perceiving the roles and functions of the white woman as a pro-slavery agent within the reproduction of slave systems – its patriarchal superstructure especially; over-emphasis upon the experiences of enslaved black women as labourers and insufficient conceptual attention upon their biological and legal function as the conduits of slavery; and the retreat from a systematic use of gender ideology in which 'woman', as a category in history, is seen as constructed and reproduced by patriarchal systems of representation.

The tendency has been to see the white woman and the enslaved black woman as constituting a bi-polarity within a fragmented notion of womanhood that assured the reproduction of the slave system. Considerations of race, however, privileged the white woman. Conceivably, labouring white women saw the slave system as an assured avenue to betterment while their elite 'sistren' understood their privileged distance from labour in much the same way. Yet, united by race and sex ', they were divided by a dichotomous gender ideology in which class was the determinant; the latter were represented as the embodiment of purity and liberty, and the former as social evidence of decay and degeneration at the colonial frontier.

At the centre of recent women's history literature, then, is the notion of the élite woman's removal from the process of sugar plantation production and her reintegration principally at the level of social reproduction – as mothers and wives within the household. From this location, she is understood to have functioned as a critical ideological subscriber to the slavery system in so far as she exerted a pro-slavery influence on infant socialisation, imposed on household divisions of labour a conservative value system, and altogether reassured the planter-merchant socio-economic model of its development integrity and leadership.

According to Brathwaite, the 'activities of these women appeared to be mainly entertainment on behalf of the establishment. They were very conscious of the establishment and their place within it. Basically, she was concerned with supporting the establishment and looking after her husband's welfare'. Quoting Mair, Brathwaite continues: 'One could not expect otherwise of the white female. She was the second sex, taking the cue from her man. The whole thrust[10] of her upbringing had been to make her 'pretty polly, pretty parrot', to add sweetness and charm to public life if she could, but not to interfere or to agitate.[11] More recent work by Beckles, Trevor Burnard, and Mary Butler, however, shows the autonomous market activities of propertied white women as significant, and indicated that the 'pretty polly, pretty parrot' representation constitutes a marked departure from known social circumstances.[12]

Logically, the 'woman', both black and white, had to be socially constructed, engineered and re-engineered to facilitate the agro-commercial enterprise and its supportive social environment. It is here that in spite of some useful starts, more intense work needs to be done by historians of Caribbean slavery. What does it mean, for example, that representations of 'woman', reproduced during the slavery period, say more about the origins and character of representation than about the actual lives, experiences, and identity of women? This is a question asked more often by historians of gender than by historians of women. But it is one that warrants no analytical or methodological contention and should inform all social history enquiries.

From the point of view of the hegemonic expansion of the slave mode of production the seventeenth century is the common place for an analytical beginning. It is a time and place generally associated with the proliferation of the sugar plantation and its revolutionary absorption of enslaved Africans. It was also a moment when propertyless white women constituted a significant element within the ganged labour force of the sugar estates. Considerable evidence suggest the slave-like social existence of these plantation labourers, and indicate that their general treatment, measured in terms of material care and loss of civil liberties, was consistent with that experienced by enslaved Africans.[13] They were considered initially satisfactory workers at the frontier, and the nature of demand for their labour both for field work and domestic duties, indicates their flexibility and versatility.

Manual labour, slave trading, and domesticity were not considered locked in contradictory orbit during the formative stages of gender representation. In fact, these practices were held together in determining the elements that constituted the images of the colonial white woman. There were many images and representations which in turn reflected the recognition of complexity and diversity in colonial social life. These are to be found in the early narratives histories, travel accounts and biographies. In them, labouring white women are described variously as 'loose wenches', 'whores', 'sluts, and 'white slaves', and designated as suited mainly to field labour.

By the early eighteenth century, however, the evidence indicates a significant shift in the ideological and social representation of the white woman. By this time the migration of white women to the islands had greatly contracted, and with the rapid expansion of the plantation culture throughout the Antilles, the question of sexual imbalance within the white community assumed new dimension. The 'shortage' of white women was said to threaten the colonial mission since it rendered the white community unable to reproduce itself naturally. Meanwhile, plantation inventories were indicating clearly that black women had become the majority in the labour gangs of Antigua, St Kitts, Martinique, St Dominique, Barbados and other sugar producing colonies. Also, references to their greater relative productivity were seeping into accounting calculations which had the effect of consolidating the idea among planters that slave women were a more profitable investment.

The white woman, then, marginalised within the culture of private capital, disenfranchised by colonial constitutions, and socially oppressed, now found herself cocooned within another system of representation that denied her social identity and right to autonomous self-expression. Eighteenth century texts in which these representations were formulated – the canon of the imperialist historiographic tradition – also indicate their mythical nature and illustrate clearly the ideological need within patriarchy for the reconstruction. The authors of these narratives – ideological engineers in their own right – were as much privately concerned with representations of this kind as they were with historical accuracy and authenticity, hence the entry of considerable fiction into the storehouse of historical writing.

The discrepancy between the social reality of everyday life and behavioural expectations embedded within these representations was often times explored (and exploded!) in quite remarkable ways. A demonstrative case can be extracted from the records of eighteenth century Jamaica. It concerns the life of Elizabeth Moore-Manning, wife of Edward Manning, Member of the House of Assembly. In 1739, Elizabeth was brought by her husband before the Legislature in an attempt to settle a divorce case. Mr Manning's case against his wife had to do with evidence surrounding (and high society's reactions) allegations that she was sexually involved with a number of black men on the estate. The 'burden of the evidence' supplied by slaves, white servants, and others, says Brathwaite, suggests that she was 'something of a nymphomaniac'.[14] This evidence indicated that the 'sheepboy', the 'watchman', the 'cookboy' and others had 'laid with Mrs M'.

Mrs Manning, of course, claimed that much of this was untrue and that she lived a 'normal' life in the absence and presence of her husband who demonstrated no sexual interests in her whatsoever. The case, which soon became an attractive 'soap opera' for Jamaican slave society, dragged on for months, with slaves – male and female – white housekeepers, managers, friends and family all having their say on Mrs Manning's sexual taste, interests and style. White males, however, made of the same social material as the distraught Mr Manning, had long considered unrestricted sexual access to the slave women as a 'right' of mastery, and the refusal to exercise it on their part was considered strange if not irresponsible.

At the same time, the social reconstruction of the black woman also began to take shape after nearly one hundred years of ideological vagueness and unspecification. As the labour gangs became increasingly female in composition, and the fertility of black women was propelled into the market economy as the key to an internal reproduction of labour, frequent references appeared in texts to the black woman as superordinate Amazons who could be called upon to labour all day, perform sex all night, and be quite satisfied morally and culturally to exist outside the formal structures of marriage and family. She was now projected by the white proslavery literary imagination as lacking a developed sense of emotional attachment to progeny and spouse, and indifferent to the values of virtue and high moral sensitivity.

The relations between the black woman's labour power and her reproductive capability were represented as exclusively confined to the culture of market forces. As property her worth was associated with productivity measurements that were calculated in terms of material output and childbearing – a child being accounted for at birth in the plantation inventories as an additional capital unit. Black womanhood and motherhood, then, existed at the same nexus of the market economy as factors in the production and reproductions process.

The predominate image associated with the representation of the black woman was that of great strength – the symbol of blackness, masculinity and absence of finer feelings. Her sexuality was projected as overtly physical (no broken hearts here!) – hence brutish and best suited to the frontier world of the far-flung plantation. Out there, social immorality, perversity and promiscuity were maintained by her on account of her possession of satanic powers that lured white men away from association with their virtuous white females – hence the existence of the mulatto community within the slave society.

Here, then, was the alleged moral crisis of slavery. A perfectly 'horrid system', says Mrs Fenwick, the English school teacher and 'reluctant' slave-owner in early nineteenth century Barbados.[15] Horrid because in no way was it conducive to the proper cultivation of white manhood and the refinement of a gentleman. The presence of black women in white households, she confessed, was the principal corrupting factor. White men simply could not resist them, bought and brought them into their beds, and produced children with them. Edward Long's eighteenth century explanation of this development in Jamaican slave society also identified the black woman as the threat to civilisation's advance:

> In a place where, by custom, so little restraint is laid on the passions, the Europeans, who at home have always been used to greater purity and strictness of manners, are too easily led aside to give loose to every kind of sensual delight: on this account some black or yellow quasheba is fought for, by whom a tawney breed is produced.[16]

Only 'a proper education' for the generality of white women, he argued, would make them more 'agreeable companions', and hence more competitive for the company of white men. The cultured upliftment of the white woman, he believed, was necessary to encourage them to reject the 'goatish embrace' of black women, and crave for 'pure and lawful bliss' with white women.[17] Coloured children, says Mrs Fenwick, born of open and shameless licentiousness, were kept in the household, raised by their white stepmother as 'pets' and on reaching adulthood dismissed to the field gangs, to labour with their mothers of whom they knew little or cared nothing.[18]

Black females, then, in eighteenth century gender representations, were not 'women' since they knew not how to nourish and care for their young, showed no loyalty and subservience to a male spouse, and could not construct a binding and building culture of domesticity. They were the 'other females' in the society whose potential claim to the status of 'woman' existed only with respect to their capacity for miscegenation with white males through which route the 'coloured' woman – liberated from the oppression of blackness – was created and idealised.

Once again, in the same texts within which these ideological configurations and structures were made, are to be found evidence of events and circumstances of a contrary nature. The textual juxtaposition produces no interpretative tension since a critical reading indicates that no close correspondence was ever expected between the two levels of communication. Representations were designed with ideological missions in mind, and they served very well such objectives, regardless of textual references to seemingly opposing evidence. This allows for an interpretation of the text as fictive, temporal discourses, rather than authoritative, objective social history.

The history of representations of women can be seen as the recreation of gendered political subjects, which allows us to redefine narrative history as the politics of a process by which power and knowledge are perpetually constituted. Indeed, the question of how power and knowledge are conceptualised resides at the core of much of the contention between those who are divided on the relative usefulness of 'women's history' and 'gender history' as analytical instruments. While historians of women demand that the real lives of women during the slavery period be carefully and systematically detailed before issues of meaning and identity are settled, historians of gender prefer to cast attention to assessing how 'woman' was redefined and reengineered under changing political and material circumstances. Historians of women are critical of the gender approach precisely because it over- emphasises the role of power which some poststructuralists attribute to language. Here, poststructualism is considered a new conceptual imperialism that negates the real world in which black women struggled against oppression and where injustice was endemic.

The politics of slavery, and women's forging of an anti-slavery ideology from experience, consciousness and identity, throw up the concept of the 'rebel woman', as used by Mair, and the 'natural rebel' as conceived by Beckles. Two separate and distinct epistemological traditions inform these seemingly similar concepts of the slave woman in politics. The rebel woman is essentially a cultural icon whose central location within the slave community – the politicised space – is derived from the ascribed matrifocality of the African social legacy. She is 'Nanny', 'Queen Mother' and 'priestess'. She is therefore culturally invested with political leadership, and the community rallies around her magical and spiritual powers. Men follow because of her claim to a vision that results from the possession of such powers. Freedom is the water that quenches the thirst, and anti-slavery is the jar from which the water is taken.

The 'natural rebel', however, is your typical 'woman in the fields, who possesses no claim to distinct individuality and is therefore one of the masses. Her identity, and the level of consciousness that informs her politics, have been conceptualised and defined by Brathwaite in his 'discovery' of the 'inner plantation'. The everyday experience of her enslavement represents the basis of a culture of refusal and resistance through which she claims a 'self' and an 'identity'. The search for the 'natural rebel', then, begins with Brathwaite's claim that the slavery system impacted upon the black women in deeper and more profound ways than was the case with black men. The slave mode of production by virtue of placing the black woman's 'inner world' – her fertility, sexuality and maternity – on the market as capital assets, produced in them a 'natural' propensity to resist and to refuse as part of a basic self protective and survival response.

From this world of ideas, attitudes, and actions flowed a constant stream of subversive missions that infused the slave community with an endemic anti-slavery ethos. Furthermore, since it was she in whom the seeds of slavery were planted and expected to germinate, she was also likely to be the conduit through whom anti-slavery flowed naturally. The affirmation in the dialectic of pro-slavery and anti-slavery forces indicates the complex nature of the black woman's experiences and consciousness. It is here, it seems, that historians of Caribbean slavery have made some headway by refusing to dichotomise the methodologies of women's history and gender history, and by insisting that the two occupy different levels of the same habitat.

The implication of this stance is clear; the analysis of 'real experience' and the theorising of 'constructed representation' constitute part of the same intellectual project in the search for meaning and truth. 'History' and 'Politics', then, may constitute coded terms for 'experience' and 'representation', respectively, but only an integrative discursive practice can adequately tackle epistemological questions arising from the notion of meaning. Furthermore, the problem for the enslaved black woman in getting the slave master off her back in the day time and off her belly in the night time was very real, and not resolvable by psychoanalysis. Rather, it had origins in the way she was historically constructed and rendered vulnerable by liberated masculinity.

Concepts of gender and race were central to how persons interfaced by the relations of slavery, established meaning that determined social order and shaped everyday life. The ideological practice of gender determination contributed significantly to managerial values that focused attention away from class conflict to gender and race differences and inequalities. Gender and race ideologies were principally at work in determining the sexual and racial division of labour and were responsible for the crystallisation of consciousness within the slave mode of production.

There is an acceptance, therefore, of Joan Scott's assertion that historians of social life should examine carefully how, at given stages in the development of a social formation, people construct meaning and how difference operates in the construction of meaning.[19] Here, we tracked down the trajectory of gender construction of white and black women during slavery and examined how the language generated by pro-slavery agents gave potency to gender ideologies. The slave mode of production was conceived and held together by an ideological defense in which a gendered and racist order was considered paramount. Gender ideology soon found an enduring home in social and moral codes, was enforced by judicial structures, and supported by the social conventions forged.

The tendency to privilege race above gender as an analytical category has no basis, therefore, in the logic and culture of the slave mode of production. Certainly, the slaveowner whose legal and ideological superstructure empowered him for unrestricted socio-sexual access to the slave woman as an expected return on capital, and at the same time imposed sexual constraints and curfews upon white women, interpreted this authority as having its roots in sex, gender, and race differences. The slave woman's location at the centre of the power pyramid of the slave order was secured essentially by sex and gender representation. It was in this politically imposed position, where the requirement of production and reproduction merged, that the black woman's experience, identity, and consciousness gave structural form to what represents the central characteristic features of the slave mode of production.

Endnotes

1 See Blanca Silvestrini, *Women and Resistance: Herstory in Contemporary Caribbean History;* Dept. of History, UWI, Mona, 1989; Rhoda Reddock, 'Women and Slavery in the Caribbean: A Feminist Perspective', *Latin American Perspectives*, Issues 40, 12:1, 1985, pp. 63-80; Arlette Gautier, 'Les Esclaves femmes aux Antilles Francaises, 1635-1848'. *Reflexions Historiques*, 10: 3, Fall, 1983, pp. 409-35.

2 See Bridget Brereton, 'Text, Testimony and Gender: An Examination of some Texts by Women on the English-Speaking Caribbean, 1770s to 1920s', a paper presented at the Symposium – 'Engendering History: Current Directions in the Study of Women and Gender in Caribbean History', UWI, Mona, 1993; Marietta Morrissey, 'Women's Work, Family Formation and Reproduction among Caribbean Slaves', *Review* 9 (1986) pp. 339-67.

3 Lucille Mair, 'Women Field workers in Jamaica During Slavery', Department of History, UWI, Mona, 1989; 'An Historical Study of Women in Jamaica from 1655 to 1844 (Ph.D, UWI, Mona, Jamaica, 1974); *The Rebel Woman in the British West Indies during Slavery (Kingston, 1975);* 'The Arrival of Black Woman', *Jamaica Journal*, 9: nos 2-3, (1975).

4 Kamau Brathwaite, 'Caribbean Woman during the Period of Slavery', 1984 Elsa Goveia Memorial, Cave Hill Campus, Barbados; Verena Martinez-Alier, *Marriage, Class and Colour in Nineteenth Century Cuba; A Study of Racial Attitudes and Sexual Values in Slave Society* (Cambridge, U.K. 1974); Arlette Gautier, *Les Socurs de Solitude; La condition feminine dans l'esclavage aux Antilles du XVIIe as XIX e siecle* (Paris, Editions Caribbeennes, 1985); Hilary Beckles, *Natural Rebels: A Social History of Enslaved Black Women in Barbados* (Rutgers Univ. Press, New Brunswick, 1989); Barbara Bush, *Slave Women in Caribbean Society, 1650-1838* (Indiana Univ. Press, Bloomington, 1990); Marietta Morrissey, *Slave Women in the New World: Gender Stratification in the Caribbean* (Kansas Univ. Press, Lawrence, 1989); Barry Higman, 'Household Structures and Fertility on Jamaican Slave Plantations: A nineteenth Century Example', *Population Studies*, vol. 27, 1993; and 'The Slave Family and Household in the British West Indies, 1800-1834', *Journal of Interdisciplinary History*, vol 6, 1976; Bernard Moitt, 'Women, Work and resistance in the French Caribbean during Slavery, 1700-1848', paper presented at symposium 'Engendering History' *op. cit.*, (1993); and 'Behind the Sugar Fortunes; Women, Labour, and the development of Caribbean Plantations during Slavery', in S. Chilungu and S. Niang (eds) *African Continuities* (Toronto, Teribi Publications, 1989).

5 Linda Gordon, 'What's New in Women's History', in Teresa de lauretis (ed) *Feminist Studies/Critical Studies*, Indiana Univ. Press, Bloomington, 1986) p. 22; See also, Louise M. Newman, 'Critical Theory and the History of Women: What's at Stake in Deconstructing Women's History', *Journal of Women's History*, vol 2, no 3, 1991; Mary Poovey, "Feminism and Deconstruction', *Feminist Studies*, vol. 14, 1988.

6 Cited in Bush, *Slave Women*, p. xii.

7 See Gautier, *Les socurs, op. cit.*; Beckles, *Natural Rebels, op. cit.*; Bush, *Slave Women, op. cit.*

8 Hilary Beckles, 'White Women and Slavery in the Caribbean', *History Workshop Journal,* issue 36, 1993; Barbara Bush, White "Ladies", Coloured "Favourites" and Black "wenches": Some considerations on Sex, Race and Class Factors in Social Relations in white Creole Society in the British Caribbean', *Slavery and Abolition*, 2, 1991, pp. 245-62.
9 Brathwaite, 'Caribbean Woman', *op. cit.*
10 Moreau de Saint Mery (1797), *Description Topographique Physique, Civile, Politique et Historique de la Partie Francaise de l'isle Saint Dominique* (Paris, 1958 reprint) p. 10.
11 See Hilary Beckles, *White Servitude and Black Slavery in Barbados, 1627-1715* (Knoxville, Tennessee Univ. Press, 1989); and 'Black Men in White Skins; The Formation of a White Proletariat in West Indian Slave Society', *Journal of Imperial and Commonwealth History, 15:1, 1986.*
12 Brathwaite, 'Caribbean Women', *op. cit.*
13 A.F. Fenwick (ed) *The Fate of the Fenwicks: Letters to Mary Hays, 1798-1828* (Methuen, Lon. 1927) p. 164.
14 Cited in Veronica Gregg, 'The Caribbean (As a Certain Kind of) Woman', p.25; paper presented at symposium – *Engendering History, op. cit.*
15 *Ibid.*
16 Fenwick, *The Fate of the Fenwicks, p. 164.*
17 Joan Wallach Scott, *Gender and the Politics of History* (New York, Columbia, Univ. Press, 1988).

Part One

Subjections

1

Black Women and the Political Economy of Slavery

Mapping the origins and itinerary of gender in Caribbean history enables us to sharpen our focus specifically on slavery as a constantly changing system of socio-sexual exploitation and control of women, and generally to penetrate its internal dynamism as a mode of labour extraction. Gender, as a social construction that determined and reflected the sexual division of labour within the slave mode of production, constitutes a clear vista through which the cultural working of patriarchy as well as challenges to it at diverse levels of everyday life can be illuminated.[1]

In some ways 'modern' slave societies in the Caribbean facilitated a revolutionary restructuring and magnification of traditional gender representations while producing unique features of their own. For sure, the institutional design of Caribbean slavery, particularly its cultural specificities, significantly affected the (re)making of gender identities of males and females. Individuals evolved self-identities within the contexts of the gender order they encountered, and often contested. A wide range of strikingly unstable circumstances gave rise to gender as organised ideology. The constant reordering and redefinitions of conditions and terms of social living – and dying – determined that gender representations were oftentimes perceived as paradoxical and contradictory. This circumstance, in turn, indicates the considerable fluidity of ideological readings of slavery, and constitutes a barometer of the turbulence internal to the construction of the gender order.[2]

The methodological approach chosen here to explore the evolution and movements of gender identities and representations, and their ideological effects, is to utilise historical evidence in order to examine the macrocosms of slavery by penetrating the microcosms within. The proposal is that visits be made to three historical sites where gender discourses seemed advanced and determining of social relations and popular perceptions of identity. First, the gender order of pre-colonial West Africa is examined within the context of pressures exerted upon it by forces endemic to the wider Atlantic political economy. Second, the ideological constitution of gender identities within the Caribbean plantation complex is explored in so far as it affected and determined the nature of work and reproduction. Third, the instability of gender representations under increasingly adverse circumstances of sugar production and the global political challenge to the legitimacy of slavery in the early nineteenth century, are presented as causes of reforms to women's relations to production and reproduction and the creation of a new gender order.

An objective of this exercise is to examine how gender relations were historically constituted and experienced, and ought therefore to be thought about. By adopting an historical approach, critical conceptual distance can be achieved to assess and alter contemporary gender arrangements. The specific empirical focus on women's history is intended to illustrate how men have succeeded in maintaining the domination of women, despite their subversive missions and visions; also, to participate in the forging of a closer analytical relation between the study of women's history and gender history within subaltern historicism.

Most slaves in West Africa during the period 1500 to 1800 were female. This was also the case in the older sugar plantation colonies of the West Indies between 1800 and 1833.[3] Prior to 1800, however, West Indian slavery was overwhelmingly male biased. The mid-eighteenth century witnessed the transition in demographic structure. There was nothing paradoxical about it; the specific focus on the female in the conception, design and reproduction of these slave systems was the result of discernible social and managerial imperatives.[4]

Sex distribution patterns within the Atlantic slave complex had as much to do with the working of gender in traditional West African societies as with modern discourses of work, gender and social life in colonising Europe. After the 1750s, the established Caribbean custom of male preferencing in the purchase and retention of slaves gave way to a pro-female trend that fundamentally transformed the sex structure and modified gender discourses. Barbados had attained the unique status of having a female majority in the slave population since the end of the seventeenth century; it shared this characteristic with the Leeward Islands by the end of the eighteenth century. Sugar planters in these colonies gradually moved towards the privileging of females as part of a revised strategic plan to promote the natural reproduction of the labour force. The effects of this demographic shift on gender representations and identities were considerable. Important insights into the causes and nature of conflict and instability in slave societies therefore necessitate the creation of gender-derived forms of knowledge.

New World slavery represented something altogether unfamiliar to African males and females. It confronted, rejected and restructured the gender attitudes and identities legitimised by their traditions. The working of labour ideologies in most West African societies distinctly gendered certain types of work and relations of power; these were exploded and reconfigured within the Caribbean context. It is therefore problematical to propose fundamental continuity in forms of slavery and legitimisation for Africans between traditional experiences and the New World encounter. The gender implications of West Indian plantation slavery for Africans furthermore were culturally transformative. Initially, the Caribbean gender order as it related to types of work was peculiar to males in part but more familiar to women in general. It is important, then, that the nature of these confrontations be identified, and their implications for gender roles and identities understood and explained.[5]

Analyses of Atlantic slavery have tended to revolve around criteria that indicate the degree of intensity and type of involuntary servility that constitute slavery. The property relations criterion in particular has received greatest attention as one way to differentiate between modernist Caribbean chattel slavery and traditional forms of slavery in Africa. In addition, notions of kinlessness, marginalisation, exclusion, and subjection to others, have been privileged by cultural anthropologists who have drawn attention to the importance of comparative treatment of the subject over space and time in different and the same societies in Africa. In neither approach, however, has it been stated that these criteria have produced mutually exclusive categories. Rather, the tendency has been to identify what may reasonably be described as 'principal' and 'secondary' characteristics within the dominant mode of production.[6]

In West Africa during the period of Atlantic slavery the majority of persons described as slaves were female. The explanation for this circumstance has to do with the function performed by women within the gender order of these mostly patriarchal societies. There was a considerable internal slave market on which the demand was mostly for women and children. Women were also traded through the Sahara into the North African Muslim labour markets, while the non-African Atlantic market was supplied mostly with males. One compelling explanation for this pattern is that West African societies did not easily absorb male slaves. A general tendency was for males captured in intercine warfare to be executed by the state; another trend was to retain limited numbers of men for military rather than agricultural or industrial purposes. As a result of warfare, and other forms of political conflict, however, the majority of captives retained and integrated into local socio-economic systems were woman and children.[7]

The development of this pattern of sex specificity has to do with the greater local demand for females as slaves. This is reflected in the prices paid for female slaves in coastal and interior societies. Philip Curtin has shown, for example, that whereas in Senegambia, African traders supplied men and women to European buyers at the same price, in the interior agricultural belt women slaves sold for twice the price of male slaves. An often stated explanation for this trend is that women slaves were preferred because of their biological reproductive functions. This is only a minor part of the explanation. African men with property did demand wives and concubines who were kinless within their immediate social space, and whose progeny had little or no property rights or status claim within the inheritance system. Such kinless women and their children however, were secured directly by patriarchal élites primarily as workers, and were maginalised mainly because of their alienability as marketable labour.[8]

The ability of the patriarchal system to absorb, assimilate, and subjugate greater numbers of kinless women is the critical part of a more systemic explanation. The more expansive the economic system, the civil society, and the state apparatus, the greater was the demand for female slaves. The wide range of possible forms of absorption of kinless women magnified the numbers any society could carry. In most West African societies wealth was accumulated principally by means of the recruitment and retention of such labour. This was as true for the state as it was for individuals. As a result there was enormous pressure upon women in most societies to maintain the 'free' status. Even within the kinship system there was significant pressure to alienate women for social offences thereby creating situations that could easily lead to their enslavement. While it was possible for some slave women to gain their freedom through gradual assimilation into a kinship system, a greater tendency existed, on account of the demand for female slaves, for free women to be denied kinship rights and marginalised into the pool of transferable slaves.

The principal objective of this process was to generate servile female labour for productive functions. Slavery, concubinage, and patriarchal dominance, assured that the woman was centred as the principal productive agency within the gender order. Women worked, and the majority of their labour hours were dedicated to agriculture. This was the case in the period of Atlantic slavery as it is now. A recent survey shows that in the sub-Saharan region women still contribute between 60-70 per cent of the labour within the agricultural sector.[9] They planted and harvested crops, looked after animals, and generally engaged in all labour intensive work such as crafts and domestic service. Importantly, women were expected to perform agricultural labour which was prescribed and understood within the dominant gendered division of labour as 'woman work'.

Since material development in most West African societies was based upon agricultural activity it followed that production and productivity expansion necessitated the aggressive integration and engagement of women slaves.

Meillassoux has shown, for example, that in these economies 'women were valued above all as workers'. Robertson and Klein have argued that increasing production depended more on acquiring female labour, since 'women's work in Africa was generally the less desirable labour-intensive, low status work'. They conclude that in these contexts 'the value of women slaves was based on a sexual division of labour which assigned much of the productive labour to women'.[10] In these societies the progeny of female slaves were claimed by their owners. Female slave owners could also secure the right to the labour of slaves' children when the fathers were outside of their sphere of legal influence. The implication of this process was not always as clear, however, when the father of children born to slave women was himself a slave owner or man of influence within the society. The biological reproduction of slaves that centred around women, therefore, was as complicated a process as its ideological reproduction within the gender order.

Such female slaves were used in miscellaneous economic activities in addition to supplying their owners with socio-sexual benefits. Many were traders, maids, cultivators, craft workers, and concubines. In addition, they were expected by male and female élites to reduce the demand for the intensive labour services of free women, and contribute towards the biological reproduction of the unfree labour force. Hard labour, then, of the intensive low status kind, came to be considered by West Africans as 'woman work', beneath men's social standing within the gender order. With respect to agricultural labour, therefore, West African men considered themselves privileged, and female slaves were gendered the 'lowest creatures on God's earth'.[11]

Caribbean slavery launched a direct assault on traditional West African gender orders. To begin with, significantly fewer black women entered the Atlantic slave trade than black men. The available records of European slave traders demonstrate this point forcefully. Klein's comprehensive analysis of the records of Dutch slave traders, who in the seventeenth century also supplied French, Spanish and English colonies, shows that only 38 per cent of Africans shipped were female. The adult sex ratio for Dutch traders was 187 men for every 100 women, and the child ratio was 193 boys for every 100 girls. Using a broader based sample of British slave trade records, Klein found a similar pattern of discrimination against females (See Table 1:1).[12]

The general pattern, therefore, was clear. Between 65 per cent and 75 per cent of all slaves shipped from West Africa were males with only slight variations across the West African coast from Senegambia to Angola. This pattern indicates the tendency for West African economies and societies to retain traditional commitments to the dominant gender order in which men were considered more dispensable to internal processes of social and economic activity.

Table 1:1 **Average sex ratio of adults shipped in the English slave trade to the West Indies, 1791-98.**[13]

Region in West Africa	*Males per 100 females*	*No. of shipments*
Senegambia	210	5
Sierra Leone	210	29
Windward Coast	208	15
Gold Coast	184	26
Bight of Benin	187	2
Bight of Biafra	138	79
Congo-Angola	217	60
Unknown	188	56
Average	**183**	**272**

The Atlantic Slave Trade, however, carried to West Indian plantations not only measurable units of labour, but also gender identities and ways of thinking about gender. On early West Indian plantations enslaved African men, the social majority, were pressed into labouring activities which for them were gendered traditionally as 'woman work'. The social implications of this development was that the Caribbean became a site that witnessed an encounter and clash of two formally contradictory gender orders – one European and one West African. Managerial power was held decisively by the European male, and the potency of African gender ideologies was tested against the background of the productive needs of colonial capitalism. The European male held clear views with respect to gender and the sexual division of labour that differed from those of the African male; both sets of men, however, shared many common gender values and attitudes with respect to masculinity and the relation of 'woman' to patriarchal power.

Europeans pursued coherence in the articulation of gender representation, categories of women, and work. White women described as 'ladies' were not expected to labour in the field or perform any demeaning physical task. This was clearly a class position since the thousands of female indentured servants imported from Europe between 1624 and 1680 worked on the cotton, tobacco and sugar plantations in gangs alongside their male counterparts, as well as with enslaved Africans. It was not until the late seventeenth century that English planters, in particular, thinking of gender more in terms of race than class, implemented the policy that the white woman was not to work in sugar plantation labour gangs. This ideologically driven initiative to isolate white womanhood from plantation field work, however, had much to do with the social needs of patriarchy to idealise and promote the white woman as a symbol of white supremacy, moral authority, and sexual purity. White supremacy, white males believed, conceptually required the social isolation of all white women, irrespective of class, from intimacy with the black male in order to minimise the 'dread of miscegenation'.

The space vacated by their departure within the labour ranks had to be filled. White men also believed that black men were best equipped for the physical task of frontier plantation construction, but suggested that black women were better prepared for the subsequent maintenance of efficient production. Critically, they did not share the black male's view that field work was female work. Colonial managers, therefore, recognising the context of the gender orders, used the brutality of the death threat to enforce a work and ideological regime upon black males that ran counter to their gender identity and consciousness. Black men found the reversal of sex roles a major challenge to their masculine identity, and reacted with both outright violence and the negotiation of demand for entry into prestigious, non-agricultural occupations. By the mid eighteenth century, most artisans and production supervisors were male slaves; so too was the visible organisational military vanguard of plantation based, anti-slavery rebellions.

As the frontier receded, the centering of the black woman within the slave complex took shape in two stages. First, by the mid seventeenth century slave owners had legislated the principle of matrilineal reproduction of the slave status. This approach provided that only the offspring of a slave woman would be born into slavery. All children at birth took the same legal status as their mothers. Womanhood, as a gendered formulation, was therefore legally constituted as a reproduction device that offered the slave system continuity and functionality.

Slaveowners were also in legal and philosophical agreement that the socially constructed white race could not be reduced to chattel slavery. This meant that the gender identity of the white woman could not be linked to enslavement, and only the offspring of black and 'coloured' women could be born into slavery. African women, then, on arrival in the West Indies, were placed centrally in the labour supply mechanism, and used as the restrictive instrument to broad based social access to freedom. By seeking ideologically to distance the white woman from the black man as a principal objective of race discourse, and at the same time socially exposing the black woman to all men, free born children from the black race would always be a very small minority.

The second stage relates to the natural reproduction of slaves as an important supply strategy. The minority status of women within the slave trade, and the fact that many of them 'had already used up some of their potential fecundity by the time they had arrived', meant that slave populations in the Caribbean 'could only have experienced a negative growth rate'.[14] This fact was not emphasised, or understood by slave owners. Over time, however, they problematised the negative growth rates of blacks and produced on the subject an expansive literature. As they debated demographic trends and patterns, and concluded from colony to colony that natural reproduction was cheaper and more politically consistent with 'progressive' managerial policies, the slave woman was further targeted and bombarded in an ideological frenzy of new gender representations.

Plantation slavery, therefore, was not all about material production and human reproduction. Work and social relations on the estates were particularly relevant to the reproduction of significant social categories such as 'male' and 'female'. Work constituted the context within which the normative expectation attached to labour was gendered. That is, the work regime had as much to do with the production of sugar and other agricultural commodities as it did with the reproduction of the gender order. Field work came to be viewed by black males as slave work, rather than woman's work, which included all blacks and excluded white women. In addition, field work, and other forms of unskilled manual labour, were promoted as consistent with the 'essential nature' of blacks, an ideological construct that finally created an escape hatch for the landless white males. This shifting of class, race and gender relations within the division of labour is indicative of West Indian planters' distinct capacity for conceptualising the nature of their social world and formulating hegemonic ways to manage it.

African arrivants, therefore, were subjected to a process of physical acclimatisation as well as re-genderisation, generally referred to as 'seasoning'. During this initial phase of two to three years, they were inducted to a new gender order and protected from the physical rigours of plantation life. The objective of this policy was to allow slaves time to recover their physical strength, build up some immunity to the new diseased environment, and learn the political economy of the gender order. It was at once an ideological, biological and labour apprenticeship.

Slaveowners in the West Indies were familiar with the gender tradition of agriculture in West Africa. They understood at once that black women could be thrown into the deep end of the labour regime, and be productive. This explains in large measure their refusal to shelter these women from the most arduous physical task, as well as the suggestion that productivity differentials did not exist between the sexes. Mature women hoed the soil, dug drains, cut and bundled canes, planted new canes, carried baskets of manure to the fields and performed other physically demanding tasks. Younger women did what was considered light work, such as weeding, grass picking, tending cattle, and miscellaneous plantation tasks. Female children, looked after stocks, carried water to the fields, as well as other tasks.

The egalitarian labour regimes women experienced provided the context within which gender ideologies were conceived as constructions designed to promote the political economy of the colonial enterprise. The gender representation of black women was formalised in ways that offered coherence to the relations between sex, labour productivity, and capital accumulation. The colonial gender discourse confronted and assaulted traditional concepts of womanhood in both Europe and Africa, and sought to redefine notions of black feminine identity. The black woman was ideologically constructed as essentially 'non-feminine' in so far as primacy was placed upon her alleged muscular capabilities, physical strength, aggressive carriage, and sturdiness. Pro-slavery writers presented her as devoid of the feminine tendernesss and graciousness in which the white woman was tightly wrapped. Her capacity for strenuous work was not discussed in relation to the high mortality rates and incidence of crippling injuries that characterised enslavement. When mention was made of such circumstances, it was done to portray her as clumsy, brutish, and insensitive to the scientific nature of bodily functions. As such, she was represented as ideally suited to manual labour as part of a wider civilising social experience. Edward Long had no doubt that she was the perfect brute upon which the plantation's future rested. Her low fertility for him was an additional feature that indicated her essentially non-feminine identity.[15]

The defeminisation of the black woman, recast as the 'Amazon', allowed slave owners to justify within the slavery discourse her subjugation to a destructive social and material environment. It was said that she could 'drop' children at will, work without recuperation, manipulate at ease the physical environment of the sugar estate, and be more productive than men. These opinions, furthermore, constituted an ideological outlook that, when articulated by white males, seemed contradicted by the evidence of commonplace miscegenation. Long's text reveals evidence of the ideological subversion that resulted from white men's sexual attraction to black women. The 'goatish embraces' invariably produced a 'tawny breed', he said, who in turn tantalised like sirens all categories of gentlemen.[16] Long was aware that the socio-sexual reality of Jamaica could readily produce a gender reading of ethnic relations that exposes the contradictory nature of the race discourse. The discursive mechanism he adopted, as a protective cloak, was the invention of white feminine degeneracy that threatened, if left unattended, the future of the white male colonising project.

Long's pro-slavery text, furthermore, could be read as part of the discussion about black feminine subversion of hegemonic representations. The sexual embrace of the black woman as metaphor speaks to the black community's claim to an irrepressible humanity that gave life to and nurtured a morally imploded conquistadorial elite. Miscegenation, of course, was a double-edged sword within the context – evidence of human sexuality to recognise itself as such and transcend crudely constructed ideological boundaries, as well as an indication of the fragility and private irrelevance of the race discourse.

Enslaved black women's protection and publication of their feminine identities, therefore, took many forms, from their insistence on procuring fine clothing and decorative jewelry, love and care for their kith and kin, pursuit of market engagements through huckstering, leadership and involvement in revolutionary struggle, to loving white men into a kind of oblivion by producing coloured children with them that took their names, and more importantly, their properties. Gender, then, was socially contested in several ways, but as a relation of power, its role in the reproduction of masculinist class and race rule was critical.

The ideological defeminisation of the black woman, furthermore, contributed to a gender order that negated black motherhood and devalued maternity. Before the 1780s slave women were given a short respite from labour in the advanced stages of pregnancy. When William Dickson arrived at Barbados in the early 1770s, he reported being:

> astonished to see some women far gone in pregnancy, toiling in the field, and others whose naked infants lay exposed to the weather sprawling on a goat skin, or in a wooden tray. I have heard with indignation, drivers curse both them and their squalling brats, when they were suckling them.[17]

The expression of hostility to pregnant women reflected planters' perception that it was cheaper to buy than to reproduce slaves naturally. This, however, is not how it was explained in pro-slavery texts. Slave-owners spoke instead about black women's disregard for motherhood and nurturing, and explained this as further evidence of their brutishness and lack of femininity. Since it was 'natural', they argued, for women to desire motherhood, black women's apparent low fertility within the context of an alleged sexual promiscuity, suggests a certain kind of moral underdevelopment rather than physical inability.

Subversive resistance to these gender representations by women invariably incurred punishments. Slave drivers had the authority to use the whip to enforce conformity to the social implications of the gender order. African-born women did not expect to work during advance pregnancy nor in the three months after childbirth. Those who resisted the new regime were punished as part of the gender retraining. Richard Ligon described the mid-seventeenth century plantation regime in Barbados:

> The woman is at work with her pickaninny at her back. If the overseer be discreet, she is suffered to rest her self a little more than ordinary, but if not, she is compelled to do as others do. Times they have of suckling their children in the fields, and refreshing themselves, and good reason, for they carry burdens on the back, and yet work too.[18]

The unfamiliarity of this labour culture to Africans contributed to the low fertility levels and high infant mortality rates that rendered the black population unable to naturally reproduce itself.

Eighteenth-century records placed depletion rates (the excess of a population's crude death rate over its crude birth rate) as high as 50 to 65 per cent, while modern historians using case study analysis place it much lower. Estate records for Jamaica in the third quarter of the eighteenth century suggest depletion rates of about 20 per cent, while slave import-re-export records suggest 30 per cent between 1700 and 1750, and 25 per cent between 1750 and 1775. The depletion rate for Barbados in the first half of the eighteenth century seemed worst than that of Jamaica; 49 per cent between 1701 and 1725 and 36 per cent from 1726 to 1750, but falling to less than 12 per cent between 1775 and 1800. The demographic experiences of the Leewards approximated those of Barbados with depletion rates of 40 to 50 per cent up to the 1760s and less than 15 per cent in the last quarter of the century. By the time of the general registration of slaves between 1814 and 1818, and the collapse of slavery in 1838, depletion rates in Barbados and the Leewards were between three and four per cent.[19]

It was commonplace for visitors to the islands in the eighteenth century, who were unfamiliar with the gender order of plantation slavery, to express horror on observing the physical brutalisation of females, and slave-owners' disregard for black motherhood and maternity. Accustomed to a gendered culture in which women were perceived as being constantly in need of social and physical protection from male tyranny, some individuals who remained pro-slavery during the debate on abolition, were moved to support policies for radical reformation of slave women's condition. To such observers, it was in relation to black women that slavery was most vile, unjust, and corrupting of civilised values. Not surprisingly, therefore, abolitionists after the 1780s used evidence of corporal punishments inflicted on females, splitting up of black families, and disregard for domesticity, to make their principal moral charge against slavery. In so doing they encouraged West Indian planters to address as a separate issue the matter of slave women's social and domestic conditions. An important effect of this political campaign was the reformalisation of gender representations. For the first time in the Caribbean, the notion of the black woman as a member of the 'gentler sex' – hence physically inferior to males – became the basis of policy initiatives in slave management.

Abolitionists, furthermore, used the rate of natural decrease, or depletion rate, as proof of the unnatural character of the hegemonic gender order. They claimed that it was hostile to slave women, their domestic lives, and destroyed their natural tendency to be mothers. Centering the slave woman within gender representations as the principal victim of nutritional deficiency, Kiple considers high infant mortality the single most important factor in explaining the high depletion rate. Mothers were often helpless as their children suffered and died of lockjaw, yaws, worms, and a bewildering array of unfamiliar infections and diseases. Most of these diseases, Kiple argued, were related to malnutrition which was an endemic consequence of consciously applied gendered policies.[20]

Bennett's account of Codrington Estates in Barbados during the eighteenth century highlights the personal aspects of women's daily social experience with high infant mortality rate. Assessing the effects of underfeeding and overworking pregnant and lactating mothers, he describes their experiences with child rearing on the estate as follows:

> In 1745, Joan's daughter was born on February 7 and died on May 12; Occo's daughter began life on February 13, and died July 13; Molly's boy was born on July 7 and died on July 14; Bennebah's daughter lived only from October 3 to October 10; Arnote's son Cudgoe, and Moll's baby daughter, Moroat, lived only to 1748. Mercy's daughter, Mary, was the only one of the seven youngsters born in 1745 who survived at least three years. One of the three children born in 1746 died in the same year. The two children born in 1747 outlived their second years, and six of the seven babies born in 1748 lived past December 31 of that year – thus ten of the twenty three children born in the years from 1743 to 1748 died before the close of the period.[21]

This account offers a glimpse into the horror experienced by enslaved women, and speaks to the emotional world of women that existed behind the aggregate statistics of depletion rates. Women watched their children die in quick succession, and buried more than those who lived to become adults. It was spiritually and emotionally crippling for many, but for most the experience enabled them to find subversive ways to survive and to maintain and define their feminine self-identities. 'Monk' Lewis, a Jamaican planter in the early nineteenth century, provides piercing insights into the family world of slave women with regards to gender identity, child rearing and motherhood. Consistent with the dominant slave owners' representation of black women in the age of 'amelioration', he describes the women on his estate as 'kind-hearted creatures' who were 'particularly anxious to rear children'.[22] He details the reaction of a woman whose child had caught cold and showed the 'symptoms of a locked jaw':

> The poor woman was the image of grief itself: she sat on her bed, looking at the child which lay by her side with its little hands clasped, its teeth clenched, and its eyes fixed, writhing in the agony of the spasm, while she was herself quite motionless and speechless, although the tears trickled down her cheeks incessantly. All assistance

> was fruitless; at noon today it expired. This woman was a tender mother, had borne ten children, and yet has now but one alive: another, at present in the hospital, has born seven, and but one has lived past puberty; and the instances of those who have had four, five, six children, without succeeding in bring up one, in spite of the utmost attention and indulgence, are very numerous.[23]

Despite the agony of high infant mortality, Lewis argued that the rearing of children, domesticity and family life, exerted a steadying and maturing influence upon black women. To him, mothers appeared more moral, less sexually promiscuous, and more politically conforming.

The caring of children, the promotion of motherhood and domesticity, were therefore raised as socio-economic adjustments to managerial imperatives. Gender representations were dismantled and reconstructed to offer coherence to new reproductive policy initiatives. By the late eighteenth century, there was widespread commitment to pro-natal policies in an attempt to encourage natural reproduction as an important method of ensuring a labour supply in the long term. This development meant that a 'woman policy' had to be conceived, formulated and implemented on the estates. Traditional managerial attitudes and actions towards slave women had to be reconsidered and reshaped in a manner conducive to higher fertility levels. It was the beginning of a broad-based initiative to celebrate and promote black motherhood that resulted in the representation of the black woman as a natural nurturer – everyone's nanny, granny and auntie.

It should be stated, however, that slave owners had no direct evidence to prove that their females had been consciously imposing restraints upon their fertility, or that hegemonic gender representations helped towards its suppression, even though some believed it to be the case. No one considered that the slave woman, constructed as 'Jezebel', could possibly practise sexual abstinence (gynaecological resistance), but some believed that they possessed deep-rooted antipathy toward child rearing in slavery, especially within the context of hostility to motherhood. Slave owners proposed to minimise the degree of female indifference and resistance to child rearing by systematically offering socio-material incentives and reshaping the ideological aspects of the gender order.

This fundamental managerial departure centered the woman as nurturer and meant that new gender ideas had to be formulated, carefully tested and evaluated. As a consequence the pro-slavery cause found itself the recipient of an upsurge in literature which addressed directly aspects of slave breeding policies. Most contributors, many of them posing as experienced authorities on slave management, sought to encourage this trend, conceiving it as representative of new progressive organisational thought. Also, successful reproduction was considered a political strategy to take wind from the sails of abolitionists who argued that the endemic ill-treatment of slave women sprang from conceptual sources deep within the gender order.

One influential work, a pamphlet published in London in 1786 entitled 'The Following: instructions are Offered to the Consideration of Proprietors and Managers of Plantations', was written by a group of prominent absentee Barbadian planters. Printed in bold, capitalised letters in the introduction is the central thesis:

THE INCREASE IS THE ONLY TEST OF THE CARE WITH WHICH THEY ARE TREATED.

The Barbadians had already achieved natural growth and were now offering for emulation the key features of their success to other less experienced planters. The critical factor, of course, was the attainment of a female majority in the slave population. Barbados led in this regard (See Table 1:2), and attributed their success to the effects of their demographic restructuring.

***Table 1:2* Slave sex ratios in the British West Indies c. 1817 and c. 1832[24] (Males per 100 females)**

Colony	*c. 1817*	*c. 1832*
Barbados	83.9	86.3
St. Kitts	92.4	91.9
Jamaica	100.3	94.5
Nevis	95.3	98.1
St. Vincent	102.1	95.2
Trinidad	123.9	112.6
Demerara/Essequibo	130.9	110.2

The pamphlet emphasised the need for planters to implement a series of pre-natal policies to assist pregnant women to deliver healthy babies. Most importantly, it stressed the need to protect fertile women from the tyranny of overseers. In addition, emphasis was placed on the need for post-natal facilities to assist lactating mothers in lowering the high level of infant mortality. These policies meant, in addition to marginal reduction of labour hours for pregnant and lactating field women, and improved material care, the representation of black women as graduant members of the 'gentler sex' whose fragility required specific policy protection. In effect, the authors recommended a significant reconstruction of the gender order.

Tinkering with gender by way of finding methods to remove as many irritants as possible from women's sexual and domestic oppression was considered necessary. Slave owners were urged to encourage young slaves to form christian-style marriages as monogamous relations were considered by them more conducive to high fertility than African polygyny. The nuclear family structure, as an institutional arrangement, was encouraged by slave owners as suitable to attaining the objective of high levels of reproduction. On many estates, then, 'married' slaves were found living in family households. Also, the use of financial incentives as stimuli to reproduction was institutionalised by slave owners. By the 1790s evidence from plantation account books shows that financial payments of this kind were commonplace.

'Monk' Lewis of Jamaica could not be satisfied with crude systems of monetary and material rewards for the creation of new life. Money was important, but for him it was insufficient and brutally inadequate when offered as an incentive to motherhood. He needed something more philosophical, befitting the nature of the new, moral, gender order. Slave women, he believed, were entitled to 'honour' as mothers in their heroic struggle against nature. Respect was due to them, and such values, he believed, were necessary to encourage fertile women who were altogether too few on his estate. Lewis outlined his woman's policy as follows:

> I then gave the mothers a dollar each, and told them, that for the future they might claim the same sum, in addition to their usual allowance of clothes and provisions, for every infant which should be brought to the overseer alive and well on the fourteenth day; and I also gave each mother a present of a scarlet girdle with a silver medal in the centre, telling her always to wear it on feasts and holidays, when it should entitle her to marks of peculiar respect and attention, such as being one of the first served, and receiving a larger portion than the rest; that the first fault which she might commit, should be forgiven on the production of this girdle; and that when she should have any favour to ask, she should always put round her waist, and be assured, that on seeing it, the overseer would allow the wearer to be entitled to particular indulgence. On every additional child an additional medal is to be affixed on the belt, and precedence is to follow the greater number of medals. I expected that this notion of an order of honour would have been treated as completely fanciful and romantic; but to my great surprise, my manager told me, that he never knew a dollar better bestowed than the one which formed the medal of the girdle, and that he thought the institution likely to have a very good effect.[25]

This 'belly-woman' initiative was just the kind of counter-offensive West Indian slave owners needed to protect their regime from the moral assault of metropolitan anti-slavery campaigners. The notion of 'an order of honour' was intended to complicate the charge of abolitionists who described 'reforming' slave owners as vulgar materialists for using sexual manipulation and exploitation as necessary approaches to finding an adequate labour supply. The offering of money to slave women for the delivery of infants was depicted by abolitionists as a more degrading action than the purchase of the mother in the first instance, and constituted proof of the cultural and moral degeneracy of the gender order within the slave owning community.

Abolitionists, therefore, also centered the slave woman with respect to their campaign strategies, propaganda, and analytical critques. The slave woman was placed at the core of a contradictory discussion that sought, on one hand to protect and prolong slavery, and on the other to undermine and destroy it. The debate was transatlantic in nature. On the estates in the West Indies increases in the slave woman's fertility was hailed the deciding factor in the 'good treatment' thesis. In Europe, the slave woman was depicted as the tragic and principal victim of the worst system of masculine tyranny known to the modern world.

Public discussion over the slave woman was part of a wider discourse involving gender that sharpened opinion on both sides of the Atlantic and focused attention on the nature of slavery as a particular kind of gender power. The promotion of the paternalist idea in Enlightenment discourse of the 'woman' as the gentler sex placed tremendous ideological ammunition in the hands of the anti-slavery movement. Campaigners sought to portray the evil of West Indian slave society as resulting from this bias, both in terms of the sex structure of labour gangs and its emphasis upon natural reproduction in the wake of the abolition of the slave trade in 1807. While some hardline pro-slavery advocates continued to defend female corporal punishment, anti-slavery forces believed that they had discovered in gender – eventually – the soft, vulnerable underbelly of the slavery system.[26]

Slaveowners found themselves placed in a difficult and paradoxical position with respect to their gender thinking. While they made claim to possession of an egalitarian ideology, within which black women were not recognised as inferior or subordinate to black men – as demonstrated in their labour productivity – there was no intention on their part of weakening the dominant patriarchy to which the black male also subscribed and was partially empowered and privileged. The subsequent conceptual imprisonment of the black woman within a restructured gender representation that promoted notions of difference and inferiority had the effect of supporting her claim to legal emancipation but at the same time deepening her victimisation within the gender order. Slaveowners, however, while promoting gender egalitarianism under the whip, sought to defeminise her in this way by inferring a sameness with males.

The abolitionist challenge, furthermore, needed to cross a few turbulent rivers before it reached a comfortable resting place with respect to the objectification of the black woman. Was she in fact a woman, and if so, what did her femininity look like? In what ways, and to what extent, was she different from the white woman? Should she be regarded as a 'sister' by white women, or subsumed within the category of chattel and brute? Was she victim not only of white tyranny but also black masculine tyranny – a kind of malehood that saw all women as 'less than', and 'other'? The answers to these questions would have policy implications for the movement, particularly with respect to issues such as the separation of children from mothers, attitudes toward family life, corporal punishments, and the general nature of sex, gender and work.

By the mid 1820s both males and female English abolitionists were satisfied that the 'woman card' was their strongest in the struggle to win the hearts and minds of a seemingly indifferent public that, according to John Bull, was 'almost sick of this black business'. Throughout England, middle-class white women formed anti-slavery organisations and campaigned against slavery by promoting the 'feminine' characteristics of the black woman who was their 'sister' in the search for a new moral, Christian order.[27] Many white female abolitionists claimed a special understanding of the plight of black women, and slaves in general, derived in part form their 'essential nature' as female. The author of A vindication of Female Anti-slavery Associations, argued that their movement was part of a general struggle against human misery, social oppression, and moral injustice. Elizabeth Heyrick, a popular anti-slavery campaigner, stated in her pamphlet, 'Appeal to the Hearts and Conscience of British Women (1828)', that the woman on account of 'the peculiar texture of her mind, her strong feelings and quick sensibilities, especially qualify her, not only to sympathise with suffering, but also to plead for the oppressed'.[28]

The strategy of the British female anti-slavery movement, furthermore, was to construct a gendered trinity composed of woman, child, and family, that slavery had destroyed and denied black people. Without the emotional, spiritual and institutional bonds to enforce the viability of this concept, they argued, civilisation was not possible in the West Indies and those responsible for its absence were guilty of contributing to the pool of human misery and backwardness. 'Hell' was depicted as a place where men enslaved and beat women, alienated them from their children, placed a market price upon infants at birth, and denied them the right to religion, education and moral guidance; and it was portrayed as a place not dissimilar from a West Indian slave plantation.

Gender, then, also resided at the core of the politics that surrounded slavery and freedom in modernity. Extracted from West Africa by the slave trade and deposited in the Americas in considerably lesser numbers than men, women constituted initially a minority in fronitier Caribbean societies. Minority demographic status gave way to numerical majorities as socio-economic formations matured and were rationalised. Significant gender implications resulted from the fact that the system of slavery was female focused, as enslaved black women constituted the conduit through which blacks acquired at birth the slavery status. As a consequence, successive gender representations of black women developed around the need to align changing sex compositions and demographic requirements with the political economy of slavery.

This much was illustrated by the empirical evidence and conceptual articulations of the late eighteenth century when slave owners shifted their labour supply policy from 'buying' to 'breeding'. As the slave woman featured centrally in changing methods of slave reproduction, gender representations reflected the rationalisations of choices. Likewise, the politics of anti-slavery in Europe privileged the gender discourse to illustrated and emphasise slave women's relatively greater exploitation and brutalisation. Abolitionists, further, used gender representations of black women to highlight the extreme moral and social oppressiveness and backwardness of societies based on slavery, and the degeneracy of elites that maintain and defend it.

The considerable turbulence in the gender journey of slavery requires that events and processes be examined and historicised with the view to obtaining critical forms of feminist knowledge about male domination. Feminist theorising is best served by readings of history that illustrate how evolving communities actually thought about gender and formed opinions within changing social, economic, and philosophical contexts. As an historical moment, slavery was characterised by considerable internal turmoil that enables us to map the contours of the complex interactions between gender and relations of race and class. An understanding of the 'Enterprise of the Indies', as a project of modernity, therefore, requires the creation and organisation of knowledge about gender as socially constructed relations of domination. The politics of gender, and liberation from its capacity to socially differentiate for the purposes of domination, then, should begin and be guided by an understanding of how and why society came, over time, to determine the things it would or would not think about.

Endnotes

1. See Hilary McD. Beckles, 'Sex and Gender in the Historiography of Caribbean Slavery' in Verene Shepherd et al. (eds), *Engendering History: Caribbean Women in Historical Perspective* (Kingston Ian Randle Publishers, 1995) pp. 125-140; also in this volume, Bridget Brereton, 'Text, Testimony, and Gender: An Examination of Some Texts by

Women on the English-speaking Caribbean, from the 1770s to the 1920s', pp. 63-94; and Rosalyn Terborg-Penn, 'Through an African Feminist Theoretical Lens: Viewing Caribbean Women's History Cross-culturally', pp.3-19.

2. Kamau Brathwaite, 'Caribbean Woman' *op. cit.*; Rhoda Reddock, 'Slavery in the Caribbean: A Feminist Perspective', *Latin American Perspective*, 40, (12:1), pp. 63-80; Beckles, *Natural Rebels*, Morrissey, 'Women's Work', *op. cit.*
3. See for the wider relevance of this discussion Hilary McD. Beckles, 'Black Masculinity in Caribbean Slavery', Women and Development Unit, University of the West Indies, Cave Hill, Occasional Paper 2:96 (1996); Lindon Gordon, 'What's New in Women's History', *op. cit.*; Mary Poovey, 'Feminism and Deconstruction', *Feminist Studies*, 14, (1988).
4. See Beckles, *Natural Rebels, op. cit.*; Gautier, 'Les Esclaves Femmes', *op. cit.*; B. W. Higman, 'Household Structure and Fertility on Jamaican Slave Plantations', Population Studies, 27 (1973) pp. 527-550; *Slave Population and Economy in Jamaica, 1802-1834* (N. Y, Oxford University Press, 1976); H. S. Klein and S. L. Engerman, 'Fertility Differentials between Slaves in the United States and the British West Indies', *William and Mary Quarterly* 35 (1978) pp. 357-374; Michael Craton, 'Changing Patterns of Slave Families in the British West Indies', *Journal of Interdisciplinary History*, X:1 (1979) pp. 1-35.
5. The protracted violent war between Africans and Europeans on the sixteenth and seventeenth century Caribbean frontier has been well documented, but the contribution of changing gender identities and roles to social turbulence and instability has not been accounted for despite the considerable evidence found in slave owners' texts. See Hilary McD. Beckles, 'Caribbean Anti-Slavery: The Self-Liberation Ethos of Enslaved Blacks', *Journal of Caribbean History* 22:1 and 2 (1988) pp. 1-19; Bernard Moitt, 'Women, Work and Resistance in the French Caribbean during Slavery, 1700-1848' in Shepherd et al. (eds.) *Engendering History, op. cit.*; Morrissey, *Slave Women, op. cit.*
6. See David Brion Davis, *The Problem of Slavery in Western Culture* (Ithaca: Cornell University Press, 1966); also, Slavery and Human Progress (New York, Oxford University Press, 1984); David Eltis and James Walvin (eds) *The Abolition of the Atlantic Slave Trade: Origins and Effects in Europe, Africa and the Americas* (Madison, University of Wisconsin Press, 1981); Thomas Hodgkin, 'Kingsdoms of the Western Sudan', in Roland Oliver (ed) *The Dawn of Africa History* (London, Oxford University Press, 1961); Jan Vansina, *Paths in the Rainforest* (London, James Currey Publishers, 1990); Philip D. Curtin, 'Africa and the Wider Monetary World, 1250-1850' in John F. Richards, (ed) *Precious Metals in the Later Medieval and Early Modern Worlds* (Durham, Carolina University Press, 1982,) pp. 231-68; John Fage, 'The Effects of the Export Trade on African Populations' in R. P. Moss and R. J. Rathbone (eds) *The Population Factor in African Studies* (University Press of London, 1975), pp. 15-23; Joseph Inikori, (ed) *Force Migration: The Impact of the Export Trade on African Societies* (London, Hutchinson, 1981); Ray Kea, *Settlement, Trade and Politics in the Seventeenth Century Gold Coast* (Baltimore: Johns Hopkins University Press, 1982); Claire Robertson and Martin Klein (eds.) *Women and Slavery in Africa* (Madison: University of Wisconsin Press, 1983); Claude Meillassoux, 'Female Slavery' in Robertson and Klein, *Women and Slavery*, pp. 49-66; Walter Rodney, 'African Slavery and Other Forms of Social Oppression on the Upper Guinea Coast in the Context of the Atlantic Slave Trade', *Journal of African History* 7: 3, (1966) pp. 431-443; 'Gold and Slaves on the Gold Coast', *Transactions of the Historical Society of Ghana* 10 (1969 pp. 13-28.
7. Claire C. Robertson and Martin A. Klein, 'Women's Importance in African Slave Systems', in Robertson and Klein (eds.) *Women and Slavery*, pp. 4-5.
8. *Ibid.*; see also Martin Klein 'Women in Slavery in the Western Sudan' in Robertson and Klein, (eds.) *Ibid*; pp. 67-92.
9. See Robertson and Klein 'Women's Importance', *op. cit.* p. 9.

10. Meillassoux, 'Female Slavery', *op. cit.* P. 49; Robertson and Klein, 'Women's Importance', *op. cit.* pp. 10, 11.
11. See Robertson and Klein, *Ibid.*, p. 18. See also, J. D. Fage, 'Slave and Society in Western Africa, c. 1455-1700', *Journal of African History* 21 (1980) pp. 289-310; M. Klein, 'The Study of Slavery in Africa; A Review Article', *Journal of African History*; 19 (1978) pp. 599-609; I. Kopytoff, 'Indigenous African Slavery: Commentary One', Historcial Reflections 6 (1979) pp. 62-77; I. Kopytoff and S. Miers,"African 'slavery' as an Institution of Marginality' in S. Miers and I Koptoff, (eds.), *Slavery in Africa* (Madison: University of Wisconsin Press, 1977).
12. Herbert S. Klein, 'African women in the Atlantic Slave Trade', in Robertson and Klein (eds.) *Women and Slavery* , *op. cit.* 29-32.
13. *Ibid.*, p. 33.
14. *Ibid.* p. 37.
15. Edward Long, *The History of Jamaica 3 vols.* (London 1774) pp. 274-276, 327-328, 330-31.
16. *Ibid.*, p. 328.
17. William Dickson, *Letters on Slavery* [1789] (Westport: Negro University Press Reprint, 1970) p. 12
18. Richard Ligon, *A True and Exact History of the Island of Barbados* (London 1657) p. 48.
19. See J. R. Ward, *British West Indian Slavery, 1750-1834: The Process of Amelioration* (Oxford: Clarendon Press, 1988) pp. 121-122.
20. See K. F. Kiple, *The Caribbean Slave: A Biological History* (Cambridge: Cambridge University Press, 1981); K. F. Kiple and V. H. Kiple, 'Slave Child Mortality: Some Nutritional Answers to a Perennial Puzzle', *Journal of Social History* X (1979) pp. 284-309; 'Deficiency Diseases in the Caribbean', *Journal of Interdisciplinary History* XI: 2, (1980), pp. 197-205.
21. J. H. Bennett, *Bondsmen and Bishops: Slavery and Apprenticeship on the Codrington Plantations of Barbados, 1710-1838* (Berkeley: University of California Press, 1958) p. 55.
22. M. G. Lewis, *Journal of a West India Proprietor, Kept during a Residence in the Island of Jamaica* (London, 1929 edition), p. 87.
23. *Ibid.*
24. B. W. Higman, *Slave Populations, op. cit.*, p. 116.
25. Lewis, *Journal of a West Indian Proprietor*, pp. 108-109.
26. Report on the Debate in Council on a Dispatch from Lord Bathurst to Governor Warde of Barbados (London, 1828) pp. 21-23.
27. See Clare Midgley, *Women Against Slavery: The British Campaigns, 1780-1870* (London: Routledge, 1992) pp. 93-117; Louis Billington and Rosamund Billington, '"A Burning Zeal for Righteousness": Women in the British Anti-slavery Movement, 1820-1800', in Jane Rendall (ed.) *Equal or Different: Women's Politics, 1800-1914* (Basingstoke: Macmillan, 1985) pp. 82-111; Bill Hooks, 'Sisterhood: Political Solidarity between Women', *Feminist Review* 23 (1986), pp. 125-138.
28. *A Vindication of Female Anti-slavery Associations* (London: Female Anti-slavery Society, [n.d.] pp. 3-4; [Elizabeth Heyrick], *Appeal to the Hearts and Conscience of British Women* (Cockshaw, Leicester, 1828) p. 3. Also cited in Midgley, *Women Against Slavery*, p. 94.

2

Property Rights in Pleasure

Marketing Black Women's Sexuality

Visitors to Britain's West Indian plantations during the last decades of slavery frequently commented on what they considered the culturally endemic and morally regressive socio-sexual practices of white creoles. Comments reflecting aspects of the moral outrage that characterised popular anti-slavery literature, tended to focus on the values of domesticity within which racial groups were forging a new social sensibility. In general, they contained informed judgements on how the ethical character and aesthetic standards of creoles were shaped within the ideological sphere of the colonial mission, and highlighted the principal interest of slaveowners in maintaining and defending comprehensive property rights in persons.

Some pro-slavery practitioners, in addition, also seemed concerned by the extreme power held by slaveowners with respect to their right to intervene and manipulate the social world of the enslaved, especially its bio-social reproductive capacity. Ideologically, slaveowners understood well that they were entitled to commodify fully all the capabilities of slaves, as part of the search for maximum economic and social returns on their investment. Properly understood, this meant, among other things, the slaveowners' right to extract a wide range of non-pecuniary socio-sexual benefits from slaves as a legitimate stream of returns on capital, and an important part of the meaning of colonial mastery.

In real terms, then, new world slavery led to the legal and customary institutionalisation of the slaveowners' right to unrestricted sexual access to slaves as an intrinsic and discrete product.[1] The circuitous route of capital accumulation within the slave system, furthermore, recognized no clear distinction between the slave-based production of material goods, and the delivery of sexual services. Production and reproduction oftentimes were indistinguishable within the market economy of slavery. With respect to enslaved women, then, household work, which ordinarily meant manual labor, also included the supply of socio-sexual services and the (re)production of children as a measurable marginal product that enhanced the capitalisation process.

An exploration into the dynamic, multidimensional system of slaveowning which focuses on slaveowners' property rights in slave sexuality is essential to a psycho-social and economic grasp of the accumulating mechanisms that emerged from slavery as a mode of (re)production. The contours of such an excavation and display, furthermore, are particularly relevant to any discursive journey into the 'inner' worlds of enslaved women whose deeper integration into the market economy remains largely uncharted on account of the undeveloped polemic on the gender implication of slaveowning.

The outer sphere of this investigation touches upon the violent access to slave women's bodies by their owners, and the sale of their persons for money upon the sex market. Laws did not allow slaves to refuse social demands made by owner, but did provide for the punishment of recalcitrant, disobedient, rebellious and unruly slaves. Rape as a form, or degree, of sexual violation perpetuated against enslaved women by males – black, white, free or enslaved – was not considered a legal offense, and evidence of it does not appear in the litigation records.

Neither colonial statutes nor slave codes, then, invested slaves with any rights over their own bodies, but rather transferred and consolidated such rights within the legal person of slaveowners. This direct translation of legal entitlement into social power and authority meant that white men especially were located at the convergence where the racial, sexual, and class domination of slave women provided a totality of terror and tyranny. This judicial patriarchy supported and buttressed the ideological representation of white mastery, and illuminated the hegemonic maleness of the colonial enterprise.

The rape of the enslaved woman was first and foremost an attack upon her as a woman. Her powerlessness enters the scene of the offense only insofar as it serves as a confirmation of the totality of enslavement. It is for this reason that Orlando Patterson, attempting to compare violent rape with the coercive mechanisms of sexual manipulation, laid bare the social reality of plantation life when he stated that rape was often 'unnecessary since the slave negress soon gave in to the overwhelming pressures and made the best of its rewards.'[2] This argument rises directly from the many assertions found in the texts of slaveowners' narratives in which rape is rarely admitted but where clear prominence is given to slave women accepting offers they could not possibly reject.[3]

The inner sphere of the investigation concerns the theme of the commercialisation of slave women's sexuality as cash-receiving prostitutes. This subject also has several important implications for the way in which gender, race , and class relations are viewed within the market worlds of the slave mode of production. The roles of slaves as mistresses and concubines, and their use as prostitutes, is analyzed in connection with the formal institutional presence of 'leisure houses'; these two processes in turn are considered against the general background of the passage and reform of slave laws and the complex ideological world of miscegenation.

Unlike the Antiguan colonial elite of the seventeenth century, Barbadian colonists did not legislate against miscegenation. In 1644, Antiguans passed a law which prohibited the 'carnal copulation between Christian and Heathen.'[4] Barbadians, however, hoped that the bio-social aspects of their white supremacy ideology, enshrined in the slave laws, would function as an adequate deterrent. The dominant ideological charge of the slave laws was that blacks were heathens and should not share the same psycho-social space as Christians. The use of dehumanising animal analogies and demonisation references to blacks were common. Blacks, therefore, were not to be integrated into the emotional and sexual spheres of whites, either as domestic equals or as leisure-seeking partners.[5]

Representations of racial inequality in this social idealism, however, could not find real-life roots in the colonial setting; here societal standards were being fashioned in a rather hurried and ad hoc manner. The social and demographic realities of plantation life oftentimes required pragmatic social approaches to race relations, which included, among other things, submission to the tendencies of human sexuality to transcend ideological boundaries no matter how firmly established. Consequently, the earliest Barbadian slaveowners came to consider it their legitimate right and privilege to engage in sexual liaisons with blacks. According to Richard Dunn, seventeenth-century plantation records indicate that 'the master enjoyed commandeering his prettiest slave girl and exacting his presumed rights from her.'[6] This is further illuminated by John Oldmixon in 1708. Reporting on the domestic lives of slaveowners in Barbados, he noted that the 'handsomest, cleanliest (black) maidens are bred to menial services in order to satisfy their masters in divers ways.'[7]

As the anti-slavery movement gained momentum after the 1807 slave trade abolition, and promoted its ideas by focussing upon the exploitation of black women and the destruction of slaves' family life, the moral authority of slaveowners came under intense scrutiny. Indicative of popular European opinion was the reaction of an English military officer, Colonel Hilton. He reported in 1816 his horror and outrage at the sight of a woman in the slave market preparing to make a purchase by examining the genitals of male slaves 'with all possible indelicacy.'[8] Likewise, F. W. Bayley, an English traveller in the 1820s, found organised slave prostitution in Bridgetown rather distasteful, but reported that white males considered the houses if 'ill repute' socially indispensable.[9] Mrs Fenwick, living in Bridgetown during the 1810s, tried desperately but failed ultimately to accept a social culture in which young white males commonly underwent their sexual apprenticeship with domestic slaves and prostitutes 'brought into the household solely and explicitly for the purpose of sex.' Fearing for the moral character of her young son, she prepared to remove him to Philadelphia, but was defeated in the effort by a 'raging fever' that took his life.[10]

Creole slaveowners seemed undisturbed by such searching critical comments on their social culture and personal struggles. In general, they considered it no evidence of degenerate taste to retain black or coloured female slaves as sexual partners. The evidence suggests, furthermore, that such social relations were popular in Bridgetown, while probably less so on the plantations, although estate owners and managers had social access to a larger number of slave women. In Bridgetown, organised prostitution, and the formal integration of slave mistresses into white households, were common enough, while on the sugar estates sexual relations with slave women took more covert forms and were less visible to outsiders.

Urban society was influenced considerably by the maritime activity on which its economy depended. Here, prostitution was as much in demand as any social activity. The large, transient, maritime personnel expected to be able to purchase sex and the greater liberal values and ideological openness of urban society allowed for the proliferation of facilities that promoted slave prostitution. Claude Levy informs us that from the seventeenth century, Barbados was one of the region's busiest entrepots, and that slave prostitution was 'an occupation which was more common at Bridgetown than in any other city in the British West Indies.'[11] With reference to Jamaica, Higman states: 'Prostitution was common in the towns but rare on the plantations. No slaves were listed in the registration returns as prostitutes. But the inns and taverns of the towns were very often used as brothels as well, and the slaves attached to them were used as prostitutes as well as domestics.'[12] Prostitution was illegal in Barbados and Jamaica, but there is no evidence to show that the laws were enforced vigorously, a circumstance which suggests that this criminal activity was condoned if not encouraged by imperial and colonial officials.

Some travellers could find no significant reason to differentiate morally between urban slaveowners who engaged slave women as prostitutes and resident mistresses, and plantation owners who use them as 'breeding wenches' in search of a greater labor supply. For them, these roles overlapped, because many prostitutes were often the kept mistresses of white males, who also encouraged them, from time to time, to have children so as to benefit financially from the sale of the child. In Fenwick's value system, slave prostitutes and resident mistresses (invariably housekeepers) constituted a subgroup within many white households – a kind of informal socio-sexual domestic service sector. According to her:

> The female slaves are really encouraged to prostitution because their children are the property of the owners of the mothers. These children are reared by the ladies as pets, are frequently brought from negro houses to their chambers to feed and to sleep, and reared with every care and indulgence till grown up, when they are at once dismissed to labour and slave-like treatment.

Domestic arrangements that sought to conceal the practice of prostitution, she added, were 'common' to both urban and rural white households, and not considered 'an enormity.'[13]

Plantation owners, however, consistently denied that female slaves were sexually abused or used for sex-related 'financial gain.' They maintained that slave women were generally promiscuous, and pursued sexual relations with white males for their own material and social betterment. With respect to Newton Plantation in Barbados, the data for the late-eighteenth century show that female slaves feared, and sought to escape sexual violence at the hands of white personnel. Slaveowners reports also indicate that domestic slaves sought sexual relations with white men, both on and off the estate. In 1796, Manager Sampson Wood informed the estate owner that one woman had fled the estate, charging sexual abuse by the overseer, but that most domestics 'either have or have had white husbands, that is, men who keep them.'[14] Yet, for this plantation the evidence of sexual coercion and rape is implicit in the same records, which show that all four field women listed in 1796 as having 'mulatto children, Membah Jubah, Fanny Ann, Jemenema and Little Dolly, were impregnated between the ages of thirteen and sixteen.'[15]

The few cases in which slaveowners conceded the occurrence of rape and sexual violence they attributed such behaviour specifically to whites whom they described as persons without 'social breeding', such as dishonoured indentured servants, overseers, and other waged labourers. In 1822, for example, William Sharpe, a prominent Barbadian planter, informed a committee of the Legislative Council:

> Illicit intercourse with the whites does sometimes take place, but it is principally confined to the inferior servants on the estates, who are young men whose circumstances in life will not admit of their marrying and supporting a family:- when a connexion of this kind takes place between them and the young black women, it is done by

> persuasion, and because they have it more in their power to gratify the vanity of the females in their fondness for dress; punishment however awaits the offender when his improper conduct is discovered, for he seldom escapes being turned out of the estates. A manager's moral conduct is a great recommendation of him: glaring instances of immoral conduct would not be tolerated.[16]

In Bridgetown, however, such rationalisations and apologies were considered unnecessary and irrelevant. White males, including planters who sometimes resided in town, made a gainful business by prostituting female slaves. William Dickson found that men would often 'lease out' their slave mistresses for the purpose of prostitution as a convenient way of obtaining cash. These women, he added, were 'rented out' especially to visiting merchants, naval officers, and other such clients, for specified periods.[17] The money paid to owners of slave women for sexual services frequently exceeded the slaves' market value.

During the period immediately after the sugar harvest the number of slave women placed on the urban market as prostitutes by rural slaveowners increased, as did the number of male artisans put out to sell their technical skills on a contractual basis. In both instances, slaveowners expected all, or a proportion of the money earned; the slaves, on the other hand, considered themselves fortunate to have a greater degree of 'control' over the disposal of their time.

The question of slave prostitution was raised before the 1790-91 House of Commons inquiry into the slave trade. Evidence submitted showed that in spite of its illegality, it was 'a very common thing' for 'female slaves to be let out by their owners for purposes of prostitution.'[18] The Commissioners heard, furthermore, that rural slaves were sent to town, and town slaves were sent to the barracks at the Garrison, in order to raise money from prostitution. The evidence suggests that prostitution posed no major problems for colonial administrators, and may have been less widespread than in the cities of Europe.[19]

Early nineteenth-century references to slave prostitution emphasised the distinction between the urban and rural contexts. In 1824, Thomas Cooper, looking at the wider Caribbean situation, stated that elite slaves on the estate, notably midwives, were frequently the suppliers of young girls to urban clients.[20] J. B. Moreton, however, noted in 1790, that urban slave prostitutes were controlled by their mothers who arranged clients and received monies. He argued, furthermore, that coloured slaves 'from their youth are taught to be whores' and to expect their living to be derived from immoral earnings.[21]

In support of his abolitionist position, Cooper attributed part of the failure of slave populations on the sugar colonies to reproduce themselves naturally to the prevalence of prostitution among young females – on the estates as well as in towns. Slaveowners, however, did not accept that prostitution had adverse effects upon slaves' domestic arrangements or their fertility.[22] Edward Long echoed the Barbadian planters' sentiments when he stated that black women were predisposed towards prostitution, and performed this function with efficiency and without moral reflection.[23]

The evidence is not always clear on the distinction in occupational terms between slave mistresses, prostitutes, and housekeepers. Certainly, housekeepers were typically selected by white male householders via the sexual relation route, which suggests the inevitability of interchangeable functions. Captain Cook, a British military officer, giving testimony before the 1790-91 parliamentary committee, illustrated the many ways that Barbados' slaveowners prostituted female slaves. His knowledge of colonial society was derived from several visits to the colony in 1780 and 1782; he knew first hand the domestic culture of whites, and was attentive to the sexual practices of creole males. He described how enslaved domestics, black and coloured, were used as prostitutes in the colony's towns, and concluded that the purchase of sex by maritime crews 'was a very common practice.'[24] Slave prostitutes, he stated, would go on board ships under special arrangements with port officials for the purpose of selling sex for money. He confessed to accepting this activity on board the ship under his command, since it was part of colonial maritime life, but seemed rather indignant when he discovered that a 'negro girl' he knew well was 'severely punished on her return home to her owner without the full wages of her prostitution.'[25]

White creoles in Barbados never accepted that organised prostitution was of any economic importance. Slave women, they argued, were frequently given time to 'work out', which meant that they were free to pursue whatever gainful employment they wished, and though many would enter the business of prostitution for quick and large sums of money, it was their own 'voluntary' choice. Hiring slave women for multifarious social purposes, then, was considered part of the urban labour market in which slaves had some autonomy. Many free black and free coloured slaveowners, following the pattern set by white slaveowners, earned their living from the wages of hire-out female slaves; these worked formally as nannies, nurses, cooks, washerwomen, hucksters, seamstresses, and general labourers. The hiring-out of women specifically for sex ran parallel to this market, and the general expectation of white males who hired female slaves, under whatever pretence, was that sexual benefits, if needed, were included. Prices for hired women invariably reflected this dual function, even when it was not made explicit at the outset.

The covert organization of slave prostitution was also a popular business activity of 'well-to-do' white women, especially widows or those without influential or financially-sound husbands. White elite colonial society insisted on the projection of images of social respectability, and as such, distanced itself from formal association with prostitution as an enterprise. For financially-insecure white women, however, it was the best they could do, and they were described as displaying their involvement without shame or remorse. In 1806, for example, a British naval officer reported that he knew a respectable creole lady who, for a living 'lets out her negro girls to anyone who will pay her for their persons, under the denomination of washerwoman, and becomes very angry if they don't come home in the family way.'[26]

John Waller, an Englishman who visited Barbados in 1808, made a similar report on the relations between high 'society' white women, slave prostitution, and the 'hiring-out' labour system. He stated in his travel book:

> In the family where I lodged, a respectable lady was regretting to the company at dinner, that a young female slave whom she had let out for several months was about to return as she would lose twelve dollars a month, the price of her hire, and besides, be at the expense of maintaining her. After dinner, I made inquiry respecting the subject of hiring slaves and learned that the one in question had been let out to an officer in the garrison, with whom she had been living as a mistress. I felt extremely shocked at the idea of so strange a traffic; but I found, a few days later, this very slave advertised in the "Bridgetown Gazette," in the following curious terms: "To let, a Seamstress, a well-looking mulatto girl, seventeen years of age, an excellent hand at the needle, etc. To prevent needless application – terms twelve dollars per month. Apply, etc." I had previously noticed advertisements of this description, and I believe that few weeks pass without them; they are, however, frequently intended only for the purpose literally expressed.[27]

The institutional framework of prostitution, however, centred on the taverns, bars, and inns of Bridgetown. By the late-eighteenth century many of these leisure houses were owned, or managed, by free black or free coloured women, who were more restricted occupationally than their white counterparts in the search for economic niches. Dr George Pinckard who frequented Barbados during the 1790s as a medical officer aboard a war vessel, provides us with insights into the practice of prostitution in Bridgetown's taverns:

> The hostess of the tavern, usually, a black or mulatto woman, who has been the favoured enamorata of some backra [white man] from whom she has obtained her freedom, and perhaps two or three slaves to assist her in carrying on the business of the house, where she now indulges in indolence, and the good things of life, grows fat, and feels herself of

> importance in society. It is to her advantage that the female attendants of her family should be as handsome as she can procure them. Being slaves, the only recompense of their services, is the food they eat, the hard bed they sleep on, and the few loose clothes which are hung upon them. One privilege, indeed, is allowed them, which is that of tenderly disposing of their persons; and this offers the only hope they have of procuring a sum of money, where with to purchase their freedom.[28]

Such taverns, according to Pinckard, were 'commonly known by the names of the persons who keep them.'[29] The most frequented at Bridgetown were 'those of Nancy Clarke, and Mary Bella Green; the former a black, the latter a mulatto woman.' The white public, he intimates, would scarcely accept the terms 'Mrs Clarke,' or 'Mrs Green,' and so a 'party is said to dine at Mary Bella Green's, or at Nancy Clarke's,' the title Mrs is reserved 'solely for the ladies from Europe.'[30]

In any of these taverns, Pinckard informs, a 'bed may be had for half a dollar per night, or three dollars per week; and, for an additional sum well understood, the choice of an attendant to draw the curtains.'[31] Prostitute girls, he suggested, 'were treated in the most cruel manner by their mistresses, whose objectives were to earn as much money from their duties as possible. My considered response to such treatment,' Pinckard says, 'was much tempered by the realisation that these women "showed" neither shame nor disgrace' in their prostitution. Rather, he added, the one 'who is most sought becomes an object of envy and is proud of the distinction shewn her.'[32]

It was generally recognised that in these taverns, slave women were offered the boon of freedom as an incentive for maintaining their enthusiasm. For any category of slave, freedom was a legal status not easily rejected.[33] There were prominent freedwomen in the business, such as Sabina Brade who was described in 1807 as 'an old, fat black woman; 'Betsy Lemon, a well-known mulatto figure in Bridgetown; Betsy Austin, whose hotel was said to offer the best in 'mental and corporeal' entertainment, though at exorbitant rates; Caroline Lee, Betsy Austin's diminutive mulatto sister, after whom the well-known Barbadian yellow sweet potato is named; and Hannah Lewis, arch-rival of Betsy Austin, also a 'brown-skin lady.'[34] Dr Walker, Englishman who resided in Barbados during 1802-03, stated that these women possessed 'considerable property, both in houses and slaves.' He stated, furthermore:

> Nor can they fail to amass large fortunes, as their houses are generally filled with strangers, who must submit to the most exorbitant charges for every article of eating, drinking, as well as for the accommodation of lodging and washing. These taverns are besides houses of

> debauchery, a number of young women of colour being always procurable in them for the purpose of prostitution.[35]

In 1837, when abolitionists, Joseph Sturge and Thomas Harvey, conducted their 'emancipation' tour of the British West Indies, many hotels and taverns in Bridgetown were still considered 'houses of debauchery where a number of slave women were kept for the purpose of prostitution.'[36] Most observers of slave prostitution in Barbados noted, like Sturge and Harvey, that coloured women, both slave and free, were more in demand than black women, and fetched higher prices for their services. Coloured women, however, were less available for this role than their black counterparts in Bridgetown, because they were more likely to be mistresses of white men or married to propertied coloured men. The records attest to the favoured status of 'yellow-skinned' women, most of whom operated from the more exclusive taverns and hotels. In 1804, for example, an English naval officer made reference to a white woman he knew who made 'a round sum' by trafficking her prostitute 'coloured' girls to Europeans as 'housekeepers' in disguise, or as she preferred to call it, 'marrying them off for a certain time.'[37]

White men publicly displayed a preference for coloured women, though black women were more likely to bear the fruit of their secretive sexual exploits. The 'mulatto' girl was paraded as the kept mistress, but the black housekeeper was more likely to be the 'invisible lover.' One contemporary explained that white men's mulatto preference resulted from their cohabiting with them 'at a very early age,' and few denied that the 'brown' or 'yellow' skin 'coloured' women, outside of respectable family relations, were socially and sexually desired – more so than were white or black women.[38]

'Bayley's observations in the 1820s were perhaps representative of the white male's norm when he spoke of the sexual attractiveness of coloured women. He described them as having 'captivated' with ease the 'hearts of English, Irish, and Scotch' men on the island.[39] He added the following statement by way of personal judgement:

> If I accord the palm of female beauty to the ladies of colour, I do not at the same time deteriorate the attractions of the fairer [white] creoles; the stately and graceful demeanour which calls upon us to admire the one, does not forbid us to be fascinated by the modest loveliness of the other; yet I will acknowledge that I prefer the complexion that is tinged, if not too darkly, with the richness of the olive, to the face which, however fair in its paleness, can never look as lovely as when it wore the rose-blush of beauty which has faded away. I know no prettier scene than a group of young and handsome colored girls taking their evening walk.[40]

From the comments of Bayley, Waller and Pinkcard it seems that white elite males possessed a sexual typology in which white women were valued for domestic formality and respectability, coloured women for exciting socio-sexual companionship, and black women for less-structured covert sexual adventurism. Generations of black women, then, produced mulatto daughters who were priced higher on the market than themselves. Waller explained the forces which led to this differentiation:

> A very respectable matron, who had shewn a kind of motherly affection for a young friend of mine who came over [from England] to settle here as a merchant, advised him in the most serious manner to look out for a young mulatto or Mustee girl for his housekeeper, urging that it would greatly increase his domestic comforts and diminish his expenses; and, in addition to this, she hinted very delicately, that, by being confined to one object, his health and reputation would be better secured, than by the promiscuous libertinism to which she seemed to consider every young man as habitually addicted.[41]

North American abolitionists, J. A. Thome and J. H. Kimball, suggested that, during the 1830s, Europeans generally took this advice on 'first going to the land.' It was in vogue, they added, for new arrivants to engage 'colored females to live with them as housekeepers and mistresses.' Furthermore, 'it was not unusual for a man to have more than one.'[42] Bayley believed that this sexual culture arose principally from slavery, which corrupted the moral character of those who depended upon it, but he was not prepared to deny the sexual attractiveness of 'the proud and haughty spirits of the coloured ladies themselves.'[43]

Black women, whether slave or free, were generally not as successful in extracting socio-economic benefits from propertied white males as were coloured women. Data for Bridgetown suggest that whereas black women remained in the 'small-time' fringe of this illicit social culture, larger numbers of coloured women successfully fashioned their socio-ideological vision around the need to entertain white males, in return for social and material betterment. As free persons, coloured women's opportunities were severely limited, so this realisation encouraged them to adopt a professional attitude towards the sex industry that brought them into intimate contact with propertied white males.

Social custom dictated that prominent white men should neither marry coloured women, nor allow them in any way to transcend white women in social respectability. In this way, coloured women's social ambitions could be kept in check without alienating their sexual usefulness. In spite of their intimacy and loyalty to eminent white males, coloured women could not be accepted as equal members of official elite society. When, for example, the newly-appointed Governor George Ricketts, arrived at Barbados from Tobago in 1794 accompanied by his mulatto mistress, it caused a tremendous uproar among his councilors and assemblymen, although many had similar social relations.[44]

Illicit social relations with white men were considered rewarding options for coloured women, the recognition of which, some observers noted, frequently drove them to reject respectable domestic life with coloured men, and to consider black men socially unacceptable. An american citizen resident in Barbados noted in 1814 that 'colored parents educated their female children for this special purpose.'[45] Likewise, Thome and Kimball, observing the social culture of urban whites and free-coloureds, took the view that coloured women were 'taught to believe that it was more honourable, and quite as virtuous, to be kept mistresses of white gentlemen, than the lawfully-wedded wives of coloured men.'[46] For Bayley, only the removal of civil disabilities that adversely affected the status of free-coloured men would enable society to affect 'the weakening of those motives which induce the colored women to live in immorality with a white protector.'[47] General emancipation, he argued, could bring about a slow 'change in this system.'[48] Even then, he insisted, moral society would have to 'contend with strong and established prejudices, and the mighty influence of long custom and habit.'[49]

While the evidence points to whites and coloured women as the primary owners of slave prostitutes, occasional references to free black women and men suggest their marginal involvement. Free blacks were sometimes wholly dependent upon 'immoral gains' to maintain their status. It was not uncommon to find runaway female slaves being harboured by such persons, who in turn arranged their prostitution in return for protection. It was at this end of the business that black owners of prostitutes were to be found in large numbers, often catering for black clients, both slave and free.

Some slave women gained legal freedom through the route of the overlapping roles of prostitution and concubinage.[50] In these ways, they earned the necessary money to effect their manumission, or came in contact with clients who were prepared to assist them in doing so. Legal freedom, however, did not always result in a distancing from these roles. It was, therefore, very common to find freed women continuing as prostitutes and mistresses. In 1811, the Rector of the St Michael Parish Church, commenting on the 'very rapid' increase in the number of slaves freed by whites since 1802, suggested that 'out of every four at least three were females who obtained that privilege by becoming favourites of white men.'[51] He was supported by Joseph Husbands who claimed that in 1831:

> By far the greater number of free colored persons in Barbados have either obtained their freedom by their own prostitution, or claimed it under some of their female ancestors who in like manner obtained it and have transmitted it to the descendants.[52]

From the mid-eighteenth century, legislators seemed determined to restrain white males from manumitting their black and coloured sex favourites. In 1739, the manumission fee had been legally set at £50 plus an annuity of £4 local currency; the annuity was insisted upon by poor law officials as one way to prevent slaveowners from freeing old and infirmed persons who could not reasonably be expected to earn their subsistence. In 1774, a bill was introduced into the Assembly which aimed at curtailing the number of females being manumitted. It was designed to raise the manumission fee to £100, but was rejected on the ground that slaveowners should not be deprived of the right to assist the 'most deserving part' of their slaves – 'the females who have generally recommended themselves to our 'kindest notice.' It was defeated by a vote of eleven to five; opposition was led by Sir John Gay Alleyne who argued that female slaves who gave their loyalty, love and service to masters should not be denied the opportunity to gain freedom.[53]

Barbadian whites debated the subject once again in 1801, following Governor Seaforth's proposed bill to limit female slave manumission, and to ensure that proper provisions were made by slaveowners for their manumitted slaves. The bill became law, and raised the manumission fee to £300 for females and £200 for males. Slave women continued to be freed in significantly larger numbers than men for the rest of the slavery period (see Table 2:1), though the 1801 Act was repealed in 1816 following the Bussa Rebellion (14-17 April), and the £50 plus £4 annuity fee for both sexes was re-established.

Against this background, the Assembly continued to be notified that too many freed black women survived on income derived from prostitution. Since the 1780s Joshua Steele had expressed concerned for free black women who were forced to subsist by 'gallantry.'[54] He was supported by Governor Parry who was earlier informed by his Council that many freed women sustained 'themselves by the prostitution of their persons.'[55] The Assembly, however, was aware that the urban economy provided few outlets for free black women, most of whom were unable to compete with slave labourers in the huckster trade, or as general labourers, housekeepers, seamstresses, and the like. It was difficult, then, for free black women to break out of the prostitute/mistress cycle, unless they were able to marry those few free black men who earned a steady income.

The socio-economic integration of slavewomen into the plantation system, allowed for their use at various points along the circuit of capital accumulation. Their contribution to the overall wealth creation process of slaveowners involved not only their roles as labourers, and reproducers of labour, but also as suppliers of socio-sexual services. The sex industry was an important part of the urban economy, and the relations of slavery, protected by slave codes, created societal conditions under which the maximum benefits offered by property ownership in humans accrued to slaveowners. The use of slave women as prostitutes, therefore, was another way in which slaveowners extracted surplus value and emphasized their status as colonial masters.

Table 2:1: **Slave Manumissions in Barbados, 1809-32**

Years	*No. Males*	*No. Females*	*Total*	*%Male*	*%Female*
1809-11	168	263	431	39.0	61.0
1812-14	88	148	236	37.3	62.7
1815-17	191	279	470	40.6	59.4
1818-20	167	245	412	41.0	59.0
1821-23	131	166	297	44.1	55.9
1824-26	126	196	322	39.1	60.9
1827-29	212	458	670	31.6	68.4
1830-32	—	—	1,089	—	—

Source: **Jerome Handler, *The Unappropriated People: Freedmen in the Slave Society of Barbados* (Baltimore, Johns Hopkins University Press, 1974) p. 49.**

For the slave women, whether black or coloured, life as a concubine or prostitute was characterised by more than the omnipresent forces of relentless sexual exploitation at the hands of slaveowners. Their life chances were shaped by socially-complex and dialetically-changing circumstances. Some of them gained materially from the relations of sex in diverse ways. Many obtained legal freedom, which for slaves was the most important social commodity. Few became slaveowners and tavern proprietors, but most gained greater social mobility than the plantation field gang women, who, according to the economic and pathological indicators, were the more dispensable and shortlived 'beasts of burden' in the productive sector.[56]

Endnotes

1 See for example, George Pinckard, *Notes on the West Indies*, 3 vols. (London: Longman, 1806), 1; 245-46; John Waller, *A Voyage to the West Indies* (London; Richard Phillips, 1820), pp 9-10,20-21; J. Thome and J. Kimball, *Emancipation in the West Indies* (New York: Anti-Slavery Society, 1838), p. 79; J. Sturge and T. Harvey, *The West Indies in 1837* (London: Hamilton and Adams, 1837), p. l; William Dickson, *Letters on Slavery* (1789; reprint, Westport: Negro University Press, 1970), p. 39; F. W. Bayley, *Four Years' Residence in the West Indies* (London: William Kidd, 1833), pp. 496-97.

2 Orlando Patterson, *The Sociology of Slavery* (London: University Press, 1967), p. 160. See

also Hilary Beckles, *Afro-Caribbean Women and Resistance to Slavery in Barbados* (London: Karnak House, 1988), pp. 77-78. Most accounts of slavery in the West Indies comment upon the use of slave women as prostitutes but do not theorize the significance of this form of exploitation for an understanding of female slavery. For example, see Elsa Goveia, *Slave Society in the British Leeward Islands at the end of the 18th Century* (London: Yale University Press, 1965), pp. 216-17; Edward Brathwaite, *The Development of Creole Society in Jamaica*, 1770-1820 (Oxford: Clarendon Press, 1971), p. 160; B. W. Higman, *Population and Economy of Jamaica, 1807-1834* (Cambridge: Cambridge University Press, 1976), p. 42

3 See, for example, the Diary of Thomas Thistlewood, Jamaican slaveowner, Licolnshire Records Office, England; for extensive references to this point, see Douglas Hall, In *Miserable Slavery: Thomas Thistlewood in Jamaica, 1750-86* (London: MacMillan, 1989); also Hilary Beckles, *Natural Rebels; op. cit.*, pp. 131-38.

4 See Leeward Islands MSS Laws, 1644-1673.CO 154/1, co 154/1/49-50, Public Record Office (PRO), London.

5 The preamble to the 1661 Slave Laws of Barbados described blacks as 'heathenish,' 'brutish,' and a 'dangerous kind of people.' The 1688 Code described blacks as 'of a barbarous, wild and savage nature, and as such render them wholly unqualified to be governed by the laws, customs and practices of [the white] nation.' Acts of Barbados, 1645-1682, CO 30/2, CO 30/5, PRO. Richard Hall, *Acts Passed in the Island of Barbados, 1643-1762* (London: Richard Hall, Jnr., 1764), no. 42; also ff. 112-13. See also Richard Dunn, *Sugar and Slaves: The Rise of the Planter Class in the English West Indies, 1624-1713* (Chapel Hill: University of North Carolina Press, 1972), pp. 240, 246.

6 Dunn, *Sugar and Slaves*, p. 253.

7 John Oldmixon, *The British Empire in America*, 2 vols. (London: Mapp, 1708), 2: 129.

8 Colonel Hilton to Reverend John Snow, 16 August 1816, Codrington MSS, Barbados Accounts , 1721 to 1838, Lambeth Palace Library, London.

9 Bayley, *Four Years' Residence, op. cit.*, p. 497.

10 The Barbados Letters of Elizabeth Fenwick are to be found in A. F. Fenwick, ed., *The Fate of the Fenwicks, op. cit.*, pp. 163-207.

11 Claude Levy, *Emancipation, Sugar and Federalism: Barbados and the West Indies, 1833-1876* (Gainesville: University of Florida Press, 1980), p.30.

12 Higman, *Slave Populations, op. cit.*, p. 231

13 Fenwick, *Fate of the Fenwicks*, p. 169.

14 Report on the Negroes at Newton Plantation, 1796, Newton Papers, M523/288, ff 1-20, Senate House Library, University ot London, London.

15 *Ibid.*

16 Evidence of William Sharpe, in *A Report of a Committee of the Council of Barbados, appointed to Inquire into the Actual Condition of the slaves of this Island* (Bridgetown: W. Walker, 1822), pp. 5-6.

17 Dickson, *Letters*, p. 39.

18 Evidence of Nicholas Brathwaite, *British Sessional Papers: House of Commons*, 1791 (34), Vol. 42, 9. 183.

19 See Bryan Edwards, *The History, Civil and Commercial, of the British Colonies in the West Indies*, 3 vols. (1793; reprint, London: G. and W. D. Whittaker, 1801), 2: 23.

20 Thomas Cooper, *Facts Illustrative of the Condition of the Negro Slaves in Jamaica* (London: Hatchard, 1824), p. 42.

21 J. B. Moreton, *Manners and Customs of the West India Islands* (London: Richardson, 1790), p. 132.

22 See *A Report of a Committee of the Council of Barbados*, pp. 4-10.

23 Long, *The History of Jamaica, op. cit.*, 2: 436.

24 Testimony of Captain Cook, *British Sessional Papers: House of Commons*, 1791 (34), Vol. 42, p. 202.
25 *Ibid.*
26 Major Wyvill, "Memoirs of an Old Officer, 1776-1807." p. 386, MSS Division, Library of Congress, Washington, D.C.
27 Waller, *A Voyage, op. cit.*, pp. 20-21.
28 Pinckard, *Notes*, 1: 245-46
29 *Ibid.*, p. 249.
30 *Ibid.*
31 *Ibid.*, p. 245.
32 *Ibid.*, p. 137.
33 Neville Connell, "Hotel Keepers and Hotels," in *Chapters in Barbados History*, ed. P. F. Campbell (Bridgetown: Barbados Museum, 1986), p. 107.
34 *Ibid.*, pp. 111-16.
35 *Ibid.*, p. 108.
36 Sturge and Harvey, *The West Indies in 1837*, p. l.
37 Major Wyvill, "Memoirs," p. 383.
38 Waller, *A Voyage, op. cit.*, p. 19.
39 Bayley, *Four Years' Residence, op. cit.*, p. 493.
40 *Ibid.*, pp. 493-94.
41 Waller, *A Voyage, op. cit.*, p. 20.
42 Thome and Kimball, *Emancipation, op. cit.*, p. 79.
43 Bayley, *Four Years' Residence, op. cit.*, p. 195.
44 John Poyer, *The History of Barbados from the First Discovery of the Island in the Year 1605 till the Accession of Lord Seaforth 1801* (London: J. Mauman, 1808), p.639.
45 Jerome Handler, *The Unappropriated People: Freedmen in the Slave Society of Barbados* (Baltimore: Johns Hopkins University Press, 1974), p. 199.
46 Thome and Kimball, *Emancipation, op. cit.*, p. 79.
47 Bayley, *Four Years' Residence, op. cit.*, p. 497.
48 *Ibid.*, p. 496.
49 *Ibid.*
50 Handler, *The Unappropriated People*, p. 137.
51 Evidence of Garnette Beckwith, December 5, 1811, *Parliamentary Papers* (PP), 1814-1815, Vol. 7, p. 478.
52 Joseph Husbands, *An Answer to the Charge of Inhabitants of Barbados* (New York; Richardson, 1831), p. 19.
53 Minutes of the Barbados Assembly, 15 March 1744, Barbados Archives, Bridgetown, Barbados.
54 Joshua Steele's reply to Governor Parry, *Parliamentary Papers* (PP), 1789, Vol. 26, p.33.
55 See Handler, *The Unappropriated People*, p. 137.
56 Both terms – 'worn out' and 'beast of burden' – were used by William Dickson to describe the condition of slave women in the late-eighteenth century. See Dickson, *Letters, op. cit.*, pp. 6, 34.

3

Phibbah's Price:

A Jamaican 'Wife' for Thomas Thistlewood

Phibbah, the creole housekeeper at Egypt sugar plantation in Westmorland, Jamaica, met Thomas Thistlewood on Monday, 16th September, 1751, the day he arrived there to take up the post as chief overseer. By this time she had already established a reputation through several friendships with whites and blacks in the wider community as a respected and influential woman. Her enslavement notwithstanding, Phibbah was at considerable liberty to live with an extensive social autonomy not generally associated with other enslaved women on the estate. Thistlewood, in contrast, was new to the community having arrived from England the previous year, and was keen to establish his name. But it was not his first Jamaican job; he had been initiated into the slave economy as a penkeeper at Vineyard Pen, in the same parish. Egypt, then, represented the site of his first exposure to the heartland of the dominant sugar plantation culture that had been Phibbah's only world.

At the end of 1753 Phibbah was labelled by Thistlewood as his 'wife'. He kept a diary detailing his Jamaican life, and indicated that Phibbah resided at the centre of his social world.[1] Douglas Hall, in an edition of these texts, describes Phibbah as 'a remarkable woman', and suggests that the intimate relationship with Thistlewood was two years in the making because she was not easily seduced nor suppressed by him, and that she had an independent mission. The relationship, once established, persisted for 33 years until his death in 1786, during which time they had a son. In his will of that year Thistlewood made arrangements for Phibbah's freedom, supported by the provision of house, land, money, and slaves. Phibbah's manumission was secured but it was a journey to freedom pursued at an enormous personal price within an environment shaped by endemic sexual terror, violent death, virulent disease, and governed by the most tragic displays of human degradation and misery that authoritarian power can produce.

Thistlewood arrived in Jamaica on the 24th April, 1750, at the age of 29, an ambitious young man in search of a West Indian fortune. He was the second son of a yeoman farmer from Lincolnshire who died when Thomas was just six years old. Thomas' elder brother John, inherited his father's farm, and young Thomas was left a mere £200. He was later educated as an agriculturalist, and traveled throughout Europe, to Brazil and India before landing at Jamaica with letters of recommendation. He had a reasonable grasp of the English imperial culture into which he stepped, and to which he had subscribed.

The degree to which Thistlewood could adjust to, and redefine colonial space and its dominant social practice, would be determined by his character and personal values. His presence in Jamaica was largely a function of the ideological interconnections of Empire. The colony represented a part of the 'Enterprise of the Indies' launched by entrepreneurial and political male elites during the late Sixteenth Century, and developed as an expression of white hegemonic ruling class masculinity. He was not a member of the English elite, more the 'lower' part of the middling classes, but he shared the West Indian dream of his social superiors of attaining riches by sugar and slavery.

When Thistlewood 'discovered' Jamaica it was considered England's prized West Indian possession. The largest of all the islands in this West India Empire with 4,400 square miles, it dominated colonial sugar production, accounting for about 20,400 tons of the 45,775 tons output. The economy relied upon the labour of over 170,000 enslaved Africans, most of who worked and died on the 460 plantations of more than 1000 acres. To manage it all, Jamaica's 18,000 whites engaged the support of some 7,000 free non-whites, most of whom were also dependent upon slave owning in order to make a living and secure their freedom.

In his first year, Thistlewood observed Jamaica from the position of overseer of Vineyard Pen, a cattle estate which kept a few dozen slaves. The greater part of his career, between 1751 and 1767, however, was spent as overseer on Egypt estate. In 1767, he finally managed to purchase his own property, not a sugar estate, but 160 acres of inferior land he called Breadnut Island Pen where he raised cattle, grew fruits and vegetables, and with the help of some 30 slaves, etched out a precarious, but moderate income. This is where he died in 1786, the outback of plantation Jamaica, unmarried, disease ridden, totally immersed in the lives and deaths of his and other people's slaves, at the age of 60.

Sketches of Thistlewood's thirty-six Jamaican years are detailed in over 10,000 pages of diary. He kept this record, maybe as an indication of the phenomenal nature of his mission, but also as evidence of an organised mind that saw importance and value in the daily occurrences that shaped and guided his search for a West India fortune. As a frontiersman, he understood the significance of his managerial roles, and engaged those around him from this perspective. His record is an account of one type of white masculinity in action, at the levels of labour management, sexual engagements, cultural education, and the authoritarian manipulation of ethnic, imperial and gender power. He was a middle sized cog in the large wheel of colonial slavery. His diary illustrates how this self awareness translated into a social life the cuts through that facade of colonial respectability and revealed slavery as a gendered form of tyranny that constitutes an early indictment against the claims of enlightenment modernity.

Thistlewood celebrated himself as a sexually promiscuous colonist. By his own record, he was a sexual sadist and a rapist. His sexual exploitation of enslaved black women was not peculiar but typical of the permissiveness that was endemic to the social culture of white slave owning males. He was confident in his violent masculinity and went to great lengths to document its social expressions. He didn't try, unlike his contemporaries, to disguise or deny his sexual interests in subjected black women. Neither did he accuse blacks of possessing sexual promiscuity as a cultural characteristic. He admitted his own, and suggested that black women volunteered to participate in this social lifestyle.

As an estate manager and slaveowner Thistlewood held enormous power over slave women, and used it effectively to extract sex from them. The power to have sexual demands met was an established right of the slave owner, and Thistlewood understood that 'love', like labour, was an integral expectation of the package of benefits derived from mastery. The idea that slaves required constant exposure to physical punishment in order to induce a 'voluntary' response to the sexual authoritarism of owners, has informed the 18th century proslavery ideology articulated in historical texts. Yet, by accepting this circumstance as given, care should be taken not to deny the existence of a considerable degree of socio-sexual autonomy achieved by some enslaved women with respect to particular relationships.

Thistlewood's Jamaican project, like plantation slavery in general, was a site of the gender discourse that codified in diverse 'images' the social relations between men and women, between and within, the black and white 'races', and where the meaning of being 'male' and 'female' was socially experienced. It was where white men displayed their possession of ultimate power – the ability to demand and to take black life as a 'right'. Slavery, furthermore, produced a legal and social culture within which the interrelations between racism and sexism promoted the black woman to a heightened visibility at the head of the pecking order of human exploitation and subjection. In its logic, 'woman' was the 'centre' sex through which the reproduction of meanings of 'free' and 'unfree' were effected. Women, as a group, were collectivised by the dominant white male 'possessor', whose institutionalised, exclusive, masculine power, 'discovered' and demanded rights to all aspects of the female sex.

The plantation was semiotically a male construction that signified managerial and ownership masculinity. It was a physical and social sphere that was fashioned institutionally by white men at the micro level, and collectively managed at the macro level. It was a space economically invented by white masculine power, shaped by its contradictions, tensions, and anxieties, subscribed to by white feminine agendas, but ultimately fashioned by black missions and the dictates of capitalist production. Profits and power went hand in hand as the motive force of slavery's operation. Profits meant consumption and social status; power meant the attainment of sexual dominance, political authority, and the right to moral determination.

Enslaved women resided at the centre of Thistlewood's personal and public worlds. His diary in fact is an extended essay on self-discovery through the vista of intimate contact with black women who, he suggests, were free sexual agents. But it was a kind of discovery that empowered his masculinity; a form of power backed by the cannons of empire, with a capacity to convert slave refusal into an arcane voluntarism that also demonstrates the folly of the concept of a slave having a vote with respect to slaveowners' use of power. The pattern of his social life among enslaved women also supports much of what is known about European patriarchy. He established a 'home' within a 'house', placed Phibbah within it as principal lover, mother of his child, confidant, servant – but always slave – while he extracted sexual pleasures and pains from as many other slavewomen as he was capable. His undomesticated sexuality followed the familiar paths that led to several slave habitations where small sums of money were left behind, evidence of his belief that slave women were free to choose.

By way of explaining his fetish with black women, or more correctly enslaved women, Thistlewood suggested that he was not alone in this regard; that his experience differed in no meaningful way from other white men, and that sexual engagements with slave women was an important part of white popular culture. While he indicates, by his silence, the infrequency of social contact with white women, no statement is made to the effect that black women were targeted because of a shortage, or absence of white women. Rather, the evidence supportive of the contrary position is substantial, since many of his white friends, colleagues, and acquaintances whose extensive sexual encounters with slave women are detailed, were either married to white women or exposed to their companionship. The message from Thistlewood, therefore, is an expression of the preference for 'enslaved sexuality'.

At Vineyard, Thistlewood was the only resident white person among the slaves. He stated on January 8, 1751, for example, that he saw a white person for the first time in three weeks. By this time he had taken Marina, a field slave, one of the 18 females on the pen, as his 'wife'. Marina lived in his house; he bought her gifts, described his sex encounters with her, and eventually built her a home of her own. It was Phibbah, however, his second slave 'wife' who dominates the images of his story; it is told through comments relating to the rearing of their son John, accounts of doctors who sought to cure their venereal diseases, as well as other slave women with whom he had sexual engagements.

While he defined Phibbah as his 'wife', and expressed considerable emotional attachment to her, Thistlewood had multiple sexual partners. He had sex with dozens of slave women, and occasionally with the daughters of these women. He described in his diary how and where he had sex, as well as the frequency. Women, and sexual encounters with them, are described in detail, with references to their ages, African origins, and the degree of his satisfaction. The women he preferred were established as regular parties in sex activity. Few references are made to circumstances that could be described as rape, and he makes it clear that coercion was unnecessary since slave women could not as a right consistently refuse him sex. If they did severe punishments would follow, some of which were life threatening.

Thistlewood was in many respects a meticulous observer of black women at Egypt. He scrutinised their behaviour, and paid particular attention to their social culture and sexual conduct. His sexual interest in them heightened his powers of observation. Significantly, he was at times, mindful, to inform his diary how blacks perceived and spoke of him in his absence. On November 1, 1751, he listed the female population at Egypt, the targets of his superpower status, as follows:

***Table 3:1* Female Slaves at Egypt Plantation, 1751**

Women		*Girls*	
Name	*Description*	*Name*	*Description*
Hagar	Mandingo	Ellin	Ebo
Celia	–	Dinah	–
Mirtilla	Ebo	Clara	–
Abigail	Ebo	Rose	Ebo
Bella	Congo	Silvia	Ebo
Avasteba	–	Cynthia	Ebo
Jenny	Nago	Dido	Creole
Hannah	Nago	Java	
Phibbah	Creole	Sibbe	
Old Phibbah	–	Children	

Women *(cont.)*		***Children***	
Name	*Description*	*Name*	*Description*
Mary	–	Accuhab	–
Margie	Ebo	Susanah	Congo
Belinda	Ebo	Quasheba	–
Chrishea	Ebo	Dido	–
Big Mimber	Creole	Franke	–
Old Catalina	–	Jenny	–
Beneba	Creole		
Agnes	–		
Little Mimber	Creole		
Sibyl	–		
Prue	–		
Yabba	–		
Betty	–		
Teresa	–		
Lucy	–		
Basheba	–		
Old Sarah	–		
TOTAL	**27**	**15**	

Over the next decade he had sexual relations with most of these females. The girls were launched into premature womanhood, and children were brought on to complete the reproduction of his sexual supplies.

From the women's view point, Thistlewood was a superpower – positioned to enforce pain and grief, or offer some respite from the horror of enslavement. They too had their own missions – part of which entailed submitting to Thistlewood's sexual demands. On Saturday 21st November, 1751, for example, he documented the sexual encounter with Ellin the Ebo girl 'by the morass toward the little plantain walk'. He also noted sex with Dido, the creole girl, who left him with a 'sore redness' on his genitals which he 'did not regard'. Most of 1752, he continued with Dido, and after an encounter with her on September 30th, he noted 'a greater redness, with soreness' followed by 'a running of yellowish greenish matter.' During the night of October 3rd, he experienced 'painful erections, sharp pricking and great torment'. The symptoms increased over the next few days, with sores breaking out on his thighs and a swelling of the 'kernels'. The linen he said, is now 'loathsome'. An entry for Tuesday 26th, November, states:

> To Mr. Joseph Horlock [MD], for curing me of the Clap, £2. 7s. 6d (yet am in some doubt if perfect). Was 44 days curing, from 11th of October to 23rd November in which time was blooded, and took some 24 mercurial pills, (purging pills) 4 at a dose; . . . besides bathing the penis

a long time in new milk, night and morning, rubbing with probes, and syringing away above 2 phials of injection water.

Doubt about the effectiveness of the medicine stayed with him but did not prove an inhibition to his sexual exploits.

Ten days after the end of his treatment, Thistlewood turns to Jenny, then back to Dido. But Jenny he favoured, showered her with gifts, partly in an attempt to secure her from the attention of 'John Filton's negro man' who she seemed to care for. In a fit of jealousy, Thistlewood quarrels with her, and on May 10, 1752, took away her 'necklace, bordered coat' and other gifts. On the 16th, he states that 'Jenny came again to me', where upon he returned the gifts. For the remainder of the year, Thistlewood would have regular sexual encounters with Jenny in his bed chamber while during the day he reported having sex about the plantation fields and buildings with Susanah, Big Mimber, Dido and Belinda. Jenny's son, 'mulatto Thomas', was not claimed by Thistlewood; no other white man was mentioned in this connection; the infant died after contracting small pox. By the end of 1753, Jenny no longer served as Thistlewood's chamber mate. This development coincided with a painful experience he had with the 'buboes' – a severe swelling of the groin that caused him considerable discomfort. Phibbah, the housekeeper, became his regular partner, the beginning of a lifelong relationship that offered her the best and worst that plantation life could offer.

Phibbah's prominence at Egypt preceded her relationship with Thistlewood. Her daughter, Coobah, lived on a neighbouring plantation, and was also the lover of a white man. They became Thistlewood's 'family'. In early 1754, he documents sex with Phibbah on the nights of February 19th, 21st, 22nd, 24th, 25th, and 28th; 'Phibbah kept away' on the 26th and on the night of March 1st, he resorted to Susanah. In order to woo Phibbah, the presents began to flow her way – both in cash and kind. Meanwhile Nago Hannah, who he had sex with in September and October, of the previous year, died while giving birth to a mulatto child. Between 1751 and 1754, before and after Phibbah took centre stage in his sexual life, Thistlewood records 265 sexual encounters with over 45 slaves. Of the 265 encounters 45 were with Phibbah in 1754. These engagements were asshown in Table 3.2.

At times Thistlewood turned his attention to documenting the sexual relations of other white men who visited or worked on the estate. He paid particular attention to John Hartnole, who arrived at the estate as a 19 year old driver, and William Crookshank, sent by Egypt's owner, Captain Cope, to assist Thistlewood. Hartnole is described by him as a young man who, far too often, over-indulged himself with food and drink, but Thistlewood seemed more concerned with his sexual relations with slave women. He tells us about

Table 3:2 **Thistlewoods Sexual Partners and Encounters, 1751-54**

1751 Name	No. of Times	Name	No. of Times	Name	No. of Times
Abba	1	Asranah	1	A- D	2
Betty	1	Chrissie	5	Dido	7
Ellin	1	Flora	1	Marvina	1
Jenny	3	Juba	1	Mary	1
Natch	1	Nago	1	Susanah	1
Peggy	1	Phibbah	1	Unknown	4
(Total = 34)					

1752 Name	No. of Times	Name	No. of Times	Name	No. of Times
Belinda	1	Abigail	1	Beneba	5
Big Mimber	2	Cynthia	1	Dido	7
Mulier	1	Jenny	18	Hannah	1
Silvia	2	Susanah	19	Violet	1
(Total = 59)					

1753 Name	No. of Times	Name	No. of Times	Name	No. of Times
Belinda	6	Bella	1	Beneba	9
Hagar	1	Cynthia	2	Clara	2
Hannah	2	Mirtilla	1	Old Sarah	1
Jenny	14	Margie	1	Phibbah	21
Waadah	1	Susanah	43	Rose	2
Unknown	1				
(Total = 118)					

1754 Name	No. of Times	Name	No. of Times	Name	No. of Times
Belinda	1	Celia	1	Mountain Susanah	2
Hanah	1	Chrishea	1	Phibbah	23
Hagar	1	Doll	1	Princess	2
Juliana	1	Ellin	2	Rose	2
Melia	1	Lucy	4	Susanah	6
Moll	1	Mimber	1	Violet	3
(Total = 54)				**Grand Total = 265**	

Hartnole's first infection with 'clap'. We hear also about his nightly quarrels with Coobah, Phibbah's daughter, and of her declaration that even though she had a husband in Dago, and a sweetheart in Tom, it was Hartnole whom she loved best. It is presumed by Thistlewood that when Coobah gave birth to her first mulatto child on Wednesday, December 14, 1768, that Hartnole is the father. He was very fond of Hartnole, frequently dining with him, and making black women available to him for casual sex. On his recommendation, Hartnole was employed as overseer on Retreive Estate, a major promotion. He died of a 'putrid fever' on 14th August, 1778, at the age of 30.

William Crookshank began his sex life with black women in much similar fashion to Hartnole. He arrives at Egypt on May 14, 1754, and the following day he took Bess as his 'bedfellow'. On June 5th, Crookshank developed 'a scalding of urine'. Thistlewood is 'afraid he has got the clap', and pondered if Bess is infected. He sends Crookshank to Dr Walker for a medical examination; he returns with a letter to Thistlewood which informs him that 'William has got a confounded clap.' Its a short-lived affair; by the end of the year he had taken Mirtilla as his 'wife'. Thistlewood complains of Mirtilla's frequent arguments with Crookshank, the 'prodigious noise' they make, but is concerned more about Mirtilla's illness during her first pregnancy. He fears that she is 'going to miscarry', and sends her home. Mirtilla was not an Egypt slave; she belonged to a Mrs. Mould who lived not very far away in Savanna. Crookshank misses her, and visits 'her there every night'. Physically exhausted by this arrangement, Crookshank goes to great length to bring her closer to him at Egypt. He persuaded Mrs. Mould to hire Mirtilla to him for £20 per annum, and he in turn sub-leased her to Egypt at a charge of 2 bitts a day for her field labour.

Thistlewood, however, influenced by Phibbah's opinion, is suspicious of the whole affair. He thinks little of Crookshank's emotional attachment, and believes that he is being taken advantage of by Mirtilla. She is always sick, he says, and 'ails at little or nothing'; she stays at home and 'only resolved to put Crookshank to a needless charge through spite'. Crookshank feels the agony of Mirtilla's illness and 'cries sadly'. He loves her, and Thistlewood considers him a 'fool' for it. During her pregnancy Thistlewood doubts Crookshank's paternity as the child is more 'probably for Salt River Long Quak', a slave on the estate. In the whole year, Thistlewood notes, she 'worked 244 days' and earned Crookshank only £15.15s – £4.5s short of her hire.

Thistlewood informed Mrs Mould of Mirtilla's work habit. Mrs Mould consequently decided to punish her by putting her neck in a yolk, even though she is pregnant. Crookshank learns of the treatment his 'love' is experiencing, and 'abused Mr and Mrs Mould in an extraordinary manner in the Savanna, at their own house; afterwards crazed went down [on] his knees and begged their pardons.' On Monday, March 15, 1756, Dr Robinson delivered her child, a mulatto girl. Crookshank visited his family, and returned home crying with joy. He names his daughter Sukey Crookshank, and continued to earn Thistlewood's displeasure for pampering both child and mother.

Only casual mention is made to the many other sexual relations between white men and slave women. He refers to John Filton, his predecessor at Egypt, and 'his negro wife'; also to Thomas Fewkes, his colleague at Egypt, who 'made up a match' with Little Lydde and was 'clapped confoundedly.' Mr Cope, Egypt's owner, had his pick of women; Thistlewood lists Silvia, jealously suspects his own Phibbah, Little Mimber, Sancho's wife, Cubbah, and Phibbah's daughter, Coobah. He suspects that Cope was the father of Coobah's second mulatto child, rather than Davie, her husband, and was 'well informed that he has been bad with venereal disease.' These encounters took place while his wife, Mrs Cope, was pregnant, and when she gave birth to a girl on 26th January, 1760, Thistlewood notes that her husband's 'passion for Little Mimber' was well known. He also referred to Barbadian Robert Gibbs, who was hired as Egypt's driver, taking Nanny as his 'wife', and to another driver, Irishman Christopher White, who 'made a match' with Susanah. When Barbadian Gibbs moved on, and was replaced by Patrick May, he too took on Nanny as a house mate, a relationship that ended when May, while drunk, wounded her with a gun shot during a quarrel.

Thistlewood's emotional insecurity in relation to Phibbah is thinly disguised. He does not deny emotional attachment, but recognises that Phibbah's independence could not be curtailed. Phibbah knows that Mr Cope, her owner, has an authority over her not possessed by Thistlewood. She plays the politics of this power relation to her advantage. Thistlewood suspects that there is a sexual relationship between her and Cope, is reluctant to explore his suspicions in case he loses both Phibbah and his employment. On December 2nd, 1759, he tells us that Cope visits the estate and Phibbah goes to his house for 'what I can't tell'. On Thursday 23, Cope again visits the estate and Phibbah is, 'I don't know where'. The following week Phibbah comes to him and he chases her away for her 'impudence'.

More often, however, are references to Phibbah rejecting Thistlewood, or just disregarding his overtures. On Sunday, 2nd February, 1754, he tells us: 'Phibbah did not speak to me all day'. The following day, he writes: 'I fetched Phibbah from her house and had words with her'; but on Friday 2nd, he notes: 'Phibbah denied me'. The bond between them, however, intensified over time. When Phibbah leaves the estate Thistlewood feels 'mighty lonesome', and she responds by sending him daily many kinds of specially cooked foods. Furthermore, on her return she brings him gifts. He never allows her to travel alone, always protected by a male slave guard, and made well comfortable. He never admits to loving her, but speaks of his 'care', 'sympathy' and 'desire' for her. But, the quarrels are constant. As the relationship grows, she complains about his infidelity and withholds her affection periodically.

There is a level at which Thistlewood's diary can be read as one very divisive and dangerous quarrel. The quarreling did not stop. The sex went on, and on, and everyone it seemed, was being infected with venereal disease. Thistlewood seemed almost celebratory in his references to men, white and black, contracting the 'clap', while appearing more pitiful in remarks about women. The 'clap', it seemed, held them all together in a pathogenic family, through the subtext of the experience, as it relates to the quarrels, is missing. Phibbah is badly infected. On January 1st, 1761, she 'complains of a violent pain at the bottom of her belly. She also has a 'running' which stains the sheets yellowish'. He gives her mercury pills at night. The evidence of the infection occasionally subsides, but flare up again causing her considerable pain.

Thistlewood, however, continues to go to Susanah, then to Princess, back to Phibbah, while complaining about 'emission painful'. He tells us that Princess has the 'clap', and so does newly arrived Simon, Chub, and many other male slaves; Cudjoe he says, is bad with it, 'again'. On Sunday, 20th November, 1774, he writes 'Sally has the clap very badly'; he had been having sex with her regularly since 1770, while noting that 'Phibbah is highly displeased'. In 1770 he had also been having sex with a field hand also named Mirtilla, a 24 year-old who was 'married' to Egypt's driver, Johnie. In May, 1771, he tells us that Mirtilla 'has got the clap and its very bad upon her'. She complains of 'violent pain in her neck'; she steals, runs away, gets drunk, and suffers with 'bad fits'. On May 21, 1773, he records sex with her, and in November he writes: 'Mirtilla has got the clap badly'.

But it is Phibbah, his 'wife', whom he seemed concerned about. Her venereal infection took a heavy toll on her health. The mercury pills, yellowish stains, pain in the belly, and countless restless nights, had also impaired her mental condition. Neither of them could rest comfortably on account of her nightly pain and discomfort. The doctors came, bled her, but it wouldn't help much. But as Thistlewood grew older, he seemed to prefer the young girls. In November, 1779, he suspects that he has infected young mulatto Sukey Crookshank, 23 year-old daughter of William, his sub-overseer. Phibbah is aware of some of these encounters. He claims and suspects, that Phibbah is not entirely 'faithful' to him, and still believes that Mr. Cope, his employer, sleeps with her occasionally.

But while Thistlewood defines Phibbah as his 'wife' he records having sex with Susanah, Nago Hannah, Aurelia, Sabina, Abba, Little Mimber, Mazarine, Warsoe, Little Lydde, Pheoba, Violet, Daphne, Amelia, Coobah, Sally, Peggy, Mirtilla, Sukey, Franke, and Bessie. Phibbah protests, and occasionally rejects him for these relations; his diary is punctuated with statements such as 'Phibbah would not come to bed – was rather too saucy'. It is a relation, conceived and nurtured within the gendered structure of superordinate male power, mediated by emotional protest, human concern, and the emergence, finally, of a subversive feminine submission. She loans him money from her earnings accumulated from sewing. He keeps her valuable goods and looks after her medical expenditures.

In April, 1760, Thistlewood and Phibbah had a son; he names him John, after his brother who lives in England. It is also a sexually active year for Thistlewood. His son could have been born to any of the 27 women listed below with whom he had sexual encounters between 1759 and 1760:

Table 3:3 **Thistlewood's Sexual Partners and Encounters at Egypt between 1759-1760**

Women	*Times*	*Woman*	*Times*	*Woman*	*Times*
Nancy	5	Beck	3	Clara	1
Egypt Susanah	29	Eve	1	Little Doll	2
Lydde	1	Little Member	20	Little Lydde	1
Mazerine	24	Moll	3	Mould's Lydde	1
Mary	1	Mountain Lucy	1	Phibbah	160
Quasheba	3	Violet	5	Rosama	6
Abbah	1	Warsoe	5	Daphne	1
Amalsa	1	Jenny	2	Ellin	2
Mountain Lydde	1	Mountain Susanah	1	Unknown	1

John is raised as an heir, sent to private school, but does not take to books which disappoints his father. He preferred the craft of the carpenter. He is apprenticed at age 15 years to Mr William Hornby, a master carpenter, under a six years indenture which cost Thistlewood dearly. John becomes a free coloured man. Phibbah is proud, attentive and protective of her emancipated son. He dies tragically at the age of 20. There was widespread speculation that he was poisoned. Phibbah had nursed him on his death bed, and watched him die with a 'putrid fever'. She mourned his passing for several months, and thereafter seemed more attentive to Thistlewood's needs.

When Thistlewood bought his own property and struck out on his own, he hired Phibbah from Cope. This was the best he could do. Cope, probably because of his own involvement with Phibbah, refused to sell her to Thistlewood, and did not consider manumitting her. Thistlewood paid a rent of £18 per year for her hire. He considered it an act of 'condescension' on Cope's part. They lived together on his property. Life continued as it was at Egypt. Occasionally their venereal disease would act up, and they would take mercurial pills for the 'running that caused stains'. On November 18, 1768, Phibbah fell ill, and Thistlewood wrote:

> About midnight last night Phibbah was so restless and violently ill of pain in her left elbow, etc., that I thought she would have died. I got up and tended her, had her arm rubbed with British oil, etc. I got no rest this night past.

When her eyesight began to weaken, affecting her sewing, he bought her a pair of spectacles'. But Phibbah's sight, it seemed, was on her freedom. Her son had secured his, short-lived though it was, and she expected hers – ultimately. Their years together were turbulent indeed, but something else seemed to hold them together.

Phibbah's charm, and the general importance to Thistlewood of her love and labour, were critical parts of the relationship. As a seamstress, she generated a steady stream of revenue for Thistlewood and herself. Thistlewood needed the cash; when he experienced financial problems, he borrowed heavily from Phibbah. His accounts of income for the year 1768 shows that 128 bitts were earned from Phibbah's sewing, compared with 124 bitts from the sale of wild fowl, 57 bitts from fish, and 322 bitts from vegetables. Phibbah, however, was not the only woman from whom Thistlewood extracted cash. During most of the 1760s Damsel was his chief higgler. She would sell a range of commodities, some made on Thistlewood's property, to neighbouring households as well as in the town of Savanna-La-Mar. Accounts for the end of financial year 1767 show that Damsel, by the sale of eggs, cake, cabbage, savoys, limes, beans and 'Indian Kale', earned him a substantial '212 bitts in all'. Thistlewood effectively organised the female labour on his Pen in a range of creative occupations. It was an intensive labour regime.

Table 3:4 **Occupations of Women Slaves on Breadnut Island Pen, 1783**

Name	Occupation
Phibbah	cook, housekeeper, seamstress
Abba	washerwoman
Bess	seamstress
Damsel	cook, stockgirl, higgler – supported by her daughter, Nelly
Sally	fetching water for Nanny
Phoebe	carrying stones and mortar
Peggy	fetching limestone
Sukey	picking up horse dung to be mixed in with the mortar
Maria	" " " " "
Mirtilla	" " " " "
Franke	selling garden vegetables in town
Mary	still 'runaway'

His 12 women worked alongside 7 men slaves – Joe the waiting boy, Dick the fisherman, Lincoln the poacher, Caesar the lime maker, Jimmy the lock cleaner, Solon who picked quasi, and Cudjoe the watchman.

While Thistlewood earned cash from the work of women slaves, and borrowed money from others, many women in turn earned sums of money from him as sex payments, transactions that contributed to the circulation of money within the slave community. On Sunday January 20, 1759, for example, he

***Table 3:5* Female Workforce at Egypt, March 11, 1752**

Little Mimber }	
Teresa }	
Jenny }	sick at home
Chrishea }	
Old Catalina }	
Ellin }	
Celia	hogstyes (disabled)
Basheba	'in Town lying'
Hanah	trash carrier
Violet	trash carrier
Old Sibyl	turner
Mirtilla	cane carrier
Lucy	cane carrier
Quamina	watchwoman
Phibbah	house
Dido	house
Susanah	house
Nague	house
Nimini	clears the gutters

gives Susanah 2 bitts after sex, and 1 bitt was paid to Mazerine on June 21st for the same reason. In the evening of the 3rd August he paid Little Lydde 1 bitt, and on the 17th, Susanah 2 bitts. Violet received 1 bitt after sex in a canefield on the 22nd, and on the 4th September Susanah received another 2 bitts, but on 8th March, 1784, Abba's daughter, Mary, received 4 bitts. Mary was at this time six months pregnant for Quacoo. The baby was born and died in June.

But long before turning to young Mary, her mother Abba, who was his washerwoman, had been a Thistlewood favourite. Entries in his diary for 1774-76 give insights into the nature of his relationship with Abba:

Wednesday, 15 June 1774	Gave Abba 2 bitts to buy rice, her daughter Jenny is Sick
Saturday, 4 February 1775	Gave Abba 32 bitts as compensation for the death of her sow, the support of herself and children.
Tuesday, 2 May 1775	Gave Abba 10 bitts, and told her to lay in and rest.
Saturday, 20 May 1775	Gave Abba 2 bitts for her honesty in bringing him some bitts he had lost out of his pocket.
Sunday, 28 May 1775	Sex with Abba under shed in New Garden.
Friday, 26 January 1776	Jeremy, a mason belonging to Mr. Johnson, 'is about to make a match with Abba.'
Sunday, 21 April 1776	Abba has a daughter name Phibbah, Lincoln claims fatherhood.

With respect to child bearing, Abba was Thistlewood most prolific 'breeder', – though many of her children did not survive. In 1770, her son Johnie died at the age of six and Thistlewood paid for the funeral and the entertainments that followed. In October 1771, she gave birth to a 'yellow' girl child that died after one week. The following year on 25th August, she produces another girl child, and shortly thereafter her son Neptune dies. In May 1773, Thistlewood suspects that she 'miscarried', and two years later, June 9, 1775, she had a son who died within the month. In January the following year, Abba is 'with child already'.

During this period, Thistlewood lists many of Abba's lovers – including Cudjoe who he claimed asked him leave 'to have her' to which he consented. While he seemed jealous of a relationship she developed with Jimmy, Thistlewood made at least 40 entries in his diary of sex with her during 1771, and over 140 altogether. In the majority of cases he indicated a payment of between 2 and 4 bitts to her. These frequent 'intimacies', and financial compensations, however, did not exclude Abba from Thistlewood's managerial wrath with respect to work performance. On 11th July, 1770, he warms her 'with a manatee strap for laziness in cleaning the house', and two days later flogged her again for 'neglect in cleaning the house'. He accused her of encouraging Jimmy in sleeping late, and neglecting his duties. On 3rd May, 1771, before sunrise, he goes to her house, 'catches Jimmy sleeping with her'. He puts them both 'in the bilboes and when light flogged them.' Meanwhile, he makes occasional visits to her daughter, Mary.

The listing of Abba's punishments indicates that Thistlewood because of his sexual interest in her, may have spared her what many others did not escape. For example, when Derby was accused of stealing cane, Thistlewood had him held down and ordered 'Hector' to 'shit in his mouth'. Likewise, when Port Royal ran away and was caught Hector was ordered to 'shit in his mouth' and a gag placed over it 'whilst full'. These two events occurred on May 26 and July 25, 1756 respectively. When, on the 26th and 31st July, Phillis was caught stealing canes she was ordered similarly a mouthful, with the gag, on both occasions.

Corporal punishment is more frequently documented by Thistlewood, and references appear in relation to a wide range of alleged offenses. In December 1752, Abigail and Bella received '100 lashes each' for disobedience. They ran away to Salt River to lodge a complaint with Mr Cope, their owner. Mirtilla and Nanny received a flogging on the 6th December, 1777, for eating badly prepared 'poisonous cassava', 'almost killing themselves'; Franke was flogged for disturbing Thistlewood's sleep with her domestic quarrel. On 23rd August, 1778, he instructed Jimmy to flog Dick, the driver, for not flogging the women in the field gang with force. Jimmy in turn was flogged for not 'exerting himself in flogging Dick'. Peggy was unfortunate, perhaps unlucky. On Wednesday 28th June, 1780, Strap, the driver, was whipping field hand Mary, and Peggy who got in the way was struck in her right eye. Mary received another flogging for contributing to the accident. She ran away to the mountains as a result. Strap was flogged and demoted from the rank of driver 'for lashing out Peggy's eye'. But before he relinquished office, he had to assist in fetching Mary, and was ordered to flog Maria 'for going in the rain to Mr. Wilson's Negro ground and getting sick'. The following year, 27th September, 1781, Mary was flogged again for running away but this time, in an effort to secure his property, Thistlewood 'put on her a steel collar with a few links of chain to it, and marked her left cheek 'TT' [Thomas Thistlewood]'.

Mary was too much of a free spirit for Thistlewood. As soon as she was released Mary 'set off for the mountain again'. Coobah, Sukey, and Maria were likewise branded, but on the right shoulder. Sally paid more dearly for her attempt at running away. After she received a flogging, and imprisonment for the night, Thistlewood wrote:

> Put a collar and chain about Sally's neck, also branded her with "T.T" on her right cheek. Note her private parts is torn in a terrible manner, which was discovered this morning by her having bled a great deal where she laid in the bilboes last night.

She is 'threatened a good deal' and confessed that while in town (Savanna la Mar) a sailor 'had laid with her'. Thistlewood undertook to have her 'doctored'. The event with the sailor occurred on August 22, 1768. On October 22, Thistlewood had sex with her, and writes: 'meam sup. Terr at foot of cotton tree by New Ground side, West North West from house (sed non bene).'

Like Mary, Sally was a free spirit who resisted and rebelled in ways she knew best, despite the regime of brutal punishments. Abigail was a habitual 'runner', and others, like Betty and Hagar, from time to time 'marched off' and had to be tracked down in the mountains and retrieved. Even Abba, with whom Thistlewood claimed intimate connection and trust, ran away from enslavement, for which he 'flogged her well'. But Sally could not be contained. Thistlewood's record of her presents a curious mixture of sex, floggings, and flight, which perhaps, represents, evidence of the most obvious contradiction to Thistlewood's claim of mutualism in sexual relations with enslaved women.

He provides some information about Sally's background. She was born in Congo, and was purchased by Egypt's owner in 1762 when about ten years of age. An attempt was made by Thistlewood to start her breeding when she was 17 years old. She was put to live with Chub, but the arrangement was not successful. From the beginning she showed herself to be a strong, survivalist character, taking every opportunity to promote her own interests above those of Thistlewood's. She was frequently flogged for taking and eating estate poultry, and for unauthorised visits to the kitchen store room. Thistlewood paints a portrait of her as a thief, and indicates that this was part of her roguish, insubordinate and rebellious nature. But she is one of his sexual favourites. He had sex with her on Tuesday, 3rd July, 1770, and Wednesday, 8th August , and in between, on the 7th August, he writes: 'As Sally steals everything left in the cookroom, and eats it if eatable, Phibbah had her tied with her hands behind her naked for the mosquitos to bite her tonight. She bawled out lustily, but before 9 o'clock in the evening broke loose and ran away.'

Sally is caught a few miles away, her hand still tied; once again, she is placed under 'lock and key'. Phibbah objects to being involved in punishing Sally, and suspects that Thistlewood is having sex with her. The sex sessions continue through October and November, and during the following year she ran away several times. Each time she is caught, flogged and a collar and chain applied. On one occasion, she is sent to the fields as part of the punishment. In between her marronage, sex with Thistlewood is recorded. During 1772 to 1774 he provides a narrative of – flight, flogging and sex. Sunday, 20th November, 1774, we are told that 'Sally has the clap very badly', and during 1775 the process of flight and flogging starts all over again.

Thistlewood did all he could but did not prevent Sally from taking flight. In April 1776, he decided to employ her at the distant Bluecastle property. She runs away, and goes underground in the town of Savanna-la-Mar. Solon finds her, takes her back to Egypt where she is flogged, collared for a week, and put to hard labour in the field. In June, the lock collar is placed 'upon Sally as she will not help herself, but attempts to run away.' Constant vigilance was Thistlewood's last resort. Quamina was instructed to keep watch on her during the day and Solon at night.

Sally's resistance is ineffective because of the very difficult and unsupportive external environment. The area surrounding Egypt was characterised by bog lands, swamps, and crocodile infested rivers. Oftentimes runaways were returned by canoes; many drowned in desperate attempts to cross rivers. The harshness of this world took toll upon runaway women especially those not schooled in the arts of fishing and hunting for survival. Most runaways returned voluntarily. Freedom was difficult to maintain in the wild; it was a lonely, precarious, and an uncertain existence that few persons could negotiate. Plantations were also sites where the joyful aspects of family life, cultural celebration, and other forms of social bonding took place.

Freedom without friends and family was for many runaways, the worst kind of 'slavery'. During Sally's time, the chances of successful flight to maroon communities had been substantially reduced. Maroons in the outer areas of western Jamaica, under the leadership of Captains Cudjoe and Accompong, had signed, and were honouring a Peace Treaty with the English administration since 1739. A critical trade off in this agreement was that the English would recognise the freedom and autonomy of maroons in return for their acceptance of slaveowners right to property in slaves. This meant in effect that maroons were asked to participate in the policing of slaves. They were also expected to capture and return runaways, and participate in the suppression of slave rebellions.

Cudjoe and Accompong had agreed to these terms, and Thistlewood's diary describes how highways, swamps, and mountains were effectively policed by maroon collaborators. References to them returning runaways, collecting rum, clothes, and other domestic items as rewards indicate the extent to which maroons had become a normal part of plantation life. They participated in the suppression of the 1760-61 slave revolt in Westmoreland, and sent a powerful signal to plantation slaves that the white community was not their only serious adversary.

Slave women in Westmoreland, therefore, encountered directly two forms of pro-slavery masculinities: overseers and property owners, like Thistlewood, and maroon military leaders and their field scouts. Flight from the former more often than not resulted in capture and return by the latter. In between these superordinate monuments of 'liberated' masculinity, they contended daily with physical and social abuse from the subordinate masculinity of male slaves who shared their degradation and psychological terrorisation. Male slaves not only whipped, chained, and imprisoned female slaves under managerial instruction, but in their domestic relations some brutalised them as a normal expression of their compromised patriarchy.

In this regard Thistlewood's Lincoln was a serious offender. Thistlewood is ambivalent in his views on Lincoln, but keeps him in good office, though not sparing him the rod occasionally for neglecting his duties. He was a little, Ebo man, described as being about 5′ 2″. His teeth were not filed, and he had yaws marks on his hands and feet. Thistlewood added to these decorations with stamping 'T.T' on each check and each shoulder, in addition to 'some weals on his back'. He worked as a house servant, driver, a fowler, and a fisherman. He was bought by Thistlewood in 1756 at about the age of 16 years. In March, 1760, he 'made a match' with Violet. Thistlewood approves, and they were allowed to share the same quarters. The relationship was not a loving one, and he beats her from time to time. Thistlewood is often called upon to mediate. He writes on Monday, 2nd June, 1760: 'Lincoln beat Violet again, and is very impudent and ill-minded.' Thistlewood, not surprisingly, already had sex with Violet, and recorded the event on as the 22nd, August, 1759. The quarrels between Lincoln and Violet were frequent, and his physical abuse of her intensified. In

October, 1760, Thistlewood claims that he 'got the clap from Doll', but Violet receives it from him.

Lincoln and Violet soon parted company, and within a few months he had taken up with Sukey. By 1767, it was Sukey's turn to receive beatings from him. On February 5th, he beats her 'terribly', and she is 'very bad'. Thistlewood find her 'speechless' and in great pain. Anticipating that he will receive a flogging from Thistlewood, Lincoln goes into hiding and cannot be found. When he returns, he is deranked, put into demeaning field labour for a while, but is later reinstated. Between 1760 and 1767, he also had sexual relations with Susanah Lucy – who produced a daughter (Mary) with him, and Abba. While mating with Sukey he also had a 'wife' at the neighbouring Prospect estate. He is Thistlewood's favourite male slave. He beats him occasionally, but punishes him mostly with deranking and extra labour. But he is always restored to favour, and is close to Thistlewood. In many respects they are similar characters.

Some women, nonetheless, like Phibbah, struck out, defended and expressed themselves in an extreme manner. Those who took life, or attacked white persons, paid with their own lives. They were many such instances, and the law did not recognise sex in handing down capital punishments. On 5th May, 1764, Thistlewood records: 'a Negro wench hanged at Savanna- La-Mar today. She was concerned in cutting out the sailor's tongue lately'. Women were gibbetted and hanged for violent offenses, and Thistlewood accounts of such events are vivid. The death by hanging of Polly, a slave belonging to one Dr Frazier, was particularly gruesome. She was forced to watch her 'husband', Stompe, a 'mial man', being burnt alive before the rope was placed around her own neck. Both were accused in June, 1768, of being party to a planned uprising of slaves in which whites were fearful of their lives.

Thistlewood, despite his slave 'wife', like many whites in Jamaica, had good reason to fear for his life. His sexual exploitation of slave women was a contributing factor. He was aware of the dangers in which he lived, and took occasional precautionary measures. The 1760 Westmoreland slave revolt may have been a special moment for him. On receiving news of soldiers being 'murdered by the negroes', and being told by soldiers themselves that he would 'probably be murdered in a short time', Thistlewood admitted to his 'fright' and employed four trusted armed slaves to 'watch over him all night.' 'I lay down sometimes with my clothes on and slept little', he noted, and seemed disturbed that one of the 19 black prisoners had vowed to 'eat the heart and tongue of one of the white people murdered'. He distrusts most of his own slaves and 'suspect something is brewing among them'. Driver Johnnie gets a flogging for drumming at night, and he 'gave strict charge to the negroes to make no noise', even during the night of Christmas Eve.

Eight years earlier in 1752 Thistlewood claimed to have discovered a plot by Egypt slaves to take his life, and had asked them if they planned to 'poison or murder' him. He was left in no doubt by the celebration that followed the death of his nephew John, who was engaged in a tragic sex encounter with Little Mimber, a female slave. He wrote: April 4, 1765, between 8 and 9 pm; 'heard a shell blow on the River, and afterwards in the night 2 guns fired with loud Huzza after each on the river against our negro houses, for joy that my kinsman is dead'. He had not forgotten that in December 1752 Bella and Abigail, watched 'but would not assist' him as he battled for his life with a runaway slave. Neither could he easily forget that five other men slaves and three women had passed by and saw the tussle, but refused to help him when he 'called out, murder, and help for God's sake'. He remembered one slave responding that 'he was sick, and others that they were in a hurry'. These experiences hardened his views towards slaves and contributed to the sadistic forms of punishment he meted out to males and females alike. He seemed to have taken pride, however, in the nickname given him by slaves – 'Abbaumi Appea', 'no for play'.

By September 1786, the 'play' for Thistlewood was fast approaching an end. Sick and in great pain, Phibbah sleeps with him on the 12th, the last reference he makes in his diary to an intimate encounter. Drs Drummond and Bell visit, but his declining strength confines him to bed – alone. He records feeling 'fit only to faint', but is keen to write his will in order to secure Phibbah's freedom. He does so on the 25th, and died five days later on the 30th. Legal procedures to settle Phibbah's manumission moved slowly, and were settled on the 26th, November, 1792. From his estate, £80 currency was paid to Dorrill Cope, Phibbah's owner, who accepted it and contracted to 'Manumise, Enfranchise and from every tie of Slavery or Servitude, set free a certain Negro woman slave named Phibbah, to hold the said Manumission, Liberty and Enfranchisement so thereby granted unto the said Phibbah and her future issue and increase . . .'.

Phibbah's freedom was the end product of a domestic mission that stands as evidence of the overriding value placed upon liberty by enslaved blacks. She might not have wished her freedom to be conceptualised in these terms, but effectively this was the case. While her family life with Thistlewood was set within the frames of an authoritarian, but flexible white patriarchy, and constitutes proof of slavery's ideological double standards on race relations, She knew, and was often reminded by Thistlewood, of the limits slavery had placed upon it. Phibbah understood Thistlewood. She, at once, accepted and rebelled against their relationship. She wrestled with his crudeness and sexual permissiveness, challenged the limits of his social control over her, and kept her autonomy by significantly determining the terms of his 'real' power.

Endnotes

Thomas Thistlewood's Diary is kept in Lincolnshire Records Office, England. It contains some 10,000 pages of folio. References quoted here are given by date of entry. See for an edition of the diary, Douglas Hall, *In Miserable Slavery: Thomas Thistlewood in Jamaica, 1750-86* (MacMillan, London, 1989).

PART TWO

Subscriptions

4

White Women and Freedom

Studies of the rise and fall of the Caribbean planter class have not paid any attention to the planter's wife as a socio-economic agent.[1] Ignored to an even greater extent is the white woman as owner of slaves, agricultural lands, and other forms of property. Emerging from the scholarship is the notion of white women's relative unimportance to ideological formation within the history of the colonial complex. The argument that white women were of marginal historical importance in fashioning the colonial complex is striking when placed alongside interpretations found within the historiography of slavery in the southern United States. Since the 1950s, historians have suggested that southern white women, particularly planters' wives, represented a kinder, gentler authority within the power structure of the plantation. Some historians went further and argued that the plantation mistress was the unifying element within southern patriarchy. It is through her, according to this argument, that slaves were emotionally and socially integrated into the white household, rather than rejected and used primarily as natally alienated, disposable chattel. Against this ideological background, the southern plantation mistress, Morrissey states, came to consider herself 'the conscience' of society, while her Caribbean counterpart is conceived within the literature as a person who 'contributed little and benefitted shamelessly from slave labour'.[2]

Recently, this perception of the Caribbean white women received an important boost from the work of Barbara Bush. In discussing the socio-sexual manipulation and exploitations of all women by empowered white males, she produces a typology in which women's societal roles were defined by race and colour, and prescribed by the ideological weight of racism within the colonizing tradition. While Bush recognises the privileges afforded white women within the slave system, many of which were predicated upon the subjection and brutalisation of non-white women, she seeks, nonetheless, to highlight the common ground where womanhood in general was the target and prey of a white patriarchy.[3]

Lucille Mair, moreover, in outlining a framework for detailed historical research, reinforced the parasitic view by stating that in Caribbean plantation society the white woman was a super-consumer.[4] Again, the diverse productive roles played by white women in the development and maintenance of the slave mode of production are peripheralised by the projection of an hegemonic, culturally moronic consumerism in which they were apparently imprisoned.

None of these approaches addresses adequately questions concerning white women as economic actors, managers of slave-based households, and conduits in the process of socio-ideological transmission. As a result, the traditional, stereotyped conception of the slave owner as male remains unchallenged, and the socio-economic limit of patriarchy not identified. Nowhere, until the work of Mary Butler in 1995, was there to be found within the historiography, a systematic assessment of white woman's autonomous roles as economic agents and positive participators in the formulation of pro-slavery values and institutions. Yet, there is no shortage of documentary evidence to show white women as accumulators of property and profits through involvement on their own account in commercial and service activities, and as ideological enforcers within the social organization of slave society.

In 1797, Moreau de Saint Méry noted, with respect to the eighteenth century developments in the French colony of St Domingue, that white women were initially the ideological victims of the male-managed colonisation mission. He argued that they acquiesced under intense social pressure to subscribe to the institution of black slavery by fashioning the plantation household and projecting it to slaves as the centre of all legitimate power and justice.[5] In committing themselves to this socio-economic role, however, they emerged over time as critical parts of its internal logic, and became inseparable from its cultural legacy. At the centre of Saint Méry's argument is a conception of white women's removal from the process of production and integration into the plantation system at the level of reproduction as mothers and wives. This analysis runs along the same course as that by Pollack Petchesky, who suggests that women with a large investment in reproductive relations tend to exert a conservative influence on gender-role attitudes and in so doing become critical to the consolidation or patriarchal structures and ideologies.[6]

It would be consistent, therefore, following Saint Méry, to state that once white women's socio-economic interest had become linked to the reproduction of slavery, their consciousness and social behaviour would be fashioned by its social laws, customs, and culture. As a result, the sight of creole white women examining the genitals of male slaves in the markets before making purchases, which offended the sensibilities of some European travellers, should not be considered necessarily as evidence of social degeneration, but rather as a feature of the dialectical relations between social and economic forces within the slave mode of production. Neither should such an action be considered contrary to their roles as good mothers and wives within the plantation household. Rather, it suggests that white women were acting fully within the epistemological framework of slavery by ensuring that rational market choices were made. The slave plantation enterprise, its defenders and promoters argued, was a principal expression of Renaissance rationality within the colonial realm.

It is important to recognise the contradictions inherent within the attempt of plantation patriarchs to import and impose elements of aristocratic and bourgeois domestic values upon the metamorphic creole culture of frontier civilization. These can be seen in their effort to insulate white women, as much as possible, from the aesthetically crudest aspects of slavery. They went about this by passing legislation and using specific aspects of social custom as moral strictures. For example, in order to protect white women from the hallmark of enslavement – field labour – Caribbean sugar planters by the late seventeenth century refused to employ white working-class women as fieldhands. By the end of the century most fieldhands in the English colonies were black women.[7] Also, from the beginning of the plantation system, laws were framed and implemented in order to disassociate white womanhood from the reproduction of the slave status by linking it solely to black women. When white women produced children with enslaved black men, which was not as uncommon as generally suggested, infants were born legally free. In this way the offspring of white women would not experience social relations as human property, nor suffer legal alienation from social freedom. White women, then, were constitutionally placed to participate in the slave-based world as privileged persons, and to adopt ideological positions consistent with this condition.

The linking of white womanhood to the reproduction of freedom meant that the entire ideological fabric of the slave-based civilisation was conceived in terms of sex, gender and race. This was the only way that black slavery and white patriarchy could coexist without encountering major legal contradictions. As a result, it became necessary for white males to limit the sexual freedom of white women and at the same time to enforce the sexual exploitation of black women as a 'normal benefit' of masterhood. In so doing white males valued black women's fertility solely in terms of the reproduction of labour for the plantation enterprise, and placed a premium on white women's maternity for its role in the reproduction of patriarchy.

The 'victim' approach to the study of white women in the slave formation, therefore, has severe conceptual limitations. These can be identified immediately by an empirical assessment of the white women's autonomous participation in the shaping of economic and social relations. The demographic data, for instance, show the extent to which slave ownership correlated to differences of class, race and sex. While white males were the predominant owners of slaves in the plantation sector, the same cannot be said for the urban sector. White women were generally the owners of small properties, rather than large estates, but their small properties were more proportionately stocked with slaves than the large, male owned properties.

In 1815, white women owned about 24 percent of the slaves in St Lucia; 12 per cent of the slaves on properties of more than 50 slaves, and 48 per cent of the properties with less than ten slaves. In Barbados in 1817, less than five of the holdings of 50 slaves or more were owned by white women, but they owned 40 per cent of the properties with less than ten slaves. White women were 50 per cent of the owners of slaves in Bridgetown, the capital, on properties stocked with less than 10 slaves. In general, 58 per cent of slaveowners in the capital were female, mostly white, though some were also 'coloured' and black. Overall, women owned 54 percent of the slaves in the town. The typology of slave owning in the West Indies as a whole shows a male predominance in the rural areas, and a female predominance in the urban areas where property sizes were relatively smaller.[8]

White women also owned more female slaves than male slaves. The extensive female ownership of slaves in the towns was matched by the unusually high proportion of females in the slave population; female slaveowners owned more female slaves than male slave owners. The evidence shows, furthermore, that in Bridgetown in 1817, the sex ratio (males per 100 females) of slaves belonging to males was more than double that for female slaveowners. The majority of slaves in the town were owned by male slave owners. The sex ratio of slaves belonging to males was 111 and that for slaves belonging to females 49. The sex ratio of slaves belonging to white females, when separated from other non-white females, was higher at 53. For Berbice in 1819, slaves owned by males had a sex ratio of 132, while those owned by females had a ratio of only 81.[9]

From these data the image that emerges of the white female slaveowner is that she was generally urban, in possession of less than ten slaves, the majority of whom were female. That female slaveowners generally owned female slaves, indicates the nature of enterprises, and hence labour regimes, managed and owned by white women. It is reasonable, then, to argue that any conceptualisation of urban slavery, especially with reference to the experiences of enslaved black women, should proceed with an explicit articulation of white women as principal slaveowners. Such a departure is an analytically necessary precondition for the correct identification of white women within the slave owning ethos, and for a more rigorous assessment of urban-rural differentiations within the slave mode of production. Furthermore, it would enhance a real situational understanding which is necessary for the theoretical interpretation of black women's slavery experience, by linking it also to the power and authority of white matriarchs.

An empirical understanding of this reality should be presented against the background of the sexual composition of white communities. Demographic structures and patterns indicated and determined the nature of white women's functions as economic and social agents. Reports for the eighteenth century, for example, illustrate significant differences in the sex-structure of Caribbean white communities. Statements ranging from the chronic shortage of white women in Jamaica to an abundance in Barbados have been used by contemporaries to account for important socio-political variations between these two colonies. In Jamaica, white women constituted no more than 40 per cent of the white community up to 1780, while as early as 1715 white women outnumbered white men in Barbados by one percent, and by seven percent in 1748, levelling off at about fifty-two per cent female for the remainder of the slavery period.

Eighteenth-century observers, such as William Dickson, argued persuasively that the white female majority in Barbados tempered the brutish frontier mentality of white men and promoted at an early stage a mature hegemonic paternalism. By 'civilizing' the white community in many respects, he suggests, that the overwhelming presence of white women tended towards the gradual amelioration of slave relations. Conversely, it has been suggested that the shortage of white women in eighteenth-century Jamaica explains in part the rapid rise of the mulatto population, and accounts for the undeveloped state of the planter households, as well as the violence endemic to relations between white and black males, much of which resulted from competition for black females.[10] More importantly, however, the larger numbers of white women in Barbados meant that many remained unmarried, untied to plantation households, and financially independent of males. As a result, there was a greater tendency for white women in Barbados to participate in the market economy as autonomous agents, and to establish independent accumulationist strategies based upon the ownership and possession of slaves.

Explaining the structure and distribution of white women's slave holdings requires, however, a precise grasp of the socio-economic forces operating within the white community. For example, it requires an understanding of the extent to which white women were subordinate to white men within the domestic economy, constitutional provisions, and social culture. Indeed, white women were not 'free', in the sense that white men were, to participate in the polity and market economy as unrestricted colonising agents. On marriage, unless complicated trust arrangements were made, their properties were legally transferred to their husbands, an alienation of resources which ensured their subordination to men and promoted their second class status within the 'free' society.

Many unmarried white women were forced to find whatever niche was available within the market economy in order to make an independent living. Generally, most of what they found was in areas that propertied white males considered inadequate, in terms of low rate of returns, or socially dishonourable. Many operated on the periphery of the urban economy, dominating the ownership and management of enterprises in the service sector such as taverns, sex-houses, slave rental services, petty shopkeeping and huckstering. Small scale urban slave rental businesses were typically controlled by single white women, who leased domestic servants for miscellaneous household tasks. These businesses operated with a greater female than male labour force which accounts for the relatively larger number of female slaves owned by white women in the towns.

Invariably, then, white women's businesses were concentrated in the informal sector, especially in those areas that bordered on the illicit and illegal as defined by white male officials. In most Caribbean societies, prostitution was illegal, but white women made a thriving business from the rental of black and coloured women for sexual services in the port towns.[11] The hiring of slave women for various purposes was an integral part of the urban and rural labour markets. Many white and free-coloured families, and quite often single white women, made their living from the wage earnings of hired female slaves who worked not only as prostitutes but as nannies, nurses, cooks, washerwomen, hucksters, seamstresses, and general labourers. The hiring out of women for sex ran parallel to these markets.[12]

Infants of slave prostitutes were owned by their mothers' owners and often sold when weaned as an additional product.[13] At the end of the eighteenth century weaned slave infants fetched up to ten dollars local currency on English Caribbean markets. The accumulation of such lump sums of capital also accounted in part for white women's preference for female slaves. The economics of slave reproduction suggests the rationality of a market preference for female slaves, since several streams of return could be derived from such an investment. The marketing of black women's sexuality, and the sale of their progeny, were therefore associated directly with the economic accumulation strategies of white women, and ought to be considered an integral part of the overall capitalist exploitation of slave labour.[14]

This evidence can be interpreted to suggest that many black women probably suffered their greatest degree of social exploitation at the hands of white women, since the direct sale of women's sexuality for accumulation purposes represents a crucial distinction between the general experience of plantation and urban slaves. It is precisely in this area that the inhumane forces of slavery entered the inner world of women with its greatest devastation. For this reason, it becomes problematic to root an empirical argument which suggests that white women might have been more humane owners of slaves.

The pro-slavery subscription of white women was seen by some contemporaries as emerging from their realisation that non-white women competed effectively for the attention, favours and resources owned and controlled by white men. White women were said to react with jealousy to patterns of white male sexuality, and invariably directed their anger against non-white women.[15] Many contemporaries suggest that white males in the Caribbean possessed a sexual preference for mulatto or brown-skinned black women over white women. One individual ironically, explained this preference in terms of white males cohabiting with coloured women 'at a very early age' under the guidance and encouragement of their mothers.[16] White women, according to this observation, played a critical role in shaping the ideological content of white male's sexual attitude towards black women.[17]

Bayley's observations in the 1820s perhaps betrayed the white male's norm when he spoke of the attractiveness of 'coloured' women.[18] Bayley and Waller, who visited the West Indies between the 1790s and the 1820s, suggest that white males fathered thousands of socially fatherless mulatto daughters, many of whom on becoming adults, 'enjoyed' levels of recognition and attention unknown to their mothers.[19] Waller wrote at length about the critical role played by white women in the reproduction of white male sexual ideology.[20] Elizabeth Fenwick's letters from Barbados illustrate the extent to which white women, even unwittingly, shared and contributed to the racist ideologies and values of the plantation world.[21] Fenwick gives detailed and critical insights into the colony's slave-based social culture. Her primary problem related to the management of domestic slaves, most of whom were females. Undoubtedly, Fenwick's judgement is that of an Anglocentric foreigner, but her keen eye renders her evidence most valuable.[22] (See Chapter 5)

Acts of extreme cruelty to black women by white women are documented in much of the eighteenth and nineteenth–century literature. European travellers seemed rather surprised and disturbed that white women should display attitudes to human suffering and impose punishments that held them indistinguishable from their male counterparts. Bayley, for instance, deplored the standard forms of torture used on slaves, but concluded from his four years' residence in the West Indies: 'I will state, however, my conviction that female owners are more cruel than male; their revenge is more durable and their methods of punishment more refined, particularly towards slaves of their own sex.'[23] If Bayley's conclusion erred on the side of popular stereotype, David Turnbull correctly located the expression of white female authority within the specific context of the overriding need for effective slave control. Reporting from his experiences of Cuban slave society, he stated in 1840:

> The mistress of many a great family in Havana will not scruple to tell you that such is the proneness of her people (slaves) to vice and idleness, she finds it necessary to send one or more of them once a month to the whipping post, not so much on account of any positive delinquency, as because without these periodic advertisements the whole family would become unmanageable, and the master and mistress would lose their authority.[24]

Such policies were consistent with the material and social interest of the white community in general, and should not be considered surprising, given that white women participated fully in the accumulationist and elitist colonial culture that depended upon the successful control of slave labour.

Mary Prince, the only West Indian female slave who, to the best of our knowledge, produced an autobiography, gave an account of her mistress that confirms impressions presented by Turnbull. She wrote:

> She taught me to do all sorts of household work; to wash and bake, pick cotton and wool, and wash floors, and cook. And she taught me (how can I ever forget it!) more things than these; she caused me to know the exact differences between the smart [inflicted pain] of the rope, the cart-whip, and the cow-skin, when applied to my naked body by her own cruel hand. And there was scarcely any punishment more dreadful than the blows I received on my face and head from her hard heavy fist. She was a fearful woman, and a savage mistress to her slaves.[25]

An important value of Prince's account has to do with the nature of relations between female slaves and mistresses. 'Both my master and mistress,' she stated, 'seemed to think that they had a right to ill-use [the slaves] at their pleasure.' This is clearly illustrated in the case of the punishment of her friend, Hetty:

> One of the cows had dragged the rope away from the stake to which Hetty had fastened it, and got loose. My master flew into a terrible passion, and ordered the poor creature to be stripped quite naked, notwithstanding her pregnancy, and to be tied up to a tree in the yard. He then flogged her as hard as he could lick, both with the whip and the cow-skin, till she was all over streaming in blood. He rested, and

> then beat her again and again. Her shrieks were terrible. The consequence was that poor Hetty was brought to bed before her time, and was delivered after severe labour of a dead child. She appeared to recover after her confinement, so far that she was repeatedly flogged by both master and mistress afterwards . . . till the water burst out of her body and she died.[26]

Throughout her narrative, Prince argues that the execution of owners' authority was not affected by their sex, and gave no indication of being surprised by the pro-slavery role of white women.

Since the plantation economy was capitalist by nature, and market forces generally took precedence over the ideological need for racial solidarity at the frontier, many white women found themselves in a labouring relationship to the planter dominated economic system. For those in the rural sector, the custom was to attempt subsistence farming on 'rab' lands not used for sugar but denied the blacks. Many of these 'poor-white' women, noted Dickson at the end of the eighteenth century, could be found tilling small patches of land without the assistance of slaves, and walking 'many miles loaded with the produce of their little spots, which they exchange in the towns for such European goods as they can afford to purchase'.[27]

The relationship between black and white female hucksters was complex, and was never far removed from legislative considerations. Dickson commented that their marketing patterns and associated customs were similar in many ways. White women typically carried baskets on their heads and children strapped on their hips in the traditional African manner, which was perhaps due to some degree of cross-cultural fertilisation between the two groups. For Dickson, this illustrated the extent to which slave women defined the behavioural patterns and customs of huckstering. He also believed that white female hucksters depended to a large extent upon their trading association with slaves, especially those who operated retail outlets in the towns.

The intimacy of relations between working-class white women and slaves inevitably found expression in socio-sexual activity and family formation. In the formative decades of slave society, when social ideologies were not yet fully rooted, the evidence of sexual relations between black men and white women was recorded. In the St Michael parish register for 4 December 1685, for example, a marriage is entered between 'Peter Perkins, a negro, and Jane Long, a white woman'. The 1715 census shows that they had a son; three other children of such relations were recorded as: Elizabeth X, a mulatto born of a white woman; Mary K, the daughter of a white woman and begotten by the extract of a negro; John L, a mulatto born of a white woman.[28]

Table 4:1 **The Inter-racial family ties of white women in the parish of St Phillip, Barbados, in 1715**

Name	*Age*	*Description given in Census*
John Goddard	40	A mulatto, born of a white woman
Jane Goddard	32	White, husband a mulatto
Elizabeth Shepherd	52	White, husband a mulatto
Thomas Goddard	30	Mulatto, born of a white woman
Ann Goddard	30	White woman, husband a mulatto
Mary Shepherd	13	Mother a white woman, father a negro
John Wake	13	Father negro, mother white
Elizabeth Wake	8}	
Simon Kitteridge	18	Son of a white woman and coloured man
Sarah Avery	15	Mulatto, born of a white woman
Charles Sergent	36	Mother white, father a mulatto
Mary Sergent	31	White woman, husband a negro
Elizabeth Sinckler	48	Born of a white woman and negro man

Source: **Census of Barbados, 1715: Barbados Archives**

During the mid-century, however, as the slave society matured, the role of racial and gender ideologies became increasingly important to the white male elite as tools of social control, and reports of such relations more or less vanished from official documents. Black men faced punishments such as castration, dismemberment, and execution for having sexual relations with white women, who in turn were socially disgraced and ostracised. In this way, the sexual freedom of white women was curtailed, and white males reported no problems with their authority system in this area for the remainder of the slavery period.

Commonplace within the historiography is the assertion that the white male sought to prevent the social access of black males to the white female in order to project her as a symbol of moral purity and ideal domesticity. Indeed, such an interpretation has contributed to the spawning of stereotypes about the lives of white women and the views of white men within the development of patriarchal ideology. Though it is unnecessary to deny the validity of such claims, emphasis should be placed upon the white male's principal concern which was to limit the size of the free non-white group within society. Since the most natural way in which this could be done was to greatly reduce the incidence of white women's cohabitation with slave men, it was logical for white men to see the white woman as an avenue to freedom for blacks that had to be blocked.

By restricting the sexual lives of white women, then, white males moved to ensure that the progeny of black males were not lost to the slave gangs, while at the same time maintaining the status of freedom as the most prized commodity within their society. Evidence of this reasoning can be found in the nature of race relations during the formative years of slavery, and in white men's indifference to black men's sexual access to white prostitutes who were considered outside of the fertility considerations of the slave régime.

The obvious influence of African social culture upon European and creole white women did not meet with the approval of visitors to the 'Indies'. Edward Long was saddened by the cultural deterioration he thought white women experienced from 'constant intercourse' with black household servants. He suggests that these women 'insensibly adopted' the dress, speech, and manners of blacks, which rendered them further removed from European culture than the colour or their skin suggests. According to Long:

> We may see in some of these places, a very fine young woman awkwardly dangling her arms, with the air of a negro servant lolling almost the whole day upon beds or settees, her head muffed up with two or three handkerchiefs, her dress loose, and without stays. At noon, we find her employed in gobbling pepper-pot, seated on the floor, with her sable hand-maids around her.[29]

Maria Nugent, the famous wife of a Jamaican Governor, reported that creole white women were 'not untainted' by their close relations to blacks, and implied, like Long, their cultural inferiority to their European counterpart.[30]

The white female voice was rarely heard on issues of this nature. They certainly did not organise an anti-slavery core within the islands, nor did they exert any special influence upon the reconstruction of social life after emancipation. Since they were excluded from holding public office and participating in political administration, their views are absent from official annals. Even when disturbing crises, such as slave revolts, surrounded and impacted upon their lives, their voices were silenced by officialdom and subordinated even to those of free non-white males. After revolts, for example, when evidence was submitted to official commissions, their views were not sought; neither was it assumed that they were in possession of a gender-specific interpretation of events that was valuable.

Since white women in the Caribbean did not emerge as part of an anti-slavery front, unlike their counterparts in the United States, it would be folly to expect manumission records to indicate that they were more active participants in the promotion of black freedom. Available data suggest that white women were less inclined to manumit their slaves than white men. These records show that the typical manumitter was a white male, while the typical manumitted slave was a female domestic. Since white women owned a significant proportion of domestic slaves, it can be inferred that white women were less inclined than white men to free slaves. Most white males who freed their female slaves did so as a result of repayment for socio-sexual services rendered. Since white women might not have benefitted from slave owning in these ways (to the same degree) part of the explanation for the divergence might also be found in the fact that white males were better able to pay the large fees involved in manumission procedures.

The images that emerged of white women as slaveowners in the Caribbean context, then, suggest that they were generally pro-slavery, socially illiberal, and economically exploitative of black women. They were assigned the primary role of symbolic matrons of the slavery culture, but were also active subscribers in their own right in the socio-economic accumulations that slavery made possible. They made valuable contributions to the development of the colonial economy and society, not only as the domestic partners of planters, merchants, overseers, and managers, but also as large and small-scale owners of slaves and other forms of property. Their participation in the consolidation and defence of the slave system, then, cannot be explained solely in terms of their dependent status – social and economic victim of patriarchy. Rather, emphasis should also be placed in their autonomous survival strategies within the unstable and socially hostile colonial culture fashioned by competitive market forces.

Finally, the theoretical discourse on the relations between race, sex, gender and class forces in slave society requires an empirically sound grasp of the process of socio-economic construction and transformation. The search for such an understanding should involve a careful assessment of the diverse and complex manifestations of patriarchal ideologies, the precise location of women within productive structures, as well as their reproductive relations within households and communities. This research should then be informed by the culturally embracing process of social creolisation in which European immigrants were transformed at the frontier into natives who possessed an increasingly distinct value system and sensibility.

Endnotes

1 Beckles, *Natural Rebels, op. cit.;*

2 See for example, Catherine Clinton, *The Plantation Mistress: Women's World in the Old South,* New York, 1982; C. L . R James, *The Black Jacobins: Toussaint L'Ouverture and the San Domingo Revolution,* New York, 1963 pp. 30-31; Morrissey, *Slave Women, op. Cit.,* p. 150. Barbara Bush, 'White "Ladies"', *op. cit.;* Joan Gunderson, 'The Double Bonds of Race and Sex: Black and White Women in a Colonial Virginia Parish', *Journal of Southern History,* 52, 1986, pp. 351-72.

3 Bush, *Slave Women,* op cit., pp. 8, 134. See Mary Butler, *The Economics of Emancipation: Jamaica and Barbados, 1823-1843* (Chapel Hill, University of North Carolina Press, 1995).

4 Mair, 'An Historical Study, *op. cit.;* The Rebel Woman, *op. cit.;* 'The Arrival of Black Women', *Jamaica Journal,* 9: 2 and 3, Feb 1975; see also Jacqueline Jones, '"My Mother was Much of a Woman". Black Women, work, and the Family under Slavery', *Feminist*

Studies, 8, 1982, pp. 235-69. Marietta Morrissey, 'Women's Work', *op. cit.*, pp. 330-67.

5 Moreau de Saint Mèry, *Description, op. cit.*, p. 10; *Slave Women*, op cit., p. 150.

6 See R. Pollack Petchesky, 'Reproduction and Class Divisions among Women', in A. Swerdlow and H. Lessinger (eds), *Class, Race and Sex: The Dynamics of Control*, Boston, 1983, pp. 221-31; Alwin Thornton and D. Camburn, 'Causes and Consequences of Sex-Roles, Attitudes and Attitude Change'. *American Sociological Review*, 48, 1983, pp. 211-27; Alwin Thornton and D. Freedman, 'Sex-Role Socialisation: A Focus on Women' in J. Freeman (ed) *Women: A Feminist Perspective*, California 1984, pp. 157-62.

7 See Hilary Beckles, *White Servitude, op. cit.*, pp. 115-68; 'Black Men in White Skins', *op. cit.*, pp. 5-22; *Natural Rebels, op. cit.*, pp. 24-54.

8 Higman, *Slave Populations, op. cit.*, p. 107.

9 *Ibid.*

10 See for the structure of the Barbados and Jamaica white population, Beckles, *Natural Rebels, op. cit.*, p. 15; *Black Rebellion in Barbados: The Struggle Against Slavery, 1727-1838*, Bridgetown, 1985, pp. 58-9; William Dickson, *Mitigation of Slavery* [1814] (Westport, Negro University Press edition 1970), pp. 439-41.

11 Parliamentary Papers, 1791, vol. 34, Testimony of Evidence of Captain Cook, p. 202; also, evidence of Mr. Husbands, p. 13.

12 Major Wyvill, 'Memoirs of an Old Officer', 1815, p. 386, MSS. Division, Library of Congress.

13 Waller, *A Voyage, op. cit.*, pp. 20-21.

14 Fenwick, (ed.) *The Fate of the Fenwicks, op. cit.*, pp. 9. 169.

15 See Bush, *Slave Women, op. cit.*, pp. 44, 114.

16 Waller, *A Voyage, op. cit.*, p. 19.

17 F. W. Bayley, *Four Years' Residence, op. cit.*, p. 493; Bush, *Slave Women, op. cit.*, p. 115.

18 Bayley, *Four Years' Residence*, pp. 493-4.

19 See Bush 'White "Ladies"', *op. cit.*

20 Waller, *A Voyage, op cit.*, p. 20.

21 Fenwick, *The Fate of the Fenwicks, op. cit.*, pp. 163-4.

22 *Ibid.*

23 Bayley, *Four Years' Residence, op. cit.*, pp. 417-8.

24 David Turnbull, *Travels in the West*, (London 1840), p. 53.

25 Moira Ferguson (ed), *The History of Mary Prince: A West Indian Slave, Related by herself* [1831], (London, Pandora 1987), p. 56.

26 *Ibid.*

27 Dickson, *Letters, op. cit.*, p. 41.

28 St. Michael Parish Register, vol. 1A, RL 1/1, Barbados Archives; see also, Richard Dunn, *Sugar and Slaves*, pp. 255-6. Census of Barbados, 1715. Barbados Archives.

29 Long, *The History of Jamaica*, vol. 2, pp. 412-13; see also 278-80. Bush, *Slave Women, op. cit.*, p. 25.

30 Bush, *Ibid.*

5

Fenwick's Fortune

A White Woman's West India Dream

Surprisingly, opportunities have not always been taken to contest, from the perspective of gender, well-known dominant concepts in the recent historiography of Caribbean slavery.[1] Debates that should arise, for example, from feminist criticisms of privileged texts, such as Richard Pares' 1950 seminal A West India Fortune, have not taken place. One result is that mythic representations of women's experiences and identities within the literature have survived as stable conceptual constructs outside the reach of critical discourse. 'A West India Fortune' illustrates this state of affairs, and is selected here as a point of departure only in so far as it illuminates an area of interpretation not visited by scholars of either women's or gender history.[2]

Pares elegantly recounts the journey of the Pinneys, a financially-broken yeoman family from Dorset in England, as they accumulate an enormous amount of wealth in the Leeward Islands from the end of the seventeenth century to the mid-eighteenth century. It is an account of the imperial white, nonconformist, protestant male as he transformed, and is reshaped by, the West Indian colonial frontier that had made black slavery the basis of all its economic and social arrangements. The Pinney men, starting with Azariah, and continuing with his son and grandson, are presented as successful representatives of England's superior entrepreneurship, as well as the creators and patriarchs of a dynamic and profitable economic system that contributed in no small measure to the revolutionary refashioning of the modern world. The Pinney women, however, are located, when identified, on the margins of the entire accumulation affair. The general thrust of the analysis, furthermore, suggests that the lure of a West India fortune, which had gripped the heart and soul of the propertied classes in English society, had engendered positive responses only from enterprising menfolk.[3]

Little is known about the motives and experiences of white women from the 'middling classes' as participants in the West India enterprise. During the seventeenth century, when the 'sugar plantation' revolution swept the islands of the Lesser Antilles, labouring white women figured prominently in the records of indentured servitude. The collapse of the white indenture system, under the impact of black slavery, meant the removal of the principal mechanism used by labouring white women to settle in the West Indies. Those who came were mostly driven by destitution, and arrived as bonded labourers without social honour and with minimal legal protection. Most of them worked on the sugar estates, and apart from the few who secured social mobility through marriage or other relations with propertied white males, they emerged from bondage only to contribute to the 'poor white' lumpen proletariat that eked out a living in the 'outback' of the plantations and inhabited the urban slums.[4] Much less, furthermore, is known of those white women who, as part of the rural gentry and urban middling classes, chose the West Indies as a place to repair broken domestic economies or pursue new fortunes.

In this chapter, the journey to Barbados in the early nineteenth century of a 'respectable', English, female-headed family is placed at the centre of the discourse represented by Pares' text. The purpose of the examination is not so much to destabilise his argument and assumptions, but to advance a proposition that speaks critically about the way social experiences of women have been historicised and how as a result the history of West Indian slave society has been written. To some extent, it is motivated by a considerable conceptual curiosity, and driven, in part, by an unshakeable suspicion about the ideological perspectives that have informed and fashioned the canon of West Indian historiography. By placing a gender history reading within the analytical 'calaloo' of race, colour, class and identity, not only is the white woman called forth – to account rather than by accounts – but also the complexities of human experiences involved in pursuing West India fortunes can be discerned.[5]

Unlike Azariah Pinney, preacher, small landowner and lacemaker, who found himself marooned in Nevis in 1685 serving a ten-year transportation sentence for his involvement in Monmouth's Rebellion, Eliza Fenwick arrived in Barbados in 1811 seeking to repair her family's domestic economy that had been shattered by the separation of her parents, John and Elizabeth Fenwick. Her father had been a business failure, leaving the family ruined and at the financial mercy of concerned friends. While he continued to fall deeper into debt to various London money-lenders, and occasionally going off to Ireland on unsuccessful business ventures, his wife, adult daughter and teenage son eventually became involved in the West India enterprise as colonists'.[6]

The collapse of Mrs Fenwick's marriage forced her to consider ways to generate an income in order to 'extricate' herself from the 'torture' of seeing her husband 'perpetually struggling against a tide that so fettered and manicled, he could not stem'.[7] She considered turning a profit from writing, but recognised that the distress caused by marital separation made this difficult. Finally, she resolved to open a school hoping to earn a living from teaching. Eliza, meanwhile, who had also considered teaching as a career, was well on her way to being a full time actress, performing at various theatres in the West End. Resolved to 'work and starve together' mother and daughter prepared collective survival strategies.[8] In 1811, after failing to secure parts for the Haymarket season, Eliza, now 23 years old, became distressed by her financial uncertainty. It was then that she encountered the colonial world in the person of Mr Dyke, a businessman from Barbados, who sought to contract her for his new theatre in Bridgetown.

The Barbados proposal, the Fenwicks thought, was far-fetched and not received with much enthusiasm. While it promised 'some remuneration in money', there was the burden of doubt about inhabiting an unknown colonial society.[9] Ireland was ruled out, but as Mr Dyke pressed his claims, Eliza and her mother soon considered themselves as having little choice. They discussed at length the nature of the Barbados undertaking, and sought counsel with London residents who knew West Indian conditions. It would be a family migration, pioneered by Eliza; her mother, and Orlando her younger brother, would follow. It would change the course of the family's life in ways unimaginable. A Bridgetown theatre was a far cry from the Covent Garden and Haymarket Eliza had idealised, but it was an opportunity to gain further experience, promote her reputation as an actress and generate a reliable income. The financial package seemed agreeable. She would be assigned exclusively to Mr Dyke's theatre for eight months and tour Antigua with the company for the rest of the year. A salary of 6 guineas per week, paid weekly, was offered, in addition to lodgings at Mr Dyke's home for 2 guineas per week. On tour to Antigua the company would pay the expense of the voyage. An undertaking was made in writing by the 'Committee of Gentlemen Subscribers' to the theatre with respect to the payment of salaries. The Committee was chaired by Judge Beckles, son of the Attorney-General for the colony.[10]

Eliza arrived at Barbados, 'the Land of Promise', 'heaven', on 20 December 1811. The theatre, 'not half-finished', was scheduled to open on the night of Saturday, 28th December, with a play entitled *The West Indian and the Spoiled Child*. She described it as a 'handsome building on the outside, but is painted within in every colour that ever was invented or thought of. In the middle of the ceiling, over the "Pit" is a great daub – King George riding in a chariot thro' the sea'. The 'prevailing colours', she noted, 'are crimson, scarlet, dark blue and dark green – very well chosen for a cold country!' Immediately, she had reason to question the details of Mr Dyke's financial calculations. The row of boxes, pit and gallery, when full, would produce £500. The green room and dressing rooms were unfinished, and would be small.[11]

These revised calculations, in addition to other unforeseen expenditures, caused Eliza to reassess her financial projections. In a letter to her mother dated 18th December 1811, she sets out her condition:

> I shall not make a fortune here the first year at any rate, if I do afterwards, I have half a hundred expenses I never dreamed of. I have been obliged to buy my bedstead. It cost 20 Dollars. There is not a bit of furniture in my room but that, a table and one chair, and I fancy if I have anymore I must buy it myself. Drawers are £40 the set, so they are put out of the question. You may suppose how much I am distress'd being obliged to keep everything in my trunk . . . Oh my money![12]

The 'seasoning period' was, however, short, and early in the next year Eliza seemed settled and surer of her financial affairs. 'Everything', she told her mother, 'turned out better than I had any hope of,' and 'I say this is the happiest period of my life.'[13] 'I am sure', she commented of Mr Dyke, 'if ever there was an honest man in the world he is one', and 'At the theatre I am the first personage and of course comfortable there., 'I am certain (I think I am),' she concluded, 'that I shall reach the top. I have here every advantage (but one), and by devoting every hour I can call my own to the serious study of the stage . . . I shall be advancing our interests better than by any present money I might gain by teaching.'[14]

Eliza was now ready to sponsor the immigration of her mother and brother. 'England has discarded us,' she proclaimed, and the choice was one of destination – America or Barbados. 'Yes, indeed, you must come here, ' she implored her mother; 'I am sure there is a fortune waiting for you here, and easily earned. I have no time to teach. You would do wonders.' She instructed her mother to bring her brother, Orlando. 'We can keep him for three years,' she advised, 'But he must never become a Manager of Slaves.'[15] Mrs Fenwick outlined the details of her daughter's proposal to her friend, Mary Hays:

> Eliza with the beginning of the new year began the project of a school in Barbados for me, upon the prudent consideration of making an experiment upon the professions of those who had loudly and long declared that if she and her mother open a school on the island, the greatest encouragement would be given, and that it must inevitably be a most profitable undertaking.[16]

She had earlier agreed to take 'a year to consider the plans', which seemed attractive bearing in mind that supporting Orlando financially was beyond her reach, and that there was hope he could 'study and practise the Laws of Courts' in Barbados.

On 28 October, 1814, Mrs Fenwick and her son arrived in Barbados.[17] Eliza was married to a Barbadian and had a daughter. She described the colony, as her daughter had done three years earlier, as the 'Land of Promise'.[18] In December, she informed Mary Hays:

> Our prospects, I am assured, are excellent, and one of the wealthiest men of the Island told me yesterday the only danger was of our having too large a school. Eliza and Mr Rutherford [her husband] are no less sanguine on the subject, but the dearness of living and the hideous expense of servants create fears in my mind ....Orlando is quite well, but I was ill-informed in London respecting the ease of placing him in a Commercial House here. There are at this moment six young men of families here waiting for a probable vacancy in a great Merchant's office, and another merchant, to whom I brought letters, tells me he is not only overstocked with young clerks, several of whom have given £100 premiums for their admissions.[19]

Notwithstanding the unfavourable prospects for settling a career path for Orlando, Mrs Fenwick shared the optimism other people expressed about her own circumstances as an educational entrepeneur. 'Prosperous I am likely to be', she professed, but the social process of wealth accumulation involved 'various and harassing changes' and a 'feeling of desolateness'.[20]

Within six months the number of pupils attending Mrs Fenwick's school for girls increased from 14 to 30, with the possibility of further increases. These were all day students, but several applications were made by parents for boarders. She was soon on the search for a suitable house to meet the demand for boarding. These developments occurred despite her admission that 'the school's prices are high, very high'. Day students, she stated, paid from 'ten to thirty or forty guineas per annum, according to what they learn'. These charges, she added, 'are much higher than the other schools (which are to me surprisingly numerous)', but they kept her 'in the higher and wealthy classes', thus securing her 'from bad debts'. The school she described as being 'in fashion', and 'those rich families who do not send their daughters to England, give them to us'.[21]

The 'Barbados project' was going well for Eliza and her mother. The school was proving a business success, and projections for the future indicated that within two years the family would be 'clear of all debt, including the money sunk into . . . passage and preparation'.[22] Orlando, now 17 years old, had finally secured a placement for three years with a young merchant in Bridgetown who had extensive business interests in other West Indian colonies. In addition, Eliza was offered '24 guineas per week and clear benefits to join the Company performing in Jamaica'.[23] In July 1815 Mrs Fenwick reported 37 pupils, including one boarder at £100 per year, and 'several others spoken of as coming'. The family had moved into 'a very fine house' in order to accommodate the boarders, and the expectation of having 50 students by the end of the year was considered reasonable. The day school was now 'bringing in nearly £800 per annum'.[24] 'Thus, my dear Mary,' Mrs Fenwick wrote, 'our experiment has been attended with the happiest results'.[25]

The Fenwick enterprise cannot be accounted for within the dominant historiographic paradigms that focus exclusively upon the financial activities and entrepreneurship of white, agro-commercial males. Negating the significance of white women as colonising agents making autonomous ideological, social and economic inputs into the colonial system has resulted in a conceptual homogenising of the white community's experiences. The Fenwicks, like other white women, played important roles in shaping the urban and rural milieu of colonial society. As slave-owners, entrepreneurs and pro-slavery ideologues, they demonstrated by their ideas and social and economic actions considerable support for the colonial mission as an opportunity for betterment.

As businesswomen, their search for autonomy within the structures of colonialism entailed the staging of various forms of contests. The militarism of empire and the patriarchal culture of plantation commercial organisations had assigned to white women a supportive, but not independent, role. These roles can be seen in the efforts of colonial patriarchs to insulate them, as much as possible, from the aesthetically crudest aspects of slavery. For example, in order to protect propertyless white women from the hallmark of enslavement, field labour, slave-owners were refusing by the late seventeenth century to employ them as fieldhands.

The society which the Fenwicks entered was already settled in its ideological representations of gender and sexual divisions of labour. Considerations of race and class had fractured any unitary concept of womanhood, and social relations were understood and shaped within this context. By the middle of the eighteenth century, most fieldhands in the English colonies were black women. In addition, from the beginning of the slave system laws were framed and implemented in order to dissociate white womanhood from the reproduction of children of slave status by linking it solely to the progeny of black women. The children produced by white women with enslaved black men, which was not as common as generally believed, were born legally free. In this way the offspring of white women could not experience the status of human property, nor suffer legal alienation from social freedom.

The linking of white womanhood to the reproduction of free status, the Fenwicks understood, meant that the entire ideological fabric of slave societies was conceived in terms of sex, gender and race. This was the easiest way for black slavery and white patriarchy to coexist without encountering major legal contradictions. They also knew that these relations made it necessary for white males to suppress and dominate white women, limit their sexual freedom, and at the same time, enforce the sexual exploitation of black women.

The 'victim' thesis that seeks to explain the experiences of white women like the Fenwicks has severe conceptual limitations. These can be identified immediately by an empirical assessment of white women's autonomous participation in the shaping of economic and social relations. The Fenwicks' were representative in many ways of the small business culture developed by white women in Bridgetown and other West Indian towns. It is necessary, therefore, to place them within its economic and social context.

The demographic and property data, for instance, show the extent to which slave ownership correlated with differences of class, race and sex. Recent work by Mary Butler has shown that the Barbados slave registers for 1834 list 27 women as owners of sugar plantations comprising 6,241 acres and at least 3,870 slaves. They accounted for 11 per cent of the 241 persons who owned estates of more than 50 acres and supervised the affairs of 11 per cent of the total of 307 plantations of that size. At emancipation, when slave-owners were compensated for the loss of their slave property, their claims accounted for 37 per cent of the total submitted. Likewise, in Jamaica, Butler shows that white women owned or controlled approximately 5 per cent of the estates, and several ranked among the island's greatest landowners, some with properties in excess of 1,000 acres.[26]

Different patterns of ownership and involvement can be discerned for the urban sector. White women were generally the owners of small urban properties and businesses, and these had higher stocks of slaves than the large, male-owned properties.[27] In 1821, the Fenwicks employed in their household eight slaves, five of whom they owned (two men, two boys and one woman) and three hired (three women). Mrs Fenwick found from experience, unlike other town dwellers, that male slaves were easier to manage, and were more productive within the domestic economy.[28]

The Fenwicks' dream of accumulating a West India fortune could be realised only within the context of this slave-owning culture. For them, three related levels of engagement with slavery can be discerned: first, the need to purchase or rent slaves for their business establishment; second, the employment of slaves within the household; third, their representation of the ideology of white womanhood and its relationship to slavery as a system of race, gender and class exploitation. Their adjustments to, and working acceptance of, this culture had to be swift and practical. If private spheres of thought and action conflicted with public expectations, they had to be suppressed.

Eliza's exposure to the social economy of slavery began immediately upon arrival. She was sent to bed, and tea was brought by the 'negroes'. She was informed by her host that the governor 'is the only person on the island who has a white servant'.[29] Slaves, she recognised, were vital to the operations of propertied families, and the craft of their ownership and management had to be acquired by heads of households. After one month's residence she located her position upon the chart of pro-slavery consciousness; 'I have never yet seen any black or coloured people in the Theatre. Out of it they look queerly enough, for some of the men and women go about the streets entirely naked'.[30] She wrote to her mother:

> I think the slaves, I mean the domestic slaves, the laziest and most impertinent set of people under the sun. They positively will do nothing but what they please . . . There are always three or four to do the work of one, and they laugh in the owner's face when reproved for not doing their duty . . . I speak principally of Capn. Soaper's slaves. They take liberties that no English servant would be allowed to do; he has two who are drunk half the day, and one female negroe who waits on Mrs.S. throws herself into fits the moment she is found fault with. They will not scour the floors that is too hard work for them, and the field negroes are sent for to do it. By the way, I am told the condition of the field negroes is deplorable enough, and the only way to make the domestic slaves do as they are bid is by threatening to send them to the plantations.[31]

On arrival in Barbados Mrs Fenwick reported being 'shocked at the alteration in Eliza'. She had been very ill, but much of her 'debility' had to do with the annoyances and fatigue in the management of the slaves that the 'mistress of an English family, with even the worst English servants, can form no idea of'. In spite of Eliza's physical condition, her mother found 'her heart and her principles still the same,' and we are told that Orlando 'had exactly the same impression'.[32] Like her daughter, furthermore, Mrs Fenwick found the black slaves necessary, distressing, pitiful and provoking. In a letter to Mary Hays dated 11 December 1811, she stated:

> Our domestics are negroes, hired from their owners, and paid at what seems to me an exorbitant rate. With our small family we are obliged to keep three, or if we wash at home four and with that number one third of the work Eliza does herself, and another third is necessarily left

> undone, as she cannot do more than her strength will allow. They are a sluggish, inert, self-willed race of people, apparently inaccessible to gentle and kindly impulses. Nothing but the dread of the whip seems capable of rousing them to exertion, and not even that, as I understand, can make them honest. Pilfering seems habitual and instinctive among domestic slaves. It is said they are worse slaves and servants in this Island than in many others because there is less severity made use of. It is a horrid system, that of slavery, and the vices and mischiefs now found among the Negroes are all to be traced back to that source.[33]

Three months later, on 21 March, 1815, she returned to the theme:

> It is a horrid and disgraceful system. The female slaves are really encouraged to prostitution because their children are the property of the owner of the mothers. These children are reared by the Ladies as pets, are frequently brought from the negro houses to their chambers to feed and sleep, and reared with every care and indulgence till grown up, when they are at once dismissed to labour and slave-like treatment. What is still more horrible, the gentlemen are greatly addicted to their women slaves, and give the fruit of their licentiousness to their white children as slaves.[34]

She strongly suspected that 'a very fine Mulatto boy about 14' who attended her school to help'wait on the breakfast and luncheon of two young ladies, our pupils', was their own brother, from his resemblance to their father. It is a 'common case', she noted, and not 'thought of as an enormity'. 'This culture', she concluded, 'gives me disgusted antipathy and I am ready to hail the slave and reject the master'.[35]

Undoubtedly social values shaped by gender ideologies did affect Mrs Fenwick's perception of slavery. She saw in the relations of slavery a clear reflection of the worse aspects of male oppression of women, but her stifled pro-slave sentiment was confined to the private sphere and posed no problem for the pro-slavery interests with which her accumulation project was conceived. We see this in opinions expressed to Mary Hays after the purchase of a male slave whom she described as one she 'could not lose': 'It will no doubt be repugnant to your feelings to hear me talk of buying men. It was for a long-time revolting to mine, but the heavy sums we have paid for wages of hired servants, who were generally the most worthless of their kind, rendered it necessary'.

Slavery, Mrs Fenwick suggested, was about the ability of the white race to enforce power over the black race in specific ways in order to secure greater material returns and social advantage. The resistance to this relation of power by the enslaved, however, was not received by her as part of an inevitable, justified political contest, but as an indication of their possession of negative ethnic characteristics which in turn, she thought, legitimised their subordination. 'Poor creatures!' wrote Eliza, 'They get terribly beaten sometimes and dare not strike a white man in their own defence even.'[36] 'An impassable boundary', her mother noted, 'separates the white from the coloured people', which was patrolled by laws, militias, and in the final instance, garrisoned soldiers.[37] The success of business activities in the white community depended upon these relations of power. The Fenwicks recognised that the fulfilment of their West India dream meant the safe negotiation of a passage through the 'nightmare' of black slavery.

The contest over slavery and freedom, however, was not being waged in the public political discourse of the white community. For some slave-owners it was a private turbulence, ultimately suppressed by a complex perception of self-interest. Mrs Fenwick expressed an abhorrence of slavery at three levels: first, it denied black women the ability to refuse white men access to their bodies; second, it impacted adversely on the private and public morals of white men; third, it denigrated the black race in ways that made its social morals and behaviour unacceptable to her. She had learnt, however, to live within its institutional and ideological structures, since this was the only way to advance her plans for a West India fortune. The blacks, who had never accepted their enslavement, were to present the first major rupture to the smooth implementation of her project.

Slave rebellion began on Sunday, 14th April, 1816. According to Colonel Codd, Commandant of the resident imperial troops, the political attitude of slaves, led by Bussa, a driver at Bayley's Plantation, was that 'the island belonged to them and not to the white men whom they proposed to destroy'. Few contemporaries, including the Fenwicks, believed that rebellion was imminent, or that a revolutionary situation existed on the island.

The rebellion began at about 8:30 p.m. in the south-eastern parish of St Philip, and quickly spread throughout most of the southern and central parishes of Christ Church, St John, St Thomas, St George, and parts of St Michael. Minor outbreaks of arson (but no skirmishes with the militia) also occurred in the northmost parish of St Lucy. No fighting between rebel slaves and the militia forces was reported from the eastern and western parishes of St Andrew, St James, and St Peter. An attempt to spread the rebellion among the slaves in Bridgetown was put down following the deployment of a party of the Fifteenth Regiment about the streets of the town. Dwellers in the town, however, felt defenceless, and were traumatised by news of spreading arson and military combat. In geopolitical terms, more than half of the island was engulfed by the insurrection.

The rebellion was short-lived. Within four days it was effectively quashed by joint offensive of the local militia and imperial troops. Mopping up operations continued during May and June, and martial law, imposed about 2:00 a.m. on Monday, 15th April, was lifted 89 days later on 12th July. The death toll, taken when the militia believed that the rebellious were finally eradicated, was very unevenly balanced between slaves and whites. On 21st September Governor Leith reported 144 slaves executed under martial law, 70 sentenced to death and 123 sentenced to transportation. The anonymous author of an account of the insurrection (written most probably in September) suggests that the governor's figures were a gross underestimation of the total fatalities. The author stated that 'a little short of 1,000' slaves were killed in battle and executed at law. Damage to property was estimated by the Assembly's investigative committee at £175,000. One white person was killed, a private in the Christ Church militia.[38]

Mrs Fenwick considered herself fortunate to have survived the rebellion, falling ill as she did with a 'slow fever' brought on by 'terror'.[39] Several persons, she said, 'lost their lives from their fatigues in the insurrection, and many more swept away by a fever brought hither by troops'.[40] It was damage to her business, however, that constituted the primary consideration:

> The insurrection caused us a quarter's loss of the income of the school, besides some delays of payment from persons who were great suffers and who before had been rigidly punctual. My illness has, I suppose, cost £100 at least, so that we have felt a share of the general calamity and shall still feel it, as some of our debtors have died, and the accounts must wait till next year. In the end, I believe, we shall not lose, and as our pupils are returned we have still good prospects before us, and should consider the late difficulties but as dusky clouds passing over the sunshine of our prosperity.[41]

Despite her optimism for the future, the adverse effect of the rebellion upon the financial success of the school would continue to be felt.

Tensions remained within Bridgetown, and the fears of 'a second insurrection' kept the 'Militia and Regulars on the alert'.[42] The expenses of the school, Mrs Fenwick admitted, increased 'enormously' after the 'devastation committed by the Negroes.'[43] In addition, the number of students began to fall 'because too many families are removing to England' on account of the rebellion.[44] To make matters worse, the former governess of the President of the Assembly opened a school exactly upon 'the same plan as Mrs Fenwick', to which her response was that 'we shall thus destroy each other, and none of us be able to do more than barely live'.[45] She maintained, nonetheless, a positive outlook on her business venture.

These developments, however, were but precursors to a more tragic occurrence. In the years after the slave rebellion Eliza's health continued to deteriorate. Unable to maintain a full time career with the theatre, she decided to teach in the family school in an effort to reduce costs and increase revenues. This activity soon had to cease on account of ill health, forcing the school to hire 'a widow lady of English birth and education', who had been left in 'narrow circumstances by a dissipated Barbadian husband', at a wage of £130 per year.[46] In addition, Eliza's husband, whose 'insatiable love of company and late hours' had seduced him 'into a habit of constant intoxication', became an embarrassment to her and had to be left to himself.[47] He too, had been a teacher in the school, and his departure resulted in Mrs Fenwick hiring an 'accomplished French woman' at an unmentionable cost'.

The loss of both Eliza's assistance and general support from her son-in-law were charges, says Mrs Fenwick, that could be measured by the business accounts. She had no way, however, of measuring the 'heaviest calamity' of her life, the death of Orlando by 'a cruel, malignant fever which spared the aged and devoured the young'.[48] Describing her condition as 'dark and desolate', she recognised that a prime motivation for continuing the 'Barbados project' no longer existed. Subsequently, her interest in the business declined. She considered closing the school and transferring its operation to England, but many of the parents who had promised to send their children to her reneged. This was a disappointment, especially for Eliza, now a mother of three boys and a daughter, who wished them settled in England so as to become 'right loyal subjects of Great Britain'.[49]

Mrs Fenwick also craved English society on occasions, when she would consider exchanging 'the luxuries' of her Barbados circumstance 'for a cottage and narrower means at home'.[50] A return to England, however, was not considered feasible. The Barbados success was at best moderate and unable to bear a return settlement. Such a 'removal', she said, would 'cost a little fortune', and the family would be unable to 'live in that decent and comfortable order which we think highly salutary to the habits and good taste of our children'.[51] At the same time Barbados, in spite of offering the family an opportunity to restore and advance their financial interests, could never be considered a place of final settlement. The fears of 'sudden ruin', of 'storms and hurricanes', and 'above all the fatal insurrection which we constantly dread', she observed, 'prevent the soothing consciousness of being at home'.[52] 'I am pleased on this account', she informed Mary Hays, 'with our project of removal [to America] because I can look to a lasting settlement for Eliza, ' as well as 'the opportunity of giving excellent educations to our boys and bringing them up to habits of industry and utility at a very moderate expense'.[53]

In 1821 Mrs Fenwick, Eliza and her four children sold their property and removed the school with six boarders to New Haven in Connecticut under the sponsorship of a gentleman from St Thomas (Virgin Islands) whom Eliza had met eight years earlier at Santa Cruz. 'I am fully persuaded', Mrs. Fenwick concluded, 'that we have done wisely. Our friends predict the most flattering success'. 'There happens to be no female school of the higher order in New Haven, though at New York', she explained, 'and it is supposed that ours would be very attractive as the principal families are now compelled to engage masters at home'.[54]

The Fenwicks' Barbados project lasted a full ten years. It was moderately successful, in much the same way that many attempts to secure a West India fortune probably were. At the end of it, however, Mrs Fenwick could boast an ability 'to live with all the comforts of a good table, in a large and handsome house'.[55] Mother and daughter had secured a reliable income and had freed themselves from husbands considered 'a disgrace and a bother'.[56] They had taken on the West Indian world, and prepared again, as single women, to further their future on the mainland. Driven by financial motives and a desire not to fall in social status they represented the spirit of adventure, courage and determination. They both left behind husbands and broken marriages with no 'prospect of amendment', as well as a trail of decision-making and ideological markers by which it is possible to challenge the dominant historical narrative.

Neither woman concentrated energies on domestic labour, childbearing or fashioning a public reputation as the social property of a husband. Their primary concerns were with the reproduction of property and the social elevation of themselves and their children. In these roles, they functioned as part of the middling property-owning classes and forged an ideological identity that was supportive of the dominant class and race order. While they subscribed to elements of patriarchal moral ideology, such as notions of 'virtue', 'decency' and 'honour', the thrust of their autonomous accumulationist activity violated and transgressed representations in patriarchal ideology of the woman as domestic capital. It was, however, an important strength of colonial society that it could survive and be reinforced by such tensions and apparent contradictions.

It is essential to refer to such 'life histories' in order to understand the varied class composition of the slave-owning community and to appreciate the significance of the white businesswoman within it. In addition, narratives of this sort are necessary in order to study the way that gender operated in society, and to give women a space and a voice with which they can challenge their historiographic exclusion. The contention here is not that women also dreamt of making West India fortunes. This is not an important fact to be established. That they went out in pursuit of fortunes as independent and autonomous agents is, however, of considerable importance. That they went about it with very much the same ideological and social instruments as men is hardly surprising. That their actual experiences were confined in large measure to small niches, or to the margins of areas of large-scale accumulation, however, is important to know since it has relevance to an understanding of the social relations of gender within colonialism as a violent male-managed enterprise. Furthermore, the presentation of such evidence can help us to focus on the material specificity of gender in order to break free of an ideology of gender that is assigned by an historical patriarchy.

Endnotes

1 See Arlette Gautier, 'Les Esclaves femmes', *op. cit.*, pp. 409-35; Bush, 'White "Ladies"', *op. cit.*, pp. 245-62; Morrissey, 'Women's Work', *op. cit.*, pp. 339-67; Beckles, 'White Women' pp. 66-82.

2 Richard Pares, *A West India Fortune* (London, 1950).

3 See Newman, 'Critical Theory', *op. cit.*, pp. 59-60; Poovey, 'Feminism and Deconstruction', *op. cit.*, pp. 52-53; Linda Scott, 'What's New in Women's History', in Teresa de Lauretis (ed), *Feminist Studies/Critical Studies*, (Bloomington, 1986), pp. 22-23. Reddock, 'Women and Slavery', *op. cit.*, pp. 63-80.

4 See William Dickson, *Mitigation of Slavery* (1814. Rpt. Westport CT. 1970), pp. 439-41; Beckles, *White Servitude, op. cit.*, pp 115-68; 'Black Men in White Skins', *op. cit.*, pp. 5-22.

5 For recent texts on women's gender history, see Beckles, 'Sex and Gender', *op. cit.*

6 The letters of Eliza Fenwick, Fenwick (ed), *The Fate of the Fenwicks, op. cit.*

7 *Ibid.*, p. 35.

8 *Ibid.*, p. 37.

9 *Ibid.*, p. 52.

10 *Ibid.*, p. 38.

11 *Ibid.*, pp. 62-65.

12 *Ibid.*, pp. 66-67.

13 *Ibid.*, p. 71.

14 *Ibid.*, pp. 71, 99.

15 *Ibid.*, pp. 97-99.

16 *Ibid.*, p. 156.

17 *Ibid.*, p. 141.

18 *Ibid.*, p. 163.

19 *Ibid.*, p. 165.

20 *Ibid.*, p. 166.

21 *Ibid.*, p. 167.

22 *Ibid.*, pp. 166-67.

23 *Ibid.*, p. 170.

24 *Ibid.*, pp 172-73.

25 *Ibid.*, p. 177.

26 Butler, *The Economics of Emancipation, op. cit.*, pp. 92-109.

27 Higman, *Slave Populations, op. cit.*,

28 Fenwick, *Fate of the Fenwicks, op. cit.*, p. 207.

29 Fenwick, *Fate of the Fenwicks, op. cit.*, p. 69.
30 *Ibid.*, p. 73.
31 *Ibid.*, pp. 75-76.
32 *Ibid.*, p. 163.
33 *Ibid.*, pp. 163-64.
34 *Ibid.*, p. 169.
35 *Ibid.*
36 *Ibid.*, p. 91.
37 *Ibid.*, p. 169.
38 See Beckles, *Black Rebellion in Barbados, op. cit.*, pp. 87-110; also, 'The Slave Drivers' War: Bussa and the 1816 Barbados Slave Uprising', *Boletin de Estudios Latinoamericanos y del Caribe* no. 39 (1986). Michael Craton, 'Proto-Peasant Revolts? The Late Slave Rebellions in the British West Indies, 1816-1832', *Past and Present*, no. 85 (1979).
39 Fenwick, *Fate of the Fenwicks, op. cit.*, p. 178.
40 *Ibid.*
41 *Ibid.*
42 *Ibid.*, pp. 193-94.
43 *Ibid.*, p. 189.
44 *Ibid.*, p. 191.
45 *Ibid.*
46 *Ibid.*, p. 190.
47 *Ibid.*, p. 193.
48 *Ibid.*, p. 183.
49 *Ibid.*, p. 212.
50 *Ibid.*, p. 205.
51 *Ibid.*, p. 211.
52 *Ibid.*, p. 212-13.
53 *Ibid.*, pp.210-11.
54 *Ibid.*, p. 210.
55 *Ibid.*, p. 191.
56 *Ibid.*, p. 193.

6

A Governor's Wife's Tale

Lady Nugent's Jamaican 'Blackies'

Much has been said by historians of the Antebellum South about the pro-slavery ideological leadership of élite white women. While it is understood that vast and significant class and race differences divided the worlds of enslaved black women and privileged white women, a general assertion is that their common 'femaleness' oftentimes engendered mediating points and moments of understanding, sympathy, and mutual support. This postulation, however, assumes the possibility of connectedness in the trajectories of their experiences at the levels of sex and gender consciousness.

Two distinct, but related centres were represented by the white women in the gender order of Caribbean slave society. The first of these has to do with the notion that they occupied, or symbolically represented, the moral core of the white community. This was not a question of her confinement to the 'soft under-belly' of the 'hard back' conquistadorial and settler project. Rather, it was a division of labour which liberated emotionally the white male to engage in the 'inevitable', socially primitive aspects of the project while securing his 'humanity' by burying it deep within the bosom of 'his' woman, thereby creating a safe haven to which he could retreat, and return, and regain a sense of wholesomeness.

Within the project of colonialism, the harsher the methods and objectives, the softer the centre was expected to be. The more the white man travelled away from his own moral centre the greater his attachment to the world he left behind. It was not possible, however, to insulate nor distance the white woman's consciousness from the nature of general operations, particularly its internal institutional formation. Also, the white man's notion of his journey as movements in the expressions of masculinity was mythical and subsumed by the fact of his physical presence in the household. The white woman was 'there' all the way, all along, and 'witnessed' his atrocities. She too engaged in criminal circumstances such as genocide, both as an ideological subscriber and a direct participant.

The second centre was the place where the white male 'secured', or anchored himself, and entrusted the white woman with social authority for the household. As a patriarchal instrument, however, the household and its ideology of domesticity, constituted a site of gender politics through which slave owning males wielded enormous power over the woman in the wider society. The white woman, as wife, was strategically imprisoned within the cult of domesticity through her assumed representation of the values of sexual purity, social benevolence, and moral virtue – all the things the white male could not afford (socially or financially) to represent. She became his self-denied self, and received compensation for her subscriber role in terms of superior material consumption, social security, and public respectability.

In the West Indies white males were aggressively engaged in the genocide of the indigenous population; society was built subsequently upon a new and most extreme model of chattel slavery; violent, bloody, anti-slavery rebellion was endemic; trans-imperial warfare the norm; and majority black communities, for most of the period, were unable to reproduce themselves naturally. Within these contexts, the white woman found it impossible to 'live' at an ideological distance and perform assigned roles with social clarity and distinctiveness. She was whipped up and fully propelled into the deep, turbulent end; she learnt how to survive, and emerged virtually indistinguishable ideologically from her husband as far as slavery was concerned. In the West Indies, unlike the US, no distinct culture of the white woman as mediator of slavery emerged; rather her subscription to slavery and colonialism led to an ideological assimilation that produced within her family considerable political sameness and symmetry.

Lady Maria Nugent's residence in Jamaica between August 1801 and June 1805, as documented in her Journal, provides a vista through which to examine an elite woman's relations to a society based on slavery. She was, in no respect, representative of Jamaican female society, but her contact with it, service on its behalf, and sympathetic support for its structures and forms of legitimisation, placed her as an ally at the centre. On arrival in Jamaica she was 30 years old, daughter of American parents of Scottish-Irish background. Her husband had applied for the job as Governor, and she tells us that he was surprised by his appointment. On leaving Jamaica to take up the post as Commander-in- chief of the army in India, he was made a Baronet and Maria became Lady Nugent. She also kept an 'India Journal', but it lacks the sociological insights and ideological construction of the Jamaica text. Both, however, marked her as a keen intellect, and an articulate voice through which the Empire spoke and was skilfully represented.

The moral dilemmas posed by slavery were many and varied. Nugent's responses included an outright denial of such dilemmas, an attempt to resolve them through private and public attempts at ameliorating the conditions of slaves, and the internalization of a self serving, but popular belief, that black people were happy with their lot and preferred their subordinate social status. She held distinct views on the subject of racial differences, black freedom, and the legitimacy of the white colonial project. In addition, she viewed these issues from a central vantage point, adopted and applied a particular vocabulary, and was unequivocal about the politics and intelligence of her postures.

Quickly learning the internal environment of imperial operations in Jamaica was top priority for Nugent. This meant coming to terms with the public management of Jamaican slave society and the private administration of her slave staff. Knowledge derived from familiarity with the latter would constitute the information base for the former assessment. Being a woman, she believed, gave her a special privilege in that it enabled her to quickly establish intimate practical relations with domestic females, and to hear the private confessions of men in public life who were often tight-lipped about the society they politically administered.

From the outset she refers to the black people as 'the blackies'. This was her principal term of description so that shortly after arrival in Jamaica she tells us on 6 August, 1801, that she 'Reflected all night upon slavery, and made up my mind, that the want of exertion in the blackies must proceed from this cause.' She stated the problem: 'I wish the poor-blackies would be a little more alert in clearing away the filth of this otherwise nice and fine house.' The blacks, she discovered, are lazy, and slavery is responsible. She is not moved to suggest a resolution to the problem of labour by means of the abolition of slavery.

Nugent, of course, placed in His Majesty's 'Kings House' – the Governor's residence – could harbour no such proposal without compromising her husband's missions, one of which was to protect the colony in the face of a real threat from anti-slavery revolution in neighbouring St Domingue. She adopted another, but also logical, option – a meaningful discussion with the enslaved. She tells us: 'Assemble them together after breakfast, and talk to them a great deal, promising every kindness and indulgence. We parted excellent friends, and I think they have been rather more active in cleaning the house ever since.' The 'blackies' then, could reason, respond rationally to incentives, and establish friendly relations. Soon, she notes: 'set the black women to work, and I hope now that the house will be clean.'[1]

There is a significant paradox, however, in Nugent's perception of the 'blackies'. The black women are perpetually being 'set to clean' the house; the house is never quite clean; but the 'blackies' are always happy , merry, and providing Nugent with a constant source of amusement. On August 4th, 1801 she writes: 'The blackies are all so good-humored, and seem so merry, that it is quite comfortable to look at them.' December 15th, she adds: 'Lord Balcarres cattle have ruined our garden; but I cannot help laughing at the rueful faces of our blackies.' January 23rd, 1802, Nugent declares her hand: 'never was there a happier set of people than they appear to be. All day they have been singing odd songs, only interrupted by peals of laughter; and indeed I must say, they have reason to be content, for they have many comforts and enjoyments.'[2]

The house, nonetheless, is never clean to her satisfaction. She is not ambivalent in her support for their enslavement; neither is she prepared to be 'closeted' with respect to the articulation of racist opinions. She recognises the specific dilemmas posed by slavery, particularly those that relate to punishment and labour productivity, but believes that direct, encouraging interaction with slaves by owners is sufficient to achieve desired results.

Nugent had much to say about all aspects of the slavery process. Slaves were imported from West Africa, and creolised through an intense labour process; they adjusted, revolted, displayed cultural preferences, and indicated a range of opinions on race relations, domesticity, gender attitudes and roles, nutrition, mortality and identity. Starting at the beginning, her general opinion is that enslaved Africans were happy to be in the West Indies; that the onset of enslavement offered no terrors for the arrivants. For her, the fanfare of arrival was one of jollity for Africans, and that caravans from the docks to the plantations seemed more of a carnival. January 22nd, 1805, she writes of a group of arrivants:

> In returning home from our drive this morning, we met a gang of Eboe negroes, just landed, and marching up the country. I ordered the postilions to stop, that I might examine their countenances as they passed, and see if they looked unhappy; but they appeared perfectly the reverse. I bowed, kissed my hand, and they laughed; they did the same. The women, in particular, seemed pleased, and all admired the carriage. One man attempted to show more pleasure than the rest, by opening his mouth as wide as possible to laugh, which was rather a horrible grin. He showed such truly cannibal teeth, all filed as they have them, that I could not help shuddering.[3]

Displays such as this were used as part of the evidence she gathered in order to construct the concept of the happy, smiling slave who needed but a measure of compassion and consideration from owners to secure their toothless loyalty.

Take, for example, her representation of the circumstances that surrounded the birth of her child. The slaves in her household, she intimates, displayed the greatest happiness on receiving news of her successful delivery. She is not surprised by this, as she is convinced of their attachment and loyalty. There is no other explanation for the slaves' conduct. It is described, recognised, and rewarded:

> In speaking of the kindness of domestics, I ought not to forget Cupid, who was the picture of woe I am told, and would neither eat, drink, nor sleep, while I was ill; and then danced and sung, and seemed half mad with joy, when my dear baby was born. And I have rewarded him, by letting him be the first of all the blackies about the house to see the baby, and he is also to be his valet-de-chambre bye-and-bye.[4]

Cupid, however, was probably not stupid. He may have danced himself into a job that offered him more than a song ever could. The narrative breaks, and the future of 'achievement' is not known.

Nugent did not dance, neither did she sing at the birth of her domestics' babies. She did, however, visit them, and took christian measures to protect their mortal souls. Her own child she described as a 'little darling'; the black children were not so fortunate; 'One of the black women produced two boys, this morning. Went to see them, and they were exactly like two little monkeys'. One of the twins died the following week and Nugent arranged for the survivor to be 'christened Philip King.' 'Margaret', one of the black maids, and two of the footmen were chosen by her, not the parents, as the godparents. These slaves, she tells us, 'appeared much flattered at being selected for the office, and promised to do the duties of it, poor thing!'

In addition to the 'cannibal- teeth' and the 'monkey looks', Nugent's 'blackies' were also unbearably odourous. The 'looks' and the 'smell' of slaves were common parts of her descriptive armour. The animalisation of blacks, as an important part of the politics of ideological representation, was an advanced narrative instrument in her text. She writes:

> We dined at 6. A large party. In the evening the house was very damp and cold . . . We had a wood fire, which I found extremely comfortable, as I am still very unwell . . . This house is perfectly in the Creole style. A number of negroes, men, women, and children, running and lying about, in all parts of it. Never in my life did I smell so many.[6]

But the 'poor creatures', smell apart, she says, 'seemed the happiest of the happy, dancing and singing almost the whole night.' They were especially 'enjoying themselves' on the day of her son's christening, toasting parents and child 'with the same vociferation – merry creatures.' Young Nugent, a few years later, 'was delighted with Johnny Canoe', the black costumed caricature, 'and with throwing money for the blackies to scramble for.' He was a 'fair' child, his mother says, without 'a darker tinge', though 'born among the blackies.'[7]

Like her infant child, Lady Nugent believed the enslaved Africans of Jamaica were comfortable with her 'parenting'. This state of satisfaction, she argued, in relation to the slaves, was the result of the fact that they were 'extremely well used.' I must say, she adds, 'they have reason to be content, for they have many comforts and enjoyments.' While accepting slavery, and defending it, the issue of the poor demographic performance of blacks remained more of a phenomenal and marginally related issue than an indictment on social and moral grounds. Her ideal expectation was for a more 'humane' slavery, and wished that slaveowners would apply more long term thinking in management strategies.[8]

Greater care, Nugent insists, was the resolution of the contradiction evident in their happiness and good treatment on one side and inability to reproduce naturally on the other. The abolitionists, she knew, had targeted the natural decline of slave population as clear proof of endemic ill-treatment. Her response to this discourse was consistent with her views on the institution as a whole. She had no time for abolitionists, and would express mild contempt in response to their arguments and programmes.

April 8th, 1802; she writes:

> Amused myself with reading the Evidence before the House of Commons, on the part of the petitioners for the Abolition of the Slave Trade. As far as I at present see and can hear of the ill-treatment of the slaves, I think what they say upon the subject is very greatly exaggerated. Individuals, I make no doubt, occasionally abuse the power they possess; but generally speaking, I believe the slaves are extremely well used. Yet it appears to me, there would be certainly no necessity for the Slave Trade, if religion, decency, and good order, were established among the negroes;... The climate of this country being more congenial to their constitutions, they would increase and render the necessity of the Slave Trade out of the question, provided their masters were attentive to their morals, and establish matrimony among them.[9]

The problems with slavery, then, from Nugent's viewpoint, resulted from its mismanagement by slave-owners. The lack of sensitive leadership by few and moral authority by many stood to weaken the institution by rendering its survival dependent upon the slave trade rather than natural reproduction. Unlike many proslavery advocates, however, she was not prepared to abolish the slave trade as part of the protection of slavery. She spoke positively of both institutions from the perspective of the slaves alleged happiness with both. The slaves' social condition, she intimated, was the best test of the moral and social legitimacy of slave trading and slavery, and she found them reconciled to both.

While in many respects Nugent expressed the pro-slavery racist sentiments of élite white women in the West Indies, she was mindful of her status as the wife of the chief colonial representative of the Imperial Monarch. In addition, she understood that elite white women were expected, within the ideological framework of the gender order, to demonstrate by example how best to extend moral benevolence to the slaves. Success in this would stand as testimony of her moral superiority, as well as the enlightened spiritual wisdom of christian compassion. By taking into consideration the spiritual needs of slaves, and linking matriarchal benevolence to a caring domesticity, Nugent sought to foreground and lead a higher, charitable jurisdiction that transcended the harshness and alienating provisions of slave codes that emanated from the male dominated legislatures.

The process of white female mediation, however, that recognised the slaves' fundamental humanity, was not expected to provide any basis for anti-slavery thought or action. Nugent was clear on the direction and depth of her attempts at amelioration, particularly as it related to her own household. The scope for reform action in Jamaica was narrow, and she understood this. Her parameters were cast marginally wider than what was comfortable for élite women who believed that on more than one occasion she had crossed the boundaries established by generations of custom. She would scoff at the rigidity of their conduct with respect to blacks, and sought to demonstrate that public interaction with them was no evidence of the abandonment of pro-slavery ideology, but proof of conscientious leadership and the affirmation of superiority.

Lady Nugent records the details of her discussions with elite white women on the location of the boundaries of 'respectable' social contact with blacks. One context was a 'servants' fete at the Governor's residence, designed by her 'to see the blackies enjoy themselves.' There is plenty of food – 'barbecued hog, jerked hog, pepper pot, yams and plantains' – and glasses of madeira is served to enable them to 'drink three toast – Massa Governor and Missis, and little Massa.'[10] Nugent starts the fete. She writes: 'As soon as that ceremony was over, I began the ball with an old negro man. The gentlemen each selected a partner, according to rank, by age or service, and we all danced.' She enjoyed herself, but the white 'misses' were 'shocked' by the sight of her dancing with a black man. 'They told me', she wrote, 'that they were nearly fainting, and could hardly forebear shedding a flood of tears, at such an unusual and extraordinary sight.' The reason they offered was that 'in this country, and among the slaves, it was necessary to keep up so much more distant respect!'[11]

Nugent's attempt at mediation, therefore, engendered a serious clash with the élite section of white female sensibility. She was as shocked by their reaction to her 'dance' as they were . Her frame of reference was different, not yet fully colonialised. The ideological script she was acting out on Jamaican soil was that of the mistress – servant relation that was common fare in ruling class English society. She admits to an unawareness of the extent of the 'misses' sensitivity on the question of physical contact with the black male, and added: I did exactly the same as I would have done at a servants' hall birthday in England.'[12]

There were no regrets on Nugent's part, though she conceded that the 'misses' 'may be right.' Satisfied that she 'meant nothing wrong', and noting that the 'poor creatures seemed so delighted' by her initiative, her confession was that she 'could scarcely repent it.' She explained her ambivalence within this context:

> I was, nevertheless, very sorry to have hurt their feelings, and particularly too as they seemed to think the example dangerous; as making the blacks of too much consequence, or putting them at all on a footing with the whites, they said, might make a serious change in their conduct, and even produce a rebellion in the island.[13]

She seemed satisfied, however, that her 'dance' was not seen by the 'misses' as a metaphor, a symbol of the legitimacy of intimate contact between white women and black men. In this regard she accepted at face value their anxieties and fears, and settled the discussion.

The space available to Nugent for effective mediation was severely narrowed, therefore, by the ideas and attitudes of white élite female sensibility. She was in fact their prisoner, a condition of which she was not altogether unaware. It was not difficult for her to understand their fears with respect to any confrontation with the rigid and punitive attitudes of their husbands. The loss of respectability and financial security was socially devastating for these women, and both conditions were dependent upon élite male approval. Nugent herself sought to be a fully pleasing and conforming 'wife' and 'home maker', quick to satisfy her husband's expectations in a range of private and public areas. Pinned down by the requirements of her 'official' domesticity, and clipped by the social mores of colonial culture, she oftentimes found release in privately mocking, and knocking, the establishment of which she was a principal pillar.

Within the contexts of a highly restricted circumstance, small victories were recorded and magnified as significant achievements. In addition, Nugent documents her satisfaction with the efforts of others at worthy reform, while expressing disgust at obvious evidence of white hypocrisy and duplicity. While, for example, she celebrated her husband's decision to choose 'a mulatto man' as 'his valet de chambre', and wished him the best with his duties, she expressed disgust in recollecting the experience of a night spent in the company of a rather dull, simple-minded 'party of white ladies.' The entire exchange she described as 'completely stupid'. 'All I could get out of them', by way of conversation, she said, was 'yes, Ma'am – no, ma'am' intercepted by 'a simper or a giggle.' She was determined, however, to ensure that her husband 'investigated fairly' the negroes' many 'complaints of their master' even though she recognised the difficulty of the situation for a Governor.'[14]

A principal act of mediation by Nugent was her offering a measure of respectability to the 'mulatto' élite, particularly the women, by inviting them to participate in social gatherings at the Governor's official residence. Coloured ladies were no threat to white patriarchy. Coloured men were, and these were kept at a greater distance. A group of coloured ladies became her friends, spending time in her bed chamber, and confiding their personal secrets in her. She would take her 'ususal levee of coloured ladies' to tea; they would help her dress for special functions, and keep her company when her husband was away. 'They are all daughters of members of the Assembly, Officers etc', Nugent states, and in many instances resemble their 'secret' fathers. These ladies are grateful for Nugent's invitation and empowerment. They cling to her, win her sympathy, and take over her house.[15]

Nugent, however, has no respect for the white fathers of these mulatto ladies who are bred from childhood as sexual objects for the satisfaction of white men. These young men she described as 'thoughtless', but her main concern is for their wives and families – not the black woman with whom they sleep. 'Advice', she says, 'is of no use, and they must stand the consequences.' She is severe in her criticism of 'white men of all descriptions, married or single, who live in a state of licentiousness with their female slaves.' Particular acerbic is her description and assessment of one such man who she met while on a guided tour of 'The Hope Estate' which was owned and managed by a woman, Lady Temple:

> The overseer, a civil, vulgar, Scotch officer, on half-pay, did the honours to us . . . I talked to the black women, who told me all their histories. The overseer's chère amie, and no man here is without one, is a tall black woman, well made, with a very flat nose, thick lips, and a skin of ebony, highly polished and shining. She showed me her three yellow children, and said, with some ostentation, she should soon have another. The marked attention of the other women, plainly proved her to be the favourite Sultana of this vulgar, ugly, Scotch Sultan, who is about fifty, clumsy, ill made, and dirty. He had a dingy, sallow-brown complexion, and only two yellow discoloured tusks, by way teeth. However, they say he is a good over-seer . . .

All white men, she suggests, who keep black women as 'wives' were either 'badly flawed' morally or physically – that is, 'reduced by circumstances'. In this regard, they were lesser men not representative of the imperial masculinity typified by her husband, and supported by women such as herself.[16]

Nugent was acutely aware of the tensions between white and black women with respect to their sexual relations with white men. Coloured women were oftentimes kept as mistresses, constituting a parallel family that demanded the commitment of white males. White women, as wives, struggled to cope with these domestic structures and manifestations of white masculinity. She tells the tragic story of Mr Irvine who kept a 'favourite brown lady': 'Mr Irvine is a married man, and his unfortunate wife has been long nearly broken- hearted, as his attachment to this "lady" has occasioned his treating her often with the greatest cruelty ever'. In a 'fit of jealousy' he killed his 'lady' and 'made his escape'. Nugent is not outraged by the murder, neither does she make mention of his being captured and brought to justice. Her closing comment is a hope 'that he may lead a life of penitence, if for the present he eludes justice.'[17]

While Nugent does not suggest that such an end was befitting the 'lady', her silence on the murder as the final injustice speaks to her ideological posture that the 'moral corruption' of white men had something to do with their exposure to such women. And it is a 'corruption', she says, that visits 'white men of all descriptions', hence the totality of slavery's embrace. Even the clergy, she intimates, are not spared the spiritual reduction and character derailment. Rev. Woodham, her friend and frequent visitor, is an example of what typified her charge. She gets 'a little disgusted with him' because he gets 'tipsy, and beats his wife.' Her disbelief, she admits, should not be, since this is Jamaica and 'he is not at all like any idea I have formed of a clergyman.'[18]

White women, of course, are not spared the cultural reach of slavery. Without the buttress of an education in England, Nugent tells us, white women's integration into the cultural creolisation of colonial society becomes complete. Most of them, she says, are dull , unintelligent, and crude but well adjusted to colonial society. They lack civility, refined manners, and are brash and cruel in their relations with slaves and other subordinates. 'They appear to me', she says, 'perfect viragos'; 'they never speak but in the most imperious manner to their servants and are constantly finding fault.'[19] She describes the experience of dinner with the Roses, a white creole family.

> The old gentleman and lady are really diverting. They never agree upon any point; but she generally gets the better, from her extreme volubility; and always, when she stops to catch breath, she exclaims, 'But now, Mr. Rose, let me speak', then off she sets again with as much vivacity as ever. The daughter seems perfectly worthy of such a mother.[20]

Neither did she spare the Sherriff family, whose coffee estate she visited: 'Mrs S.', she tells us, is a 'fat, good-humoured creole woman, saying dis, dat, and toder; her mother a vulgar old Scotch dame; and Miss C. [Cumming – a visitor to the home] a clumsy awkward girl.' Such people she says typify white Jamaican womanhood.

The lack of a cultured civility among Jamaican elite white women is coupled, Nugent says, by speech patterns that resemble more those of their African slaves than Europeans. The white men she can ignore, but finds the women most intolerable. It is not just a matter of over-exposure to Africans; it has more to do with the drift of colonial society from its metropolitan mores. The 'women who have not been educated in English' cannot be retrieved.[21] They speak a 'creole language' that is 'not confined to the negroes.' It is 'a sort of broken English', she says, 'with an indolent drawling out of their words, that is very tiresome if not disgusting.' She gives an example: 'I stood next to a lady one night, near a window, and, by way of saying something, remarked that the air was much cooler than usual; to which she answered: "Yes, ma-am, him rail-ly too fra-ish".'

Nugent is aware that linguistic cross-fertilisation has taken place; that white women's speech has given way under the strain of daily contact with black women in much the same way that white men capitulated under the 'domination of their mulatto favourites.' But these white women, language apart, consider their domestics 'as creatures formed merely to administer to their ease, and to be subject to their caprice.' Nugent has no doubt that they are consumed by empty 'conceit and tyranny', but find their excessive material display quite comical, and oftentimes absurd.[22] Her description of ladies, with 'a cavalcade of blackies', going to town is offered as an example:

> It was curious to observe, when we were entering any town, the number of trunks, band-boxes etc. that were hurrying to the country again, and all on negroes' heads; for whenever the ladies go to town, or are to appear in society, their black maids and other attendants start off with their finery in cases, or tin boxes, on their heads. Trunks of any size are carried in the same manner. In short, everything is put upon the head, from the largest to the smallest thing; even a smelling-bottle, I believe, would be carried in the same way. I have often, on our tour, seen twelve or fourteen negroes in one line of march, each bearing some article for the toilet on his head.[23]

Such conduct, Nugent concludes, is quite 'extraordinary' and is attributed to the 'immediate effect that the climate and habit of living' in the colony have 'upon the mind and manners of Europeans.'

Children, furthermore, are socialised by parents into accepting as normal these values and patterns of conduct. Nugent finds the children of elite families quite spoilt, in fact, little tyrants. Slaves are fearful not to satisfy any caprice they may have. Given Jamaican social culture, she is determined that her infant son does not acquire such attitudes. 'It will be difficult', she says, 'to prevent him from thinking himself a little king at least, but she rather him 'loved by all, and not feared.' Her resolution is that he won't be 'injudiciously treated' nor 'absurdly indulged' as 'the poor young things' are in Jamaica.[24] The ill-parenting of the 'ladies', then, constituted 'a good lesson' with respect to her 'dearest little George.'

The expectations of white élite motherhood stand in stark contrast to what was projected by the political economy of slavery for black maternity and womanhood. Nugent moves from one aspect of the discussion to the other with considerable ease and dexterity. She debates with a Mr C., the economics of black reproduction and tells us that he 'gave two dollars to every woman who produces a healthy child.' The over-indulgence associated with the raising of white infants, vests alongside the expenditure in producing black infants as a discursive device that enables Nugent to distinguish between black and white women, and also to locate the mulatto woman as a middling sort to be encour- aged as an ally within the wider political project of keeping the blacks enslaved.[25]

Earlier, Nugent, as colonial signifier, is identified by her reference to black infants as monkey-like. A subsequent description of a 'little black girl' as 'remarkably thick-lipped and ugly' points to the depth of her Eurocentrism and marks her as a racist and negrophobe. Her discourse with Nelly Nugent, her friend, on the procreational capacity of black and coloured women sets up the hegemonic race-gender stereotype of the white woman as frail, sensitive, and fragile – not at all suited to the 'labour' of colonial reproduction and production:

> Nelly Nugent remarked, however, that it was astonishing how fast these black women bred, what healthy children they had, and how soon they recover after lying-in, She said it was totally different with mulatto women, who were constantly liable to miscarry, and subject to a thousand little complaints, colds, coughs, etc. Indeed, I have heard medical men make the same observation."[26]

The astonishment with regards to black women fertility and the health of their infants, she tells us, should be understood within the context of the labour regime to which both mother and infant are subjected:

> Saturday and Sunday were allowed for them to work in their own gardens, and to raise provisions for themselves. The smallest children

> are employed in the field, weeding and picking the cane; for which purpose they are taken from their mothers at a very early age. Women with child work in the field till the last six weeks, and are at work there again in a fortnight after confinement. Three weeks in very particular cases are allowed, but this is the very longest time.[27]

Observations such as these were derived from visits to estates, especially those that were owned and managed by white women. Female planters fascinated her and won her respect.

'The Hope estate is very interesting for me', she says, 'as belonging to dearest Lady Temple, and I examined everything very particularly.' The sugar estate was considered a show piece by Jamaican proslavery elements; her friend, Anne Eliza, had married Lord Temple, elder son of Lord Buckingham, and owner of the property. On his death, Lady Temple continued with the operation with considerable success, making an effort to ameliorate slave conditions, and to 'modernise' the labour process with the technology available in England.[28] She was also very fond of Mrs Sympson, owner of a prime sugar estate called 'Money Musk':

> Mrs. Sympson is a widow for the second time, and has an estate of ten or twelve thousand a year, which she manages entirely herself. They say she is an excellent planter, and understands the making of sugar etc., to perfection. She has had many proposals, but finding all her admirers 'interested', she has wisely declined taking a third husband. The widows Henckell and Bailey were staying with Mrs. Sympson. Alas! how often in this country do we see these unfortunate beings! Women rarely lose their health, but men as rarely keep theirs.[29]

Such women, won the admiration and respect of Nugent. They were entrepeneurial, independent, and determined. They 'owned' and managed things, and had acquired skills and expertise. She enjoyed their company, as she did that of the 'mulatto ladies', but in a different way for altogether separate reasons. Outside of this select group she found Jamaican women not to her taste, though the closeness of the relationships with the mulattoes seems somehow, at times indicative of something politically correct. But there was more to it than this. Perhaps she admired their survival skills and loyalty. It should not be trivialised, the fact that when it was time for her infant son to be innoculated her private physician, Dr Clare, used 'a nice little mulatto child, from whose arm [her] dear baby was vaccinated in both legs.'[30]

If, however, Nugent's legitimisation of the 'mulatto ladies' constitute an act of mediation which she found pleasurable and self-serving, her efforts with 'the blackies' proved frustrating and time-consuming. She was determined, however, to make an effort at saving their souls, and 'civilising' them as an act of private amelioration within her household. Her assumption of moral responsibility for domestic slaves was fully tested by their cultural resistance – a willingness to see life through their own ontological vistas, particularly as it relates to the relative benefits of labour productivity. She found her blackies 'lazy' and 'cunning', and tried to remedy these alleged defects of character; hope and salvation were found in the precepts of christian morality that recognised their humanity and demanded their conformity and loyalty.

The christianisation of her black domestics, became Nugent's principal, immediate, energy-consuming private project with respect to the management of household slavery. 'Previously to their being christened', the 'blackies, she said, had to be exposed to studies on the exposition of the Catechism to enable them to fully understand 'what they undertake in becoming Christian.' On November 5th, 1801, she states:

> After the usual breakfast, gave my last lecture to the blackies, and finished my Christian Story. I consider them now so well acquainted with their expected duties, that I have appointed the Rev. Mr. Warren to be here tomorrow, at 12., for the purpose of baptizing them."[31]

The following day, as planned, we are told: 'Twenty-five of our black domestics were made Christians, and I trust will be so indeed.' After the ceremony, 'cake and wine, in large pieces and glasses were served' for the 'newly made Christians.'

Nugent was proud of her creations, and had good reason. On the 15th November, she 'went to Church with the staff' and was 'delighted to see the black servants look so well, so orderly, and they behaved so properly during the Service.' It was her fourth wedding anniversary, and she 'assembled them all afterwards, and gave them each a dollar for a wedding present.' In turn, the 'blackies' wished that General Nugent, and herself 'might live happy together', until their hair is 'as white as their gowns.'[32]

For the remainder of her Jamaican sojourn, Nugent would 'teach the blackies their catechisms', one she had specially prepared for them, a copy of which was 'sent to Mr Wilberforce.' Her days were spent 'as usual, driving out, reading, writing and teaching the blackies.' Occasionally, she would meet planters who shared her opinion on black christianisation. In 1805, she had a long conversation with one Mr Vaughan, the owner of Plumstead estate in Trelawny on 'the subject of making Christians of the negroes, and of his experience of the advantage of teaching them their consequent duties.' She detailed Vaughan's policy as follows:

> On his estate, he has christened all his negroes, and has induced many of them to marry, and lead regular lives. He says, they have in consequence improved in all respects; are sober, quiet, and well-behaved; and the last year twelve children were born of parents regularly married. The new negroes are attended to, the instant they arrive on the estate, and are taught their prayers most zealously by the oldest black Christians, and those best instructed and most capable. How delightful this is! I wish to God it could be made general, and I am sure the benefits arising from it, in every point of view, would be incalculable.[33]

Sensitive to her 'political' station, and aware of the controversial nature of the project, she did not publicly campaign on its behalf other than give 'little books' made for the blackies, to the already converted, like Mr Vaughan.

While the blackies seemed more prepared to go along with the christiansation project, as launched by Nugent, she reported less success and enthusiasm amongst them with respect to the marital aspect. Nugent placed their reluctance to marry squarely at the door of white men, who by their public conduct, had discredited the value of married life by their open adulterous behaviour with black and coloured women. She offers no comments about the contest amongst blacks between traditional polygyny and European christian style monogamy, but present examples of the higher fertility of slave families living christian marriage. One such couple she heard about had 'fourteen grown up children, all healthy negroes.'

Nugent subscribed to the economic belief that christian marriage among slaves paid off in higher fertility and healthier infants, both of which impacted positively on the demographic performance of the slave population. Any action that would reduce or eliminate the slave trade was progressive, she believed. White men, she says, were too busy taking up the enslaved women in large numbers, and living promiscuous lives to the detriment of morality among the blacks. She reports the response of a male slave to a statement of encouragement to christian marriage: 'Hi, Massa, you tell me marry one wife, which is no good! You no tinky I see you buckra no content wid one, two, tree, or four wives'.[34]

Expressions of slaves' autonomy and self determination were experienced daily by Nugent, and challenged her stereotype of the 'loyal', 'good-natured' African. She lived in a 'rebellious' time, the age of revolution, and was surrounded, at home and overseas by black insurrectionary warfare. Daily, her life was shaped by ambivalent expressions of anti-slavery struggle; she records acts of revolt, but these are presented as paradoxes and contradictions within elite representations of blacks. There is difficulty, then, on her part in understanding how a slave could show anger or vengeance. Since the 'blackies' are generally 'merry', and happy with their condition within Nugent's construction, such expression for her would only result from deviance and recalcitrance, and therefore indicative of a flawed personalty. Her encounter with the boatman is illustrative of a conceptual refusal, despite a recognition of evidence, to initiate a discourse of an endemic black anti-slavery ethos:

> The sea was rather rough this evening, and I took a walk with the Little ones, instead of a row. We met a horrid looking black man, who passed us several times, without making a bow, although I recollected him as one of the boatmen of the canoe we used to go out in, before we had the 'Maria'. He was then very humble, but tonight he only grinned, and gave us a sort of fierce look, that struck me with a terror I could not shake off.[35]

The disrespect and audacity of the boatman, she notes, contrasted with his prior expression of subordination. Her linkage of his refusal to bow with a mentality of freedom struck a damaging blow. The boatman in her consciousness, was transformed from 'sambo' into an agent of evil and savagery, the equivalence of personal freedom and collective degradation respectively.

Nugent's full exposure to the praxis of black self-liberation was facilitated by the popularity within the black community of the Haitian Revolution. Everyday, news would reach her household on developments in Haiti. Her husband placed her at the centre of British imperial policy; she knew the shifting nature of British political opinion, and reflected this in her recollections. When the British government's position was supportive of Toussaint she tells us that 'he must be a wonderful man . . . intended for very good purposes.' When, however, news of 'the massacre of three hundred and seventy white people' was reported, the entire project led to Toussaint being represented as 'dreadful', 'savage' and 'barbarous.'[36]

For obvious reasons, however, her principal concern was with the impact of the Haitian Revolution upon Jamaican slaves. 'What an example to this island', she noted, 'how very imprudent, and what must it all lead to! Jamaica', she said, was now 'full of brigands' who from their mountain hideouts were harassing the English Troops, murdering 'every white man they meet as well as 'any black man they suppose to be attached to the French cause.' No place was isolated from the reach of the black revolution. Her very household, she tells us, was infested with interest among the blacks. While the Governor's guest at dinner debated the nature of the revolution, her 'blackies in attendance seem so much interested, that they hardly change a plate, or do anything but listen.'[37]

Lady Nugent was taking no chances. The presence of revolutionary blacks in Jamaica 'tampering with the negro slaves was indeed most frightful.' At bedtime, officers of the guard were placed at the 'front door of King's House . . . All the staff, too, were on the alert, and, as the nursery door did not lock well, it [was] nailed up for the night.' No one, she says, can 'describe the anxiety', and the 'thousand horrid ideas' that pressed upon her mind, and how she 'suffered' in light of the fact that 'various reports have been made . . . of the alarming state of the negro population'. Yet, in spite of it all, she was occasionally left alone with the 'awful' circumstance of having 'only the poor blackies' as her guard.[38]

The 'poor blackies' protected her, and gave the reassurance, in a way that only slaves can, that she had nothing to fear. She wished neither love nor kindness from them, just labour and loyalty; and this she got. But there was no trust with the loyalty, and no enthusiasm with the labour. She spoke of a distance, a sensation of difference, that prevented a perfect understanding of the 'blackies.' A crude assessment was what she made, and it was exposed under the circumstances. She tried the best she could to suppress conceptual inconsistencies, but it was ineffectual. Nothing she wrote indicated that the behaviour she experienced among the 'blackies' was shaped by relations of power, and reactions to it. Context was not privileged as an informer of conduct but with her the blackies had an essential character. She wrote a narrative of 'difference' but never understood, nor took time to consider, differing views within alternative narratives.

Nugent's text, stands as testimony to the need for caution, and concern, when sex is invested with a perception of inherent gender uniqueness. Womanhood in no significant way distinguished her from dominant patriarchal values and ideologies with respect to slavery and the society built upon it. She does not inform us of any important issues on which she shared a different opinion from her husband. Her class values certainly were not sex sensitive; she had no time for women and men who she considered to be lacking advanced formal education and social grace. Furthermore, she was a racist and an imperialist. Her notions of mediating slavery were specific and designed to deepen rather than relax the grip of the enslaver. The blacks in her household were mirrors in which her whiteness was understood; through them she also saw clearly the values of marriage, domesticity, and motherhood. She was a 'good Christian', a mother, and wife – and the 'poor blackies' had nothing to do with it because they were 'like children' without an opinion of their own that could be committed to a diary.[39] This is why she feared Toussaint L'Ouverture's project.

Endnotes

1 Maria Nugent, *Lady Nugent's Journal of her Residence in Jamaica from 1801 to 1805*, ed. P. Wright (Kingston, Institute of Jamaica, 1966), p. 47.
2 p. 53.
3 p. 220.
4 p. 125.
5 pp. 45, 125.
6 p. 76
7 pp. 98, 178, 188.
8 pp. 53, 86.
9 pp. 86-87.
10 p. 156.
11 *Ibid.*
12 *Ibid.*
13 *Ibid.*
14 pp. 51, 55.
15 pp. 66, 78.
16 pp.29, 87.
17 p. 182
18 pp. 173-74.
19 pp. 55, 82.
20 p. 80.
21 p. 98.
22 pp. 98, 168.
23 p. 98.
24 p. 146.
25 p. 26.
26 p. 69.
27 *Ibid.*
28 p.28.
29 pp. 58-59.
30 p. 177.
31 pp. 18, 38.
32 p. 39.
33 pp. 48, 53, 54, 242.
34 p. 87.
35 p. 277.
36 pp. 33, 40, 179.
37 pp. 40, 118, 198.
38 p. 187.
39 p. 226.

7

A Planter's Wife's Tale

Mrs A. C. Carmichael's Proslavery Ideology

Mrs A.C. Carmichael (she doesn't give her christian names) spent the first half of the 1820s in the West Indies – between St Vincent and Trinidad – and wrote a strident political account of her experience, published in two volumes, entitled "Domestic Manners and Social Condition of the White, Coloured and Negro Population of the West Indies". The text appeared in 1833, received wide circulation in Britain and the United States, and was hailed as a seminal polemical contribution to the pro-slavery cause. The political reputation her 'voice' quickly acquired pleased her, largely because the text was written with the intention of defending the world slaveholders had made and were seeking to preserve against the charges and campaigns of reformers and abolitionists. She entered the emancipation debate with an impressive amount of conceptual vigour and empirical observation, and considered herself highly qualified to do battle with metropolitan critics of the West Indian planter. She emerged, furthermore, as an articulate defender of the sinking 'slave' world as designed by planter-merchant masculinities in the glory-days when sugar was 'King'.[1]

St Vincent and Trinidad, where her husband, a Scottish planter, owned slaves and considerable landed property, were not located at the centre of the old sugar plantation world. The former colony was at best a backwater, while the latter would have sufficed with a description as England's newest West India frontier. Metropolitan abolitionists, however, were painting the colonial canvass with a broad brush, and Carmichael showed righteous indignation at this apparent disrespect for detail, the hallmark, she said, of the trampling political mind of abolitionists that had no real regard for the promotion of truth and justice. The 1820s, she knew , was a time when the spirit of triumphalism was felt by those on the side of anti-slavery, and the backs thrown against the wall, including her husbands, were the ones she sought to liberate. The English had abolished the slave trade in 1807. Slaves in neighbouring Barbados –

considered by the English the most stable slave colony – had revolted in 1816, and Parliament in 1820, when she arrived in the West Indies, could not be sure, for the first time, that slavery would survive the decade.

Carmichael's opposition to abolitionist criticisms of the slaveowning élite, and of the institution itself, was keenly contested and passionately expressed. She was not an outsider to the slaveowning culture, and saw her gendered insider location as a privileged wife as an integral part of her husbands's legitimacy. Conscious of her womanness, she judged and evaluated effects of slavery upon all participants, and spoke to the diversity of social and political reactions. In many ways the logic and lessons of her arguments in defense of the slave holding élite deny any obvious claim to a unique, exclusive woman's perspective or sensibility. She recognises no issues on which her opinions diverge from those of her husband.

Her principal project is to critique abolitionists and their political supporters in government. The state, she believed, had been hijacked by rabid, anti-slavery opinion, and had lost clear judgement with respect to its relations with the colonial élite. In her opinion, an act of political immorality was being committed by the state because the colonial élites had played more than its part in the advancement of England's national interest. It had done yeoman serv-ice, she suggested, in the development of domestic trade and industry, and imperial and metropolitan authority and leadership. The 'West Indian planter', in her opinion, was about to be betrayed by the new liberal political leadership, which from her perspective lacked the moral integrity it was seeking to promote by virtue of its duplicity. Her text, then, represents an acerbic but effectively reasoned assault upon anti-slavery lobbies in government, and a defense of the 'misrepresented' and, in her opinion, unfairly treated West Indian slaveholder.

Carmichael begins with the question of slavery's origins in the West Indies, Barbados to be exact, where sugar and slavery emerged as a phenomenally profitable expression. She argues that it was not the design of the colonial entrepreneur to develop and rely upon African slavery. They were quite prepared, she maintained, to deal with other forms of labour, including white indentured servitude, but that the English government in order to secure profit and power in relation to imperial competitors, pressured colonists to restructure productive institutions and open the door to a relentless flood of enslaved African. She tells us:

> The details which I present are far from being meant as conveying any apology for the slave trade, as it existed before the abolition; indeed I never heard the slave-trade mentioned with half the horror in Britain that I have heard it spoken of in the West Indies: and never let it be

> forgotten that Britain began the slave-trade, – not the colonists; and it is a fact which admits of no denial, that the British government forced the colonists to cultivate the islands by the labour of negro slaves imported from Africa; nay, it is a fact that the colonists of Barbados were decidedly averse to this; but the mother country insisted upon compliance.[2]

The purpose of this 'fact', she notes, is 'to show that the first and criminal part of the whole transaction rested upon the government alone, and not upon the colonists.' Colonial laws are mentioned as evidence of this coercion; property holders were penalised by imperial sponsored legislation for not keeping 'a certain number of slaves according to the proportion of acres they wished to cultivate.'[3]

The imperial government, furthermore, used its enormous influence to ensure that slaveholders were not weaned off their appetite for more slaves, thus fostering the West Indian dependency that it now wished so conveniently to cure. The West Indian slaveholder, she says, merely did what was necessary and possible under the adverse circumstances, and tried to humanise and modernise social relations within the government-sponsored slave system. What followed was not so much an arcane apology for the evils of slavery but an articulation of the belief that the slaveholder, a victim initially of imperial policy, constructively advanced by means of the routinisation of social policy, the condition of slaves, and produced among them a general state of happiness and sense of progress. Far from it, then, that the slaveholder should be held up as a representative of moral regression and social oppression. Slavery, she argued, in the care of enlightened owners, had already produced the desired states of consciousness and social existence clamoured for by its critics and abolitionists.

Building the case of the 'improved', 'happy', enslaved African was necessary in order to counter abolitionists claim that the slave plantation represented an imaginable living hell, particularly with respect to the abuses and degradation of women and children. The allegations of daily rape, sexual plunder, and corporal punishment, projected by abolitionists as evidence of the moral and social crisis of the plantocracy, were confronted by Carmichael who argued that slavery was consistent with Enlightenment idealism and that the gentleman planter was effectively its emissary. This was the case, she said, despite the prolonged slave trade which was admittedly one of several 'national iniquities'. 'I feel convinced', she concluded, 'from the consistent details of many native Africans, examined at different times and even in different colonies, that the situation of those who were removed to the West Indies, was very greatly improved in every respect.'[4]

The case study approach is utilised by Carmichael in order to amass the data necessary to arrive at this conclusion. 'My desire is, only to state truths', she says, and truth ought to be stated, whatever may be the consequences to which it leads'. Her first witness is 'F', an Ebo woman 'of uncommonly good character, but not at all clever; – a common field negro.'[5] She is questioned at length by Carmichael about her enslavement and concept of freedom:

> *Carmichael*: 'How were you taken?'
>
> *'F'*: 'Misses, Ebo go war wid a great grandee massa; him take Ebo . . . take me mamma too; she be one nice nigger, fat so; they take her, kill her, boil her, fry her, yam [eat] her every bit all: they bring her heart to me, and force me yam [eat] a piece of it . . . ."
>
> *Carmichael*: 'Did you know you were going to be sold to a white man?'
>
> *'F'*: 'Yes, misses, me happy at dat; nigger massa bad too much, white massa him better far, Africa no good place, me glad too much to come a white man's country.'[6]

Carmichael's construction of the interview ends with an explicit declaration by 'F' of her happiness with both slavery and removal from Africa.

Carmichael tells us, furthermore, that 'F' 'had been many years ago offered her freedom as a reward for her faithful services, but declined it, saying she preferred remaining as she was.'[7] Abolitionists, Carmichael insists, are guilty of conferring upon blacks the love of freedom which Europeans cherish and are seeking to universalise. 'F' was in many respects 'savage', says Carmichael, because 'she despised and refused all the comforts of civilised life'; preferring to sleep on the floor 'without any clothes', using a hand rather that a spoon for her calalou soup', and relished 'rum and water' as a favourite beverage. Her appearance 'was anything but pleasing', but at times 'almost disgusting'. When asked about her appearance and manner, according to Carmichael, 'F' would reply: 'No tease me, misses, me one very good nigger; let me be.'[8]

Why, then, Carmichael insists, should this 'poor negro's owner' be held up to public criticism and shame for her brutishness? He is not responsible, she says, for her savage condition, and the English public should know of the 'utter impossibility of convincing her that cleanliness, a few clothes, and eating her victuals like a civilised being were real comforts.'[9] The fact is, she says, that in general slaveowners were committed to improving the moral and social conditions of slaves, but the exercise was fraught with resistance. It was not that blacks were opposed to material and cultural progress; rather, it was that they did not understand the concept and had no idea of the constituent elements of civilised conduct.

Carmichael's other female witnesses offered but minor variations on these themes and their testimonies are set out in a manner that confirms the ideological integrity of pro-slavery rationalisations. 'I', a Guinea-Coast female, and field labourer, says that she arrived in the West Indies a grown woman leaving behind a husband and child. To the question, 'were you not very grieved when you found yourself away from them?', she replied that her husband used to beat her everyday, and that she was happy to be away from him and Africa; also, that her white 'massa' was there to prevent such an eventuality. With respect to her African child she says that in slavery she now had seven children, a significant improvement. Africa, she concludes, is no 'good country', and that only 'no good people' say that it is.[10]

Slavery, then, says Carmichael, was progressive, civilising, and morally uplifting in that it bred 'good negroes' by developing their character. The issue, she believed, should be dealt with within the slavery discourse was not whether slavery was a backward or modern institution, but whether or not it promoted good character among the blacks. 'Good negroes', she argued, were the norm, and that 'bad negroes' were, more often than not, the results of excessive brutality by white overseers and managers whose lack of intelligence and good breeding in no way corresponded to the quality of slaveholding gentlemen found throughout the islands. Abolitionists, she insists, knew little of these details, and spoke from ignorance in asserting that slavery was corrupting and degrading of negro character.

Carmichael, it should be emphasised, was impressive in the attempt to present empirical and conceptual arguments. The concept of good and bad negroes was set out for polemical clarity, but used also as an instrument of social analysis and to judge the importance and value of slave testimonies. Accordingly, she says:

> When I use the term a good negro, I wish my readers to understand it as we do in the West Indies – industrious, civil, with some sense of his own dignity, and a wish to retain a place in the good opinion of his master and all around him. This is the usual acceptance of the term, a good negro; such a man is seldom altogether proof against occasional deceit and theft, to an extent that would ruin the character of a servant at home; but compared with the majority, 'he is a good negro'.[11]

A bad negro, then, was 'a runaway, a thief, or a liar' whose 'testimony would not be regarded' in the West Indies, but who was not set apart from 'good negroes' by persons in England seeking the political discredit of the colonial élite.[12]

'Good negroes', according to Carmichael, did not agree with the thinking nor the objectives of anti-slavery reformers, and certainly had no desire for the 'freedom' abolitionists so fervently tried to impose. Ameliorative reforms which were imposed by Parliament upon colonial Assemblies between 1823 and 1826, and associated with the political successes of anti-slavery leader, Thomas Buxton, were targeted by Carmichael insofar as slaveholders considered them the final undoing of the world they had made. Buxton, she tells us, was far from being a slave hero, but was considered by them as an interfering outsider aggravating the acceptable circumstances of their daily lives. When news of reforms reached the slave yards, Carmichael says, it was a common refrain for slaves to say: 'I wish dat Massa Buxton would come and see a we nigger, and no send out dat law.'[13] Despite the legal disruptions to amicable master-slave relations, furthermore, 'the good negroes', Carmichael concludes, 'were less shaken in their affection, and less changed in conduct.' Always prepared to speak 'with regret of the number of "bad niggers" in their midst', the more 'faithful creatures' were eager to calm her fears and reassure her of loyalty.[14]

Abolitionists, Carmichael asserts, were the common enemy of slaveholder and slave alike, and viewed as 'dangerous' by both on account of their 'injudicious harangues made in parliament' and 'impracticable theories.' 'Deeply have the colonies suffered', she says, 'from the promulgation of wrong-headed plans', and from abolitionists' 'intemperate zeal and mistaken kindness.'[15] The political debate surrounding the abolition of corporal punishment is presented as an example of Buxton's misunderstanding of slavery as a social relation of power.

She admits that on arrival in the West Indies, laden with irrelevant moral idealism, she was 'inimical' to 'all corporal punishment.'[16] While recognising that 'corporal punishment is a dread, and tends to keep bad characters in order', it would have an effect upon 'good negroes' of driving them to suicide. But that aside, she declared, while the drivers on the estate does daily 'cracks his whip three times loudly', she 'never saw a whip used, either by a driver or by any other person.' Neither, she said, 'did I ever hear a negro complain of such a thing, although I used often to make inquiry.' What she did see, however, during her walks about the estates, were slaves at work 'cheerful and happy.'[17]

The West Indian planter, Carmichael says, knows this and makes the distinction between 'negroes possessing fine feelings' and the incorrigible thieves.'[18] Abolitionists make no distinction; the declaration of an end to corporal punishment on her properties 'produced a perfect revolution in the establishment.' The fact is, she stated, 'my domestics and negroes were daily becoming bolder and bolder in wickedness.' This forced her to agree to find alternative forms of punishment. 'Solitary confinement' in the stocks, she found, was much appreciated by 'bad negroes' who she heard saying that they were 'much obliged to massa for letting them sit down easy.' 'I tried for two years to have no recourse to corporal punishment', she said, 'but finding at length, after a course of kindness, indulgence, and instruction, that my [house slaves] became notorious for insolence and misconduct, and abhorring the alternative of corporal punishment, I had them all sent to the estate...' During this time, she says, her household was in 'absolute anarchy' under a 'reign of unpunished wickedness.' Imprisonment in the stocks [a wooden surface on which hands and feet are chained and padlocked], she concluded, was smiled upon by slaves who say it as a useful respite from employment.[19]

Slave Women, in particular, says Carmichael, took full advantage of the reprieve from flogging. The centering of women in anti-slavery rhetoric about corporal punishment focused Carmichael's attention on the significance of gender. In her opinion British political and moral discussion needed to disavow itself of the perception that slave women were members of the gentler sex deserving of social protection by legislators. A 'masculine-looking woman' was a West Indian norm, she professed, which posed very special problems for slave management.[20] She tells us, furthermore:

> I regret to have it to say, that female negroes are far more unmanageable than males. The little girls are far more wicked than the boy: and I am convinced, were every proprietor to produce the list of his good negroes, there would be, in every instance, an amazing majority in favour of males.[21]

The employment of a discriminatory gender strategy by abolitionists, then, bore no relation to West Indian reality in Carmichael's opinion, and confirmed further their ignorance of, or disregard for, the circumstances of plantation management.

The whip, though rarely used, and only with considerable restraint, should remain a deterrent, Carmichael reasoned, 'until a radical change be effected, by mental instruction.' The fact was, she argued, the blacks were not ready for the types of liberal reforms proposed, and required considerable advancement in their morals and culture before they could rise to meet the expectations set out by abolitionists. The use of psychological punishments would be ineffective, she suggest, because blacks have at best low sensitivity to non-physical stimulation. 'The mind must have made considerable progress in civilisation before mental punishment will be found productive of the slightest benefit' she concludes, and the brutishness of the blacks, particularly the women, is everywhere manifested in their social conduct.[22]

Carmichael argued the case of blacks' unpreparedness for social reform and civil rights by pointing to the state of affairs within their domestic lives. She was particularly keen to establish the charge that the black woman was a bad mother and non-feminine. Child rearing attitudes, she thought, could be used as evidence of both counts of the charge. 'Negro mothers', she said, 'I have found cruelly harsh to their children; they beat them unmercifully for perfect trifle omissions ... I have frequently seen mothers flog their children severely for forgetting to say yes or no ma'am, to them.' The black family, she tells us, was marred by violent interactions; mothers against children, brothers against sisters, and fathers against mothers. She presents evidence of this spiral of violence in households in graphic detail, and concludes that order and proper conduct is established in the black family only when some white person intervenes and punishes the principal offenders.[23]

While Carmichael is opposed to the sale of children and the forceful separation of the black family, she makes no reference to the impact of this tradition upon the nature of domestic relations. That mothers were expected to wean their children as quickly as possible, as an act of preparation for sale, did not temper her assertion that the black woman was not supportive of maternity. She presents several cases to indicate black women's disregard for infants, all of which point to the opinion that abolitionists perception of their special suffering under slavery was mythical, and that their resistance to the principles of motherhood was evidence of their general brutishness. The case of 'H' is a typical Carmichael construction:

> H. had a baby about two months old; she had nothing to do but to take care of it (being a domestic); the child was not in the estate nursery, as it would have been had the mother been a field negro. This infant fell sick, and the doctor attended it three times a day; but as the mother was stout and well, we considered that a sick nurse was unnecessary. She did not wash or cook either for herself or baby, but she always looked sulky when asked to attend upon her child. The third evening of little W's illness, I went down with the doctor to see him, but I was astonished to find the poor baby crying and rolling about the floor alone. I instantly called A., and asked where H. was. 'Misses, I don't know': every servant denied knowing anything of her, until I sent for their master, when N. said 'she saw H. go out some little time since in full dress; she believe she must be for a dance.' To pacify a poor sick baby of two months old until two in the morning, I found no easy task: at that hour the mother arrived, astonished that massa and misses 'should make such a work about the child, for he'd cry, and when done he'd go sleep.'[24]

As soon as the babies are standing upright, Carmichael says, mothers believe they have a right to begin the regime of physical abuse. As a result the common experience, she stated, was for little children to flee their mothers and throw themselves into her protection while screaming 'Oh! Massa, misses, me mamma go murder me.'[25]

Carmichael also relished the role as mediator in the conflicts between children, and was cognisant of the assumption of parental authority involved. Since mothers were negligent and incompetent, and fathers marginalised and disregarded, Carmichael believed that this function established her as the super parent of slave children. The children, she says:

> got into the habit, whenever they disagreed among themselves, of coming up to Misses . . . and then the whole evidence is heard. I made a point of first hearing all the complainant had to say, and his witnesses, one after another; and then the defendant, and his witnesses. I seldom failed in being able to pronounce a verdict to please all parties; because as they said, "come up to misses; it all one to she, who right and who wrong; she no love one pick-a-ninny more den anoder.[26]

Parents, she says, were incapable of dispensing this kind of ordered justice within households, additional evidence, she asserts, that the firm guiding hand of white civilisation was necessary in order to secure 'mental improvement' among the blacks. Without this development, says Carmichael, the planter's wife must of necessity 'watch over the negro children daily', 'see them swallow their physic', 'reward the good, and admonish the bad', 'visit the sick and encourage them', 'listen to all the stories of the . . . young, old and middle aged', and generally take 'an interest in all that concerns them.'[27]

Acceptable conduct in black domesticity, argued Carmichael, will originate in white intervention. She idealised the model of child rearing established by slaveholders that enabled sugar production and slave breeding to proceed with efficiency. It is a West Indian system that articulates production and reproduction in order to maximise labour productivity. It involves four socio-economic policies: (a) the effective separation of mother and child in the post-natal period; (b) the mobilisation of 'old', 'superannuated' women to function as surrogates for unweaned infants ; (c) the alienation of fathers from the child rearing culture; (d) the immediate integration of weaned children into the labour regime. The slave family, as a household, is seen as secondary to the demands of sugar production, and granted no autonomy as an institution. Rather, it exists at the pleasure of the slave holder and derives it structure from whatever policy is developed.

The 'nanny', as the critical child rearing institution, enabled the slave holder to continue the exploitation of superannuated field women by extending their working lives. 'Children who are too young to be employed, are all brought up' by nannies 'whose sole office is to take care of them', returning to their mothers, says Carmichael, 'at night, but not until then'. The nanny, she says, 'keeps them together all day in a building appropriate for them, out of the sun. It is her business to keep them clean, and to see that no chigres [sandflea which penetrate under the skin of the feet] are permitted to remain on them, so as to produce sores.' The important observation for Carmichael is that 'these women are kinder to the children' than their mothers, with the result that the 'infant invariably shows more affection for the nurse than for its parent.' Altogether, Carmichael concludes, 'the arrangement of the children upon a West Indian estate is most gratifying, for every want and comfort is minutely attended to.'[28]

In this regard, says Carmichael, the blacks in the West Indies cannot be said to live in the kind of oppressive slavery so 'wildly' described by abolitionists. Not only do they prefer life in the West Indies to Africa, subjection to white rather than black masters, but they live in a state of material provision and comfort in excess to what the English labourer is accustomed. With respect to the charge that slaves are overworked in order to keep hopelessly unprofitable estates in business, she sets out an argument which suggests that the contrary is true:

> If there be one sentiment respecting the colonies more erroneous than another, it is this; for although I arrived in the West Indies fully convinced that I should find, and indeed almost determined to find, every slave groaning under oppression, yet I was not one month in St Vincent, before I was compelled from my own experience of negro character, to be somewhat sceptical, whether it were possible to overwork a negro, – and I now feel no doubt upon the subject: the fact is, they are so perfectly aware that you must give them all the necessaries of life, that if they determine not to work, or at least to do little, how are you to proceed in order to make them do more? For even if punishment, corporal punishment, were resorted to, it is not dreaded by them half so much as work. Employment is their abhorrence – idleness their delight; and it is from having so minutely watched their dispositions, habits, and method of work, that I have come to this conclusion – that to overwork a negro slave is impossible.[29]

While 'far the greater number of the slave population are occupied in the culture of the cane', Carmichael adds, the hardest part of this regime is in the annual 'holing' of the ground to plant young canes. But this infrequent exercise, she says, 'is literally nothing, when compared with many of the necessary operations in the agriculture of Great Britain; such as ploughing, reaping corn, or moving hay.' The weight of the hoes used in this exercise, says Carmichael, is not 'heavy for a grown man or woman, and none else are employed in this work.' The plough cannot be effectively used as a labour relieving device, she adds, because 'the ground is so steep and rocky' in 'many of the West India colonies' as 'totally to preclude the possibility of such an attempt.'[30]

The slaves, without ploughs, have managed, says Carmichael, to reduce the labour of hoeing to a gentle canter, and not even the crack of the drivers' whip could produce any acceleration:

> The work of holing is slowly performed, and a band of Scotch potato hoers would not gain one meal a day were they to proceed in the same leisurely manner; you see the negroes often two and three at a time standing for many minutes looking about them, and never raising their hoe. When so engaged, they are usually cheerful, telling laugh-able stories to each other, and singing songs, or rather choruses. I never once heard any of them complain of the work as too hard; but I have heard very many of them express themselves pleased when it was about to commence, because they had their additional rum and water. There is a person regularly appointed to carry water to the field, the whole year through, whatever they are engaged in; always three times; and if the weather be particularly hot, it is carried five times a day. When rum is not given, Mandango sugar or molasses is used; indeed the women seem at all times to prefer sugar and water. This is universal.[31]

Work on the sugar estate, for slaves was more agreeable than for labourers on an English farm, concludes Carmichael. The slave, therefore, was not oppressed by excessive labour, cruel drivers, endemic malnutrition, frequently injury, and the psychological terror of it all. Rather, Carmichael, shows, much of this was crudely exaggerated and misrepresented by abolitionists and 'bad slaves' whose dislike of work was well known.

Slave housing, furthermore, was in general superior to what the labouring classes of England inhabited. 'Bad slaves', she says, did not care about their habitations, but 'good slaves' did, and their houses were impressive for the range of comforts and conditions achieved:

> I have paid great personal attention to the manner in which negroes are lodged, because it seems to be thought in England that they are in this respect quite neglected. After having visited negro houses without number, I do not hesitate to say that negroes are more comfortably lodged than the working classes of either England or Scotland. You cannot fail to remark upon every estate, that the work peoples' houses are placed in the healthiest situation, never so elevated as to be cold, nor so low as to be damp: the drains round them,

> or water paths, as the negro calls them, are watched with the greatest care, and kept clean, and noting that could create damp is suffered to be near their houses. No inhabited house is ever allowed to be out of repair; neither is it left to the negro to ask for what may be necessary; the houses are examined very frequently by the white people, and during their master's time, they are employed in making all tight and comfortable before the rainy season commences.[32]

The matter, then, revolved around the character of the individual slave rather than the policy of the slaveowner. If the 'slave have not some household furnitures', for example, Carmichael says, 'it is because he is indifferent to the comfort of it' or prefers to spend his money in fine clothes or jewellry. The options, it seems, were many, and available to slaves to make rational choices. 'Good slaves', she said, made rational choices, while 'bad slaves' paid no attention to their general health, cleanliness, nor habitation.[33]

Aware, however, that material preferences may be explained in terms of cultural attitudes and economic circumstances, Carmichael retreated into comparative analysis but only to advance the idea that ultimately the matter is settled in terms of the degree of 'civilization' attained by individuals and the capacity of their labour to sustain it. She made both arguments in this way:

> There is no more absurd error than to suppose that men in all classes of society, and in different countries, require the same things to render them comfortable. The Tong merchant prefers his chop-sticks to your silver forks; the English labourer prefers his own beer to the squire's claret; the Andalusian would sooner stretch himself on boards, than sink into a down bed; and the negro neither understands the refinements of a gentlemen nor requires the comforts of an European. Negroes are well off, according to their ideas of comfort and the climate in which they reside: they are abundantly supplied; and I am by no means sure that we should be conferring any benefit by introducing European fashions in the colonies – so that, while I would labour to civilize and inform the negro, which will by and by produce all its effects – taste, among others – I would also studiously avoid suddenly introducing, or unnaturally encouraging artificial wants; which, although originally luxuries, become in time necessary to comfort.[34]

No matter how she twists and turns, Carmichael comes down with the explicit assertion that 'many negroes are utterly unfit for the rights of civilised men' because they remain savage by nature. 'I could enumerate numerous facts', she says 'all tending to prove' this fact, but suffice to state as an example that 'I have seen negroes, upon the slightest provocation, snatch up any weapon at hand, and inflict a deep gash on whatsoever part of the body first presented itself, of a wife, husband, or child.' Furthermore, she adds, the argument of their savagery should be settled by reference to their 'great relish' for eating raw animal flesh.[35]

The outpouring of sentiment by abolitionists in favour of slaves, in Carmichael's opinion, was entirely misdirected, and would have served a more deserving cause had the interests of the labouring poor of Britain been similarly promoted. Slaves were already well catered for, she tells us, and abolitionists could have found richer pastures for their evangelical zeal within the inner zones of industrial cities and towns. There, at least, were not to be found idle, pampered workers that so abound on the sugar plantations. The slaves, she says, lived in an idyllic welfare state; the British workers knows no such subsidy, and are forced to confront an unfavourable competitive circumstance in order to secure a living:

> The slave may be perfectly idle, and yet he is supported. The British labourer strains every nerve to live. The slave is provided for without anxiety on his part; the object he has in view is not to live, but to save, and get rich. A wife and family are often a serious burden to the British labourer, and in order to support them he is frequently obliged to seek pecuniary aid from the parish. A wife and family have been the greatest possible advantage to a slave, for his master supplied them with every thing: his wife washes and cooks, the children soon begin to assist the mother, and they all work in their garden and grounds, and reap a great annual crop of different kinds.[36]

Furthermore, slaves were happy and contended with their condition, and had no desire to encourage the radical politics of the 'African Society' whose members considered themselves their advocates and protectors.

As it was 'not possible to overwork a negro', a true victim of plantation labour, according to Carmichael, was the white woman – both the planter's wife and those forced to work on their own account while carrying the burden of whiteness. In addition to managing the daily affairs of lazy blacks, the planter's wife was required to sew, wash, go to market, attend to stocks, cater to her husband, and do it all without the reward of material comforts associated with metropolitan living. Carmichael was aware that her colleagues in Barbados, Jamaica, and the older sugar colonies do no such work, but in St Vincent, a struggling little colony, all hands were called upon.

As a household manager, Carmichael found domestic work exhaustive, and complained bitterly about it while pouring condemnation upon abolitionists for identifying the planter-family with greed and vulgar consumption. 'It is utterly impossible', she says, 'for those who have not gone through such scenes, to comprehend the unnecessary accumulation of work thus thrown upon the mistress of a family.' Furthermore, she adds, 'let those who talk of the luxuries of a West India life, judge whether they would exchange their home in Britain, however poor it may be, to undergo all this.'[37]

Carmichael's description of life for white women in the 'outback' of struggling West Indian colonies, did not deal exclusively with the world of work and consumption. For her, many white women were abandoned by modernity and stranded among negroes – left to decay morally and culturally. As an example of this 'kind of slavery' she described a group of white women whom she met at a plantation dinner in St Vincent. They are 'distinguished' only for their 'listlessness' and 'meagreness of conversation', but she attributes their 'uninformed minds' to the 'constant domestic drudgery of a female's life in the West Indies, married or unmarried'. For the European woman plantation life is 'desolate and miserable'. Her husband is frequently away, in town or elsewhere, and the best they could do for conversation and companionship, says Carmichael, is to associate with the 'coloured' women who consider themselves well above the station of negroes. But 'no woman of decent moral habits', she says, 'can make a friend of any of the coloured population'. 'Slavery operates prejudically on the higher classes', she states, and the white woman carries the greater share of this cost.[38]

The white man at least, says Carmichael, did elect to associate sexually with coloured or black women, and when discreet, kept his reputation. She does not see these relationships as based on free choice, but consider them the result of white men being 'deprived in a great measure of white female society.' Such a crisis makes the white man vulnerable and they are 'easily ensnared by these handsome and attractive young women' whom they soon come to prefer over 'their country women'. Such young women, she says, are not victims of white masculinity, since they queue in order to 'allure young men who are newly come to the country'.[39]

For these reasons, then, white 'ladies' did not expect each other to keep company with coloured women. They were sexual competitors for the passion and property of the white male. Carmichael suggests that the white woman wins outs when the man is cultured and of good family, though the victory is never complete – nor lasting. The coloured woman of means knows well the terrain of her struggle, and takes measures to strengthen her case – she secures slaves to protect her from hard labour, dresses expensively, and associates with the Methodist church as additional evidence of respectability. Their commitment to slavery, Carmichael admires, but notes that blacks consider them harsher owners than whites. This is their colony, she admits, and will never be 'home' to the European woman whose greatest fear remains the possibility of rape by black men in the heat of revolt.[40]

But abolitionists, according to Carmichael, did not understand these things. They had no sympathy for white women and their children, outnumbered and out of reach on remote plantations. Having portrayed the slaves as 'happy, contented, poor creatures', the spectre of large scale revolt should not seem a possibility in Carmichael's world. But there were the 'bad negroes', who were capable of violence against both 'good negroes' and their owners that concerned her. She worried that the 'good negroes' might be outnumbered and unable to defend the whites in the event of an uprising. While her husband is called to militia duty the white woman 'is left with her children in a state of alarm beyond description: surrounded on all sides by negroes . . . left entirely in their power'.[41] On this note Carmichael addresses women at home with thinly disguised sarcasm:

> I am afraid some of those females, whose delicate sensibility has been so much affected by the bare name of West India slavery, would, notwithstanding their amiable belief in the gentle and harmless disposition of the negro, have been not a little nervous, had they found themselves placed on a wild West Indian estate, with a house so open as they all must be, and perhaps watching over a young family, alarmed for the safety of absent husbands; and either surrounded by domestic slaves, in whom they have no rational ground of confidence, or else, as is usual at such times, deserted by their domestic slaves altogether.[42]

The West Indian night, she concludes, is not only about beautiful moons and starry skies; 'one half of [it] is frequently passed in listening, rising out of bed, and ascertaining whether or not all is quiet'.[43]

But this fear, in Carmichael's narrative, is not a rational response to the evidence seen daily by whites. Her 'bad negroes' apart, she should have no reason to assume that a mass uprising was possible. The planter, she says, is responsive to all the slaves needs, and the slaves do not wish for freedom – largely because they do not know what it is, and in any event they wish for nothing but to serve their massas and misses. Slaves who run away are those of 'decidedly bad character', and 'good' slaves reproach them for the expense and inconvenience they cause in their capture and return. Such bad fellows were not held up as heroes in the slave yards, says Carmichael, but are avoided and disregarded.[44]

The fact is, says Carmichael, that the blacks do not wish freedom, and the abolitionists have constructed a political discourse around the myth that planters were denying them all forms of liberty. Slaves requesting freedom was something 'I never heard of in St Vincent', she says, 'unless by the term free, be understood "free time", with all the allowances of a slave'. 'The greatest boon that could be conferred on a St Vincent slave', she concludes, 'was to let him remain a slave with all his allowances; his grounds, house, clothing etc., and have his "own free time"'. 'The really good negro is wonderfully little impressed' by the idea of freedom, but for the 'lazy and the bad' negro, freedom is prized by them, not for the sake of personal liberty in the British sense of the word, but as they have invariably told me, "to sit down softly". Freedom, so given and so used, will never be productive of civilisation or Christianity'.[45]

Carmichael's campaign to establish that 'all good negroes are contented and happy, and attached to their masters', rests upon the proposition that it would be 'absurd to suppose that two or three white men could have kept up any authority on estates where there is always such a majority of negroes' if they wanted freedom. She pays no attention to the wider aspect of white power – armed militia, imperial regiments, and naval fleets – that confronted slaves, neither did she interpret the evidence she amassed with respect to slaves' uncooperativeness and subversion as expressive of an anti-slavery consciousness. Her aim is to establish blacks' unpreparedness for 'the boon of freedom', with the warning that with such an event they would 'fall back again to the habits of savage life'. Emancipation, she believed, would not be beneficial but injurious to blacks – 'both spiritually and temporarily'.[46]

Conceptual inconsistencies, however, are found in Carmichael's narrative on the question of slaves' perception of freedom and their everyday conduct. She tells us that the few slaves who could read presented interpretations, 'distorted and mangled', of Parliamentary debates on slavery to the slave community. The effect of slave yard discourse 'was instantly visible. There was a total change of conduct'. She felt this shift in consciousness on her estate, and believed that her 'slaves' were saying to her 'plainly enough – take care what you are about, for if you dare find fault with me, I'll make you smart for it'. In this section of her polemic, Carmichael's concern is to strengthen the pro-slavery argument that West Indian society was profoundly destabilised by anti-slavery speeches made in Parliament, and that the slave revolts which took place after the Slave Registration Bill of 1814 can be attributed to this source.[47]

The shifting sands of slave consciousness, were recognised and recorded by Carmichael in a manner which suggested she knew that her 'good' and 'bad' negroes could very well be the same people. Evidence of this is found in her admission that she never had 'perfect confidence in the slave population', and that she was aware of their determination 'to be influenced by no treatment however kind; and who shewed in their every action that they looked upon [her], being their proprietor, as necessarily their enemy'. She recognised, also, that those very 'good slaves' who she 'devoted a certain portion of time to their religious and moral instruction' and in whom she 'had to a great extent gained their confidence', turned out to be 'the most worthless and disreputable of all characters'.[48]

Abolitionists, Carmichael tells us, had completely corrupted the character and subverted the moral training of perfectly good slaves with their rhetoric about freedom and social justice. The Blacks, she says, rapidly arrived at the conclusion that the freedom to be given them by 'Massa King George' entailed his purchase of 'all the estates' for distribution among them, and 'a total exemption from regular work'. Freedom, then, meant land distribution, abolition of all 'massas', and deregulation of the work regime. The anti-slavery movement, she argued, should take full blame for this 'disastrous' state of affairs, since at no time did its members propose the case for 'some preparatory course'.[49]

Carmichael knew, at the time of writing, that she had backed a losing cause, and that slave emancipation with slaveholder compensation was inevitable. She did not believe the slaves sufficiently advanced in 'civilisation and religion' to benefit from freedom. Neither did she think that they would 'work like freemen' – giving five consecutive days per week of honest work.[50] Without slavery, she maintained, the West Indian world could not supply the quantity of produce needed to justify it as an imperial project. She claimed that the planter had been sacrificed on the alter of misdirected liberal political opinion, and the West Indies would follow in the disastrous path blazed by the blacks of Haiti.

As a polemic, Carmichael's text was a highly spirited promotion of the West Indian planter. Her obvious familiarity with the arguments and strategies of the abolitionists and their supporters sharpened the focus of her critique of their politics, and set it apart as a vital feminine link in the pro-slavery ideology of the early nineteenth Century. Few educated women were willing to take up the planters' cause in this way; it was more likely that they would rally around the wider network of opinion that came to support anti-slavery legislation.

Endnotes

1 Mrs. Carmichael, *Domestic Manners and Social condition of the White, Coloured, and Negro Population of the West Indies*, 2 vols. [183] (Negro Univ. Press, N.Y. 1969).

2 vol. 1, p. 300.

3 pp. 300, 301.

4 *Ibid.*

5 pp. 301-302.

6 pp. 304-305.

7 p. 302
8 *Ibid.*
9 p. 303
10 p. 306
11 vol. 2. p. 31.
12 vol. 2. p. 30.
13 vol. 2, p. 216.
14 vol. 2, pp. 216-217.
15 vol. 1, pp. 249-250
16 vol. 2, p. 6
17 vol. 2, p. 4
18 vol. 2, pp. 6-7.
19 vol. 2, pp. 6, 8, 11.
20 vol. 2, p. 12.
21 vol. 2, p. 11.
22 vol. 2, pp. 6-7.
23 vol. 1, pp. 27-70
24 vol. 1, pp. 275-276.
25 vol. 1, p. 276.
26 vol. 2, p. 153.
27 vol. 1, p. 21.
28 vol. 1, pp. 186, 188.
29 vol. 1, p. 96.
30 vol. 1, pp. 97-99.
31 vol. 1, pp. 99-100.
32 vol. 1, pp. 132-33.
33 vol. 1, p.138.
34 vol. 1, pp. 138-39.
35 vol. 2, pp. 198-99
36 vol. 1, p. 180.
37 vol. 1, pp. 22-23.
38 vol. 1, pp. 39, 62.
39 vol. 1, p.71.
40 vol. 1, pp. 75, 78.
41 vol. 1, pp. 56-57.
42 vol. 1, p. 58.
43 vol. 1, p. 58
44 vol. 2, p. 26.
45 vol. 2, pp. 106, 194.
46 vol. 2, p. 195.
47 vol. 1, p. 244.
48 vol. 1, p. 245.
49 vol. 1, pp. 246-47.
50 vol. 2, p. 285.

PART THREE

Subversions

8

Old Doll's Daughters

Slave Élitism and Freedom

Most eighteenth-century accounts of slave societies contain fairly detailed descriptions of the life experiences of groups of so-called 'privileged' or 'élite' slaves. Generally, these accounts contrast the 'superior' life-styles of skilled and supervisory slaves with those of the slaves in field gangs. The social conditions of field slaves are portrayed as materially impoverished, intensively monitored and restricted, and socially dishonorable. More often than not, contemporaries explain that this difference among the slaves was rooted within two distinct but related developments: the occupational and technological complexity of plantation production, and the ability and willingness of slave owners to grant some slaves special material benefits and social liberties commensurate with their perceived economic and social worth. Old Doll's family in Barbados was one such group, some of whom came to see themselves as more free than enslaved.

Historians of slavery, in turn, have generally recognised the heterogeneity of the labour force, and have acknowledged the relation between slave occupation and social status.[1] Social structure studies, however, as well as other more specific inquiries into slave life, rarely contain discussions of status differentiation that are set out in terms of family achievement and identity. Through a close examination of occupational status among the female slaves in a Barbados family, with reference to their different life experiences, this chapter explores how gender, work, and social relations were connected.

It is no longer contentious to suggest that analyses of social stratification among slaves which ignore the roles of gender and occupation are not likely to reflect the realities of plantation life. Although colonists in the West Indies perceived their slaves in broadly equalitarian terms while framing legislation for their control, considerations of gender fundamentally influenced their social attitudes and managerial polices. Consequently, slaveowners' records show that both the sex and the occupations of slaves noticeably influenced their access to material resources and social betterment. A number of recent studies on Caribbean female slavery have acknowledged the connection and have called for a major reassessment of the literature about slave production and social life.[2]

Marietta Morrissey, for example, has argued that while slave men, by virtue of their greater access to certain resources (skilled positions, hiring out, provision gardens), had status and authority over slave women and children, slave women had greater access to other resources, including manumission, domestic work, intimate unions with nonslave persons, and the potential for bearing free children.[3] While Morrissey and others have given us a better understanding of the social structure of the slave community, there is still need for more research into the extent to which specific slave families and occupational groups developed and expressed distinct identities and consciousness.[4]

If occupational and status differentiation within the slave 'class' should be explained within the context of the technical and social organization of work, perhaps more attention should be paid to the structure of labour processes than to the general theme of slave treatment in owner-slave relations. Some observers of slave society clearly understood this. William Dickson, anti-slavery advocate, wrote in 1789 that although 'slavery, properly speaking, admits of no distinctions of rank, yet some slaves live and are treated so very differently from others that a superficial observer would take it for granted they belong to classes of men who hold distinct ranks in society, so to speak, by tenures essentially different.'

The groups of slaves Dickson described as the 'privileged few' were the 'porters, boatmen, and fishermen' in the towns, the 'black drivers, boilers, watchmen, mechanics, and other black officers on estates,' and 'above all, the numerous and useless domestics, both in town and country.' These slaves, he stated, live in comparative 'ease and plenty' and do not 'feel any of the hardships of slavery, but such that arise from the caprices of their owners.' Dickson noted, however, that 'truth obliges one to say that the great body of the slaves, the field people on sugar plantations, are generally treated more like beasts of burden than like human creatures.'[5]

Dickson's general comments about domestics were not typical of those made in the eighteenth and early nineteenth centuries, though some household slaves were frequently described as ill-disciplined and living in excessive material comfort under an easy work regime. Elite white households, in particular, were described as over-staffed as a result of the planters' propensity to emulate the European gentry. Dickson reported a case of a lady he knew who 'retained about fifty of the idlers.'[6] In 1780 there were just over 5,000 slaveholders in Barbados. The average slaveowning household employed three domestic slaves, which gives an approximate total of just over 15,000 of these slaves. In that year, a Select Committee of the House of Assembly reported that about 25 per cent of the 62,115 slaves in the colony (15,529) were employed in 'menial' domestic service. More than half of these 15,529 domestics were female, and about 20 per cent (3105) were housekeepers. It would not be unreasonable, then, to suggest that 5,000 slaveholders in 1780 employed 3,105 slave housekeepers out of a total of 15,529 domestics.[7] Barry Higman found that in 1817 about half of all slaves in Bridgetown were domestics and that 70 per cent of all domestics in plantation households were female.[8]

Slave Women achieved their highest status and greatest socioeconomic rewards through household occupations. Some women did achieve limited status in the production system as drivers of the 'subordinate groups' comprised of children and young adults. There is no evidence they were ever made drivers of the first or 'great' gang. Women were also discriminated against in skilled artisan trades, with the exception of sewing and related crafts. While they also worked in the industrial sector of the plantations, they were generally associated with mundane, unskilled tasks, such as feeding canes to the mills and assisting boilermen.

Plantation records commonly grouped female domestics together under the title 'women in office' or 'house women.' Such lists were headed by the housekeeper and included cooks, nannies, nurses, maids, seamstresses, and laundresses. An inventory (21 May 1796) of slaves on the Lower Estate of John Newton in Christ Church parish lists elite slaves (as shown in table 8:1 below). In addition to women in office, a group of superannuated women were said to work at miscellaneous tasks about the house. These women were retired and infirm fieldworkers who were called upon to do light tasks about the plantation yard where the manager's house was located.

The origins of the integration of slave women into domestic service in Barbados date back to the crisis of white indentured servitude during the early colonising period in the mid-seventeenth century. During the 1660s suitable white female servants were hard to come by, and the planters considered those arriving from Britain expensive and undesirable. The stereotype of these such female servants, as deported convicts, 'debauched' and 'disease ridden wenches,' served also to discourage many householders from employing them as domestics.[9] By the 1670s, planters expressed a distinct preference for Amerindian and black women as domestics. Barbados planters perceived *Slave Women*, unlike white servants, as having no interests or rights that transcended those of the plantation. They were considered to be economic investments that also offered non-pecuniary benefits.

In 1675 John Blake, who had recently arrived on the island, informed his brother in Ireland that his white indentured domestic servant was a 'slut' and he would like to be rid of her. He could not do this immediately, however, as his wife was sick. But recognising that 'washing, starching, making of drinks and keeping the house in order' was no 'small task to undergo' in the colony he reasoned that 'until a niger wench I have, be brought to knowledge, I cannot... be without a white maid.'[10] John Oldmixon, an English historian of the British Empire in America, noted in 1708 that Barbados planters rarely kept white servants and that the 'handsomest,' 'cleanliest' 'black maidens' were 'bred to menial services' in and about the households.[11]

Of all domestic slaves, housekeepers were the only females invested with authority in household matters. They were expected to be domestic supervisors, confidantes to the owners, and nannies to their children. Unlike domestics such as cooks, washerwomen, and maids, who were frequently advertised for sale in the island's newspapers, housekeepers rarely changed hands. When retired, housekeepers tended to maintain close relations with household authority which formed the basis of their social status. Dickson noted that Barbados housekeepers were often fed from the family table and that their victuals were well dressed and of good quality.[12] One visitor to the colony commented on their familiarity during household events and seemed concerned that they should be 'occupied listening to any good stories and laughing at them much louder than any of the company.'[13]

***Table 8:1* Principal Female Slaves at Newton Plantation, Barbados, 1796**

Women in Office

Name	*Occupation*
Doll	Housekeeper
Dolly	In the house
Betsy	In the house
Jenny	In the house
Mary Thomas	In the house
Mary Ann	In the house

Source: **Newton Papers, 1796, m. 523/225-92, Senate House Library, University of London**

Karl Watson has made much of the apparent intimacy that existed between housekeepers and owners in Barbados. For him, the houskeeper was regarded as part of the emotional core of the planter's household, being treated as a member of the family. To support his contention, he used the correspondence of the Alleyne family, prominent members of the ruling oligarchy. He cited an 1801 letter written by John Foster Alleyne while visiting England with his wife, who had gone there to give birth. Alleyne addressed the letter to Richard Smith, his estate manager, indicating that he expected his housekeeper and other 'faithful domestics will rejoice in hearing that their mistress had a very favourable time in her lying in.' According to Watson, Alleyne had taken Meggy, his housekeeper, to England on an earlier trip and had sufficient confidence in her to believe that she would celebrate the birth of his child.[14]

In some cases, however, the evidence which illustrates such elements of mutual trust and confidence in the relations between housekeepers and owners also reflects a different experience for other domestics. Unlike housekeepers, who were valued for their supervisory training, other domestics were not considered skilled workers. This attitude was reflected in their market value and in the nature of their work.[15] Not all commentators agreed with Dickson that domestics were idlers treated with a degree of indulgence that frequently warranted their visitation by 'jumpers' (slave whippers).[16] Many suggested, to the contrary, that the work conditions of some domestics were little better than those of field slaves. Dr George Pinckard in late 1790 described the labour of washerwomen and maids and found them no better off than field slaves. He drew attention to the several 'callous scars' that could be found on their bodies, the result of 'repeated punishments.'[17]

F. W. Bayley in the 1820s, supported Pinckard's observations. Bayley noted that the arduous nature of the work of some domestics, particularly the water carriers, was comparable to that of first-gang *Slave Women*. He saw the water carriers making serveral trips to distant streams and rivers, 'bending under the weight of wooden cans of water' which they carried on their heads.[18] Such evidence suggests that the work of various categories of domestics should be carefully differentiated so that the role and status of housekeepers can be conceptualised in terms of their co-opted submanagerial status.

Elizabeth Fenwick's experiences with her domestic slaves in Bridgetown during the early nineteenth century reflect other dimensions of the complex arrangements and conditions under which female slaves worked and expressed their consciousness.[19] Even more than Dickson before her, Fenwick was able to capture the dialectical relations between slavery and resistance, subordination and power, as they occurred in everyday life.[20] This judgement, however, did not mitigate her responses to the horrors she experienced as a mistress of domestic slaves, whom she accused of being responsible for her negative attitudes to the colony and of continuously threatening to drive her away.[21]

Hired-out domestic slaves were more likely to treat their employers, rather than their owners, in a contemptuous manner. Several contemporaries commented on this, and inexperienced slaveholders soon learned that the best slaves were not hired-out but kept for their owner's purposes.[22] Domestics were employed to cook, wash, and clean, and they often also purchased household items from stores.[23] These shopping errands presented domestics with opportunities to express general insubordination. They never returned on time, using the 'better part of the day' walking the streets and visiting friends. Disturbed by the high wages of hired servants and distressed by their performance, householders would often decide to purchase slaves.[24]

Apart from the general character of domestic slavery, white female householders were also concerned with wider social domestic matters.[25] Many spoke about the 'evil' of white males and considered their domination of slave women the disgraceful part of black enslavement.[26] This culture, Fenwick believed, not only corrupted masculine values but also subverted public morality. She was intensely concerned when her young nephew, Orlando, arrived in Barbados from England. She hoped that he would not 'acquire those vices of manhood' which males openly displayed in promiscuous relationship with domestics.[27] She recognised, however, that owing to the subordinate and powerless condition of domestic slaves in relation to white men, many of these slaves pursued sexual relations as a mission of betterment. She considered both slaves and masters victims of slavery and condemned it as a 'disgraceful system' not consistent with the cultivation of 'excellence of character.'[28]

Though housewomen sometimes experienced great psychological stress because of their close proximity to white authority, and many lived in fear of sexual abuse and loss of their lives at the hands of owners and managers, they still preferred housework to fieldwork. While many domestics ran away, the dread of being sent to the field gangs, which they considered a most severe punishment, was frequently sufficient to force many to conform to the wide ranging demands of owners. If, according to Dickson, 'a house negro ever chose, or seem to choose, to go into the field, it is to flee from unsupportable domestic tyranny.'[29]

Some of these generalisations can be tested, using evidence from the Newton estate papers. These documents contain information on such matters as the material and social achievements of *Slave Women*, the nature of their social and sexual relations, their pursuit of freedom, and the considerations which shaped their social consciousness. From the mid-eighteenth century to the closing years of slavery, one slave family of five women – Old Doll, her three daughters, and her niece – dominated domestic service on Newton's estate in Barbados. This family of 'special status' was listed separately from other slaves in managers' reports. They succeeded in acquiring the use of slaves for their own domestic work, some amount of integration within white society, literacy, and property of their own.

During the early 1790s, Elizabeth Newton handed over her estate to two cousins, Thomas and John Lane. One condition of the transfer was that Old

Doll, her long-serving housekeeper, and Old Doll's family were to continue to enjoy the standard of living to which they had been accustomed under her management. This meant, among other things, that they would continue to dominate the key role of housekeeper on the estate. They were definitely not to work in the fields nor perform any arduous manual task. The new owners made a conscientious effort, in spite of complaints from their managers, to comply with these requests. One interesting result was that Old Doll's family became the centre of social and labour disputes on the estate for over a decade.

In 1796 Sampson Wood, the Newton estate manager, sent Thomas Lane, in London, a 'Report of the Negroes.'[30] This extremely detailed document provided information about the slaves' ages, places of birth, occupations, family patterns, sex, and market values. Included in the report was a list of the members of Old Doll's family, with descriptions of their character and general behaviour. Old Doll is listed as about sixty years old; she 'does nothing,' having been superannuated after some forty years as the estate's housekeeper. Two of her daughters (Dolly, aged twenty-eight, and Jenny, aged thirty) were described as 'doing little' about the estate.

Wood outlined the problem of keeping Dolly, Jenny, and their cousin Kitty Thomas in 'high office,' yet not idle. He explained that when it was possible to 'just catch at a little employment now and then for them, we do so, such as cutting up and making negro clothing, but this is but once a year and but for a few days.' Dolly, he added, who attended him in sickness, was 'a most excellent nurse,' for which he had 'some obligations to her.' Wood felt that while Old Doll and her mulatto sister, Mary Ann, should be excused on account of their long service on the estate, but Jenny and Kitty could not be treated similarly because they were 'young, strong, healthy, and have never done anything.' According to Wood, these women had been 'so indulged' that any hard work on the estate 'would kill them at once.'

William Yard, his predecessor, had 'put them into the field by way of degradation and punishment,' but this only caused Old Doll's entire family to resent Yard's management and to try their best to undermine it. During this time, 'they were absolutely a nuisance in the field and set the worst examples to the rest of the negroes.' When Wood later brought them back into the household, it was a major victory for the family in its struggle to maintain its privileged status. Mrs Wood, mistress of the estate, put Dolly to needlework and Jenny to the more prestigious occupation of housekeeping. Kitty was also brought into the house, but no account was given of her precise role. Wood later complained that Dolly had told him in conversation that 'neither she nor Kitty Thomas ever . . . swept out a chamber or carried a pail of water to wash'; Old Doll had other slave assistants to do that sort of work. 'What think you Sir, of the hardship of slavery!' the exasperated Wood declared in his report.

Old Doll's family not only had access to slave attendants, but they also 'owned' slaves who waited on them.[31] This situation accentuated their élite status in the eyes of whites and blacks. Thomas Saer, the white sexual mate of Mary Ann, had willed her a female slave named Esther. By the time of Wood's report, Esther had five children living, two boys and three girls who, though legally belonging to the Newton estate, were by custom in Mary Ann's possession. Esther's children 'slaved' for Old Doll's family, and this relationship meant that Jenny, Kitty, and Dolly were raised to consider themselves 'more free than slave.' Ultimately, the plantation house was the only place where they could work on the estate that was consistent with their social standing and consciousness.

The women in Old Doll's family aspired to sociosexual relations with free men, particulartly whites. Success in such ventures was symbolic of achievement and status. It was an index by which the whole society of black and whites would judge them, and it was also a way to minimise the possibility of their (and their children's) relegation to field labor. By systematic 'whitening' of children through conscious selection of mates, these women sought to diminish the threat of servitude. Mary Ann had four children by Saer, a white man. Wood described these children as being 'as white as himself.' Importantly, their colour immediately absolved them from field labor.

Dolly was the mistress of William Yard when he managed the estate, and she frequently used the relationship to gain access to plantation stores from which she and a cousin supplied dried goods to the family. Wood noted in his report that all the girls 'either have or have had white husbands, that is, men who keep them.' Mary Thomas, daughter of Mary Ann, whom Wood described as 'extremely heavy, lazy, and ignorant,' had a long-standing sexual relation with the white bookkeeper, with whom she had a son. Jenny also had sexual relations with white men. The records do not show that either Mary Thomas or Jenny had intimate relations with slave men, which was unlikely because of their perceptions of elitism, authority, and self-esteem.

Élite slaves, then, went about the establishment and consolidation of their distinct social identities in a self-conscious and systematic manner. They pursued and valued the measure of recognition that white society gave them. This was the most effective way, for such slaves, of distancing themselves from the harshness of slavery and increasing their chances of attaining social freedom. One important way such recognition was conferred, was for whites to address them as 'miss' or 'mister.' Another, was when owners paid them money wages for certain tasks or as an incentive to perform special duties. Artisans, drivers of the first gang, and housekeepers occasionally achieved these two objectives.

Old Doll's Family, 1798: Newton Estate

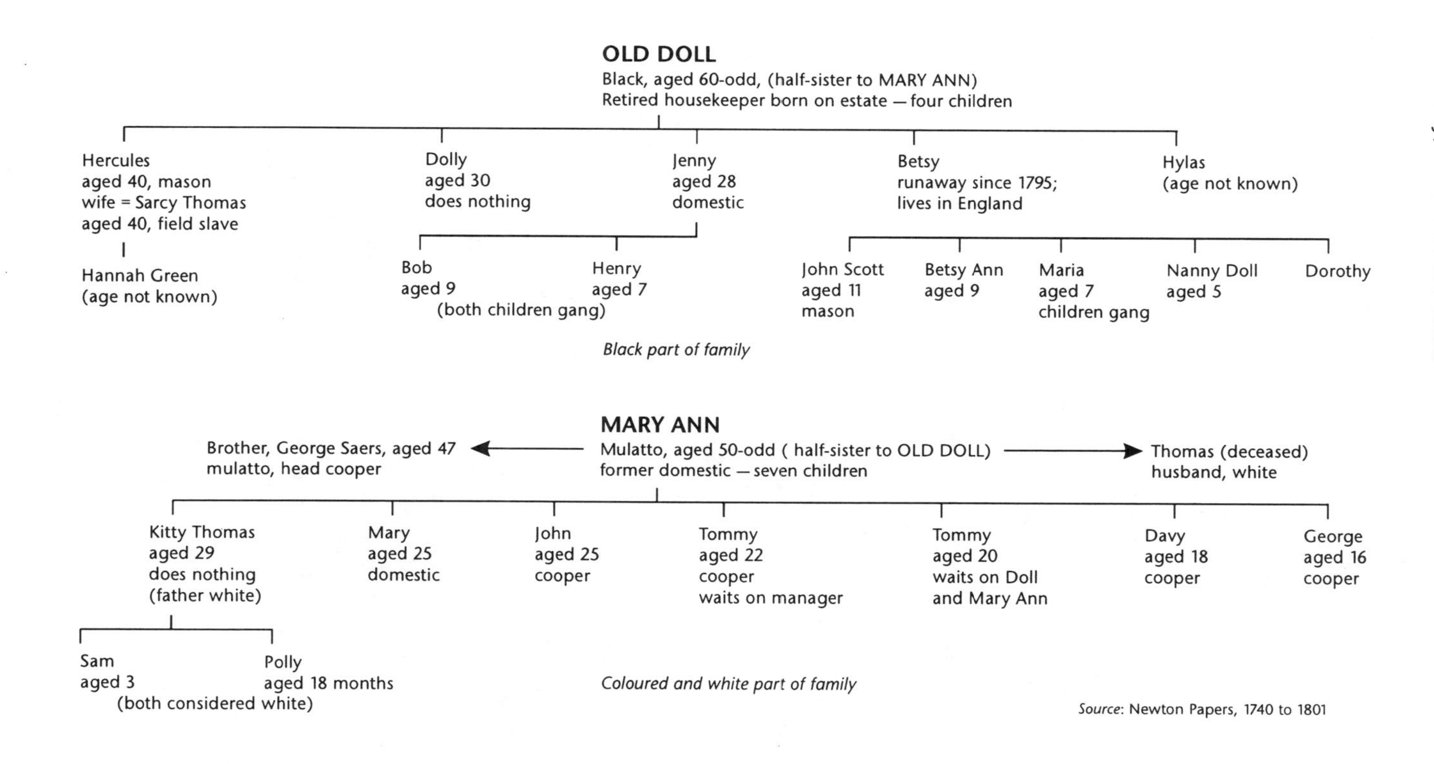

Slaves considered literacy and the attainment of professional skills to be critical in their pursuit of status and betterment in general. Michael Craton has suggested that no more than 2 per cent of British Caribbean slaves were literate in the early nineteenth century, and that most of these were likely to be housekeepers and other élite slaves.[32] Old Doll and her daughters were literate. Dolly and Jenny were therefore able to successfully petition their absentee owner for their children's manumission between 1804 and 1818. It became increasingly common for élite slaves to pay literate members of their community to act informally as teachers, though whites opposed policies that facilitated formal schooling for the children of élite slaves.

At Newton's estate in 1795, Old Doll attempted to persuade manager Wood, to allow her two grandsons to attend school. In his report to Thomas Lane in 1796, Wood stated: 'Doll wants me to put two of her grandchildren (Jenny's children) to school to learn to read and write. I told her I should put them to some trade as soon as they were set for it, but as to putting them in school to read and write, I must consult you about, which I do now.' Wood added, 'If you ask my opinion about it, I shall tell you that I shall be glad to add to the little knowledge of anyone whatsoever, and it is almost a cruelty when it is in our power to indulge them, to withhold it from them.' Wood, however, had some reservations, in that 'inclination must give way to policy.' He believed that 'it is a bad one in their situation to bestow on them the power of reading and writing. It is of little good, and very frequently producer of mischief with them.'[33] Wood got his way on this occasion, but the evidence about Old Doll's family show that overall, domestics struggled with some success to improve the social and material lot of their famlies against restrictive plantation policies and other constraints imposed by the wider slave system.

Several features of Old Doll's family are emphasized by the plantation records dealing with the genealogical patterns of slaves: first, the low profile of men as fathers – neither Doll's father nor husband(s) are explicitly mentioned; and second, the predominant role of women in decision-making and other leadership aspects of family life. As a former housekeeper, Old Doll was retired with security, and occupied her remaining years protecting and directing the lives of her children and grandchildren – both males and females. As head of the extended family her authority was respected by all, including her younger mulatto half-sister, Mary Ann, who was married to a white man and had seven children.

Mary-Ann, in turn, used her influence to ensure that her younger brother, George, the estate's head cooper, made provisions for the professional training of her young sons. Uncle George took all four of his nephews under his wing as apprentice coopers, including ten-year-old George. All of Doll's and Mary Ann's sons were trained as craftsmen and their daughters protected from the scourge of field labour as adults. Certainly, the family was very successful in ensuring the perpetuation of élite status among its members at the expense of other less fortunate families. With severe competition for the few highly prized occupations on the estates it was to be expected that élite families would close ranks and reinforce their advantage.

Even though colour was a critical factor in status achievement and social experiences, and also enhanced ideological differences between the black and coloured communities, Old Doll's family, in spite of its clear colour division, held together closely and struggled as one. This can be attributed mainly to the intimate relations between Doll and Mary Ann, but the growing 'élite' consciousness of the colony's slave labour aristocracy was also an important factor. That this family should function in this manner suggests that perhaps within families, colour as a divisive social force was not as potent a factor as in the wider social order. Old Doll was frequently brokering on behalf of her sister's 'white' children, while her sister's slaves worked for both parts of the family. It was certainly Doll's social authority that held the family together as a surviving unit rather than Mary Ann's status as grandmother of 'white' children. Furthermore, the weak image of men that emerges from the documents enhances Old Doll's stature as head of the family, and thereby reinforces the fact that women were by no means 'second class' individuals within the slave yards.

Manager Wood's 1796 'Report' is also particularly detailed on marital patterns and family size. He stated at the outset that 'all negroes that have neither father or mother attached to their names have none alive, and all women whose husbands' names are not mentioned, having children, their husbands are men who do not belong to the estate'. These data point to the significant extent to which nuclear-style families were part of the plantation's slave community. When Old Doll died, many white persons, some of prominent families, attended her funeral. Her body was taken to the burial place on a horse-drawn hearse, accompanied by solemn music, and interred by an Anglican clergyman. For a housekeeper, Old Doll had unquestionably achieved superior social standing.

Probably the most perplexing duties of female slave domestics were breastfeeding, weaning, and caring for their owners' white children. Popularised images of black wet nurses with their own child on one breast and that of their mistress on the other, though representing, in part, a romanticised image of *Slave Women*'s ultimate subservience, were not unreal. In his notes on Barbados, Pinckard recorded his reaction on seeing a slave nanny breast-feeding a white child in the home of a prominent planter. At the time, the planter and his wife were entertaining other European guests. As the child needed to be fed, the nanny was called upon. The planter's guests were most embarrassed by the sight of a white child sucking the black breast. To make matters worse, some 'respectable' creole ladies began to assist by 'slapping, pressing, shaking about and playing with the long breasts of the slave, with very indelicate familiarity . . . without seeming to be at all sensible that it was, in any degree, indecent or improper.[34] Élite white women in Barbados commonly preferred black nannies to nurse their children, and nannies were also responsible for the children until they became adults.

While black nannies, whether maids or housekeepers, socialised their own children as slaves, they also assisted their owners in raising their children in support of slavery. Within this complex orbit of psychological expectations, slave nannies moved cautiously in clear appreciation of the dangers involved. But the situation also sometimes caused slaveowners much discomfort. Many lived with the fear that nannies would murder their children, and as a result, infant mortalities were commonly enveloped in suspicion of foul play. As white doctors rarely detected poisonings, slaveowners knew that their greatest security lay in the cultivation of amicable relations with domestic staff. For some *Slave Women*, however, this condition of slavery was in itself unacceptable, and whites who recognised this never felt completely safe. In 1774, a 'favourite' slave nanny in Barbados was convicted for poisoning her owners' infant. Her confession revealed that it was not the first time she had poisoned an infant in the family.[35]

Many whites believed that the experience of house women varied in accordance with the character, class and race of their owners. Pinckard asserted that from observing a domestic's physical appearance it was possible to judge the status of her owner. Sickly looking domestics were thus generally owned by poorer planters.[36] Bayley believed that the free-coloureds treated their black domestics more harshly than did whites, probably because they saw in these women the origins of their own slavery background.[37] Dickson's emphasis was more on the character of slaveowners. Many women, Dickson stated, suffered at the hands of masters who were 'miscreant drunkards and desperados.'[38] He acknowledged, however, that it was difficult to generalise on this matter, and he offered two opposing cases as evidence. In one, a master attempted to chop off his domestic's ear with a cutlass because he believed she had overheard and publicised, to his detriment, an intimate family matter. In the other, he described how masters he knew deliberately fostered intimate sexual relations with domestics, whom they treated exceptionally well, as one way of obtaining information about rebellious designs.[39]

It was no easy matter to differentiate between the use of black women as prostitutes, mistresses, or domestics.[40] Domestic slaves, however, considered themselves better placed than field women to survive slavery. Not only were their life experiences more varied, but their chances of manumission were considerably greater. Higman's analysis of plantation slave mortality rates by sex and occupation shows that, next to head drivers, female domestics had the greatest chance of reaching sixty years of age; also, that urban domestics had the lowest mortality rates among all slave occupational groups.[41] Field women, of course, fared worst; hard labour, regular childbearing, malnutrition, and poor medical care did not make a formula for longevity.

Within the slave community, domestic slaves, particularly housekeepers, were part of a socioeconomic elite whose lives differed from those of field hands in fundamental ways. But their special status also carried elements of an extreme form of social exploitation because of close domestic association with the rulers of the plantation world. Some women were victims of their visibility, while others used their situation to improve significantly their social and material welfare – as well as that of their families. Not all of them developed a mentality of fearful submission to the slaveowners' commands. Some expressed an aggressive consciousness in pursuit of their missions, in spite of disapproval from their owners. Whatever the nature of their condition, few if any would have preferred life as a field hand. Of all the slaves, female housekeepers were the most likely to obtain legal freedom during the years of slavery.[42]

Endnotes

1 See, for example, Elsa Goveia, *Slave Society in the British Leeward Island at the End of the Eighteenth Century* (New Haven: Yale University Press, 1965), pp. 229-33; Brathwaite, *The Development of Creole Society, op. cit.*, pp. 154-62; M. Craton, *In search of the Invisible Man: Slaves and Plantation Life in Jamaica* (Cambridge: Harvard University Press, 1978), pp. 191-223; Higman, *Slave Population, op. cit.*, pp. 187-211; Patterson, *The Sociology of Slavery, op. cit.*; K. Watson, *The Civilised Island: Barbados, A Social History, 1750-1816* (Bridgetown, 1979), pp. 69-76.

2 See Bush, *Slave Women, op. cit.*; Beckles, *Natural Rebels*, op cit.; Morrissey, *Slave Women, op cit.*, 339-67; Reddock, "Women and Slavery", *op. cit.*, pp. 63-80. For comprehensive United States analysis, see D. G. White, *Ar'nt I a Woman? Female Slaves in the Plantation South* (New York: Norton,1985) .

3 Morrissey, *Slave Women, op. cit.*, pp. 64-69.

4 Edited collections have appeared recently with important cross-cultural and comparative treatments of black women's historical experiences in plantation America. See R. Terborg-Penn, S. Harley, and A. Rushing, *Women in Africa and the African Diaspora*, ed. (Washington, D.C: Howard University Press, 1989); ed. F.C. Steady, *The Black Woman Cross-Culturally* (Cambridge, Mass.: Schenkman, 1981); G.Y. Okihiro, *In Resistance: Studies in African Caribbean and Afro-Caribbean, History*, ed. (Amherst: University of Massachusetts Press, 1986); ed. S. Harley and R. Terborg-Penn, *The Afro-American Woman: Struggles and Images* (Port Washington, N.Y.: Kennikat, 1978).

5 Dickson, *Letters, op. cit.*, p. 6.

6 Mrs. Carmichael, whose observations of English West Indian slave society in the early

nineteenth century historians regard highly, noted that the Englishman who could easily suffice with four servants at home in the management of his household demanded fifteen in the Caribbean; see Carmichael, *Domestic Manners, op. cit.*, vol 1, p. 120.

7 *A Report of the Committee of the Council of Barbados, appointed to Inquire into the Actual Conditions of the Slaves in this Island* (Bridgetown, 1822), p. 8; W. Dickson, *The Migration of Slavery, op. cit.*, p. 453; Watson, *Civilised Island, op. cit.*, p. 75.

8 Higman, *Slave Populations, op. cit.*, pp. 191-384. See also Morrissey, *Slave Women, op. cit.* pp. 64-65.

9 See Beckles, *White Servitude, op. cit.*, pp. 138-39; A. Smith, *Colonists in Bondage: White Servitude and Convict Labor in America, 1607-1776* (Chapel Hill: University of North Carolina Press, 1947), pp. 1-15; D. Souden, "Rogues, Whores and Vagabonds: Indentured Servant Emigrants to North America and the Case of Mid-Seventeenth-Century Bristol," Social History 3 (1978): 23-41; Dunn, *Sugar and Slaves, op. cit.*, p. 77.

10 John Blake to brother, November 1, 1675, in Caribbeana: Miscellaneous Papers Relating to the History of the British West Indies, ed. V. Oliver, 2 vols., British Library, vol. 1, pp. 55-56.

11 J. Oldmixon, *The British Empire in America* (reprint, New York: Kelly, 1969), vol. 2, p.129.

12 Dickson, *Letters, op. cit.*, p. 14.

13 'Observation upon the Oligarchy or Committee of Distant Saints in a Letter to the Rt. Hon. Viscount Sidmouth, by an Hereditary Planter', London, 1816, p. 47, British Library.

14 Watson, *op. cit., Civilised Island*, p. 76.

15 Sampson Wood stated in 1796 that the field slaves, the majority of whom were women, were 'the most valuable.' At Seawell estate in Christ Church parish, an 1803 inventory shows that the average value of the thirty-four field women in the great gang was £85.80. At Newton estate in the same year, the average value of women in the great gang was £100, while for the six housewomen it was £85.80. At Newton estate in the same year, the average value of women in the great gang was £114 and the average value of the eight housewomen £76. While the highest value for a Newton housewoman was £150, the highest value for a field woman was £175. At Seawell, where seventy women worked in the fields, the highest value for a field woman was £160, while the highest value for a housewoman was £120. "A Report on the Negroes at Newton Plantation, 1796." Newton Papers,

16 Dickson, *op. cit., Letters*, pp. 6, 39; Watson, *Civilised Island, op. cit.*, p. 75.

17 Pinckard, *Notes, op. cit.*, vol. 1, p. 258.

18 Bayley, *Four Years' Residence, op. cit.*, p. 68.

19 Elizabeth Fenwick to Mary Hayes, December 11, 1814, in Fenwick, *The Fate of the Fenwicks, op. cit.*, pp. 163-64.

20 *Ibid.*, pp. 164-68.

21 *Ibid.*, p. 175.

22 *Ibid.*

23 *Ibid.*, p. 189.

24 *Ibid.*

25 *Ibid.*, p. 207.

26 *Ibid.*, p. 213.

27 *Ibid.*, p. 170

28 *Ibid.*, p. 169.

29 Dickson, *Letters, op. cit.*, p. 7, footnote.

30 Newton Papers, M 523/288, ff 1-20: K. Watson, "Escaping Bondage: The Odyssey of a Barbados Slave Family," paper presented at the Conference of Caribbean Historians, Barbados, 1984.

31 Newton Papers, M 523/381.

32 M. Craton, "Slave Culture, Resistance, and the Achievement of Emancipation in the British West Indies, 1738-1828," in *Slavery and British Abolition, 1776-1848* ed. J. Walvin (London: Macmillan, 1982), p. 104. See also H. Beckles, "The Literate Few: An Historical Sketch of the Slavery Origins of Black Elites in the English West Indies," *Caribbean Journal of Education* 11 (1984): 19-35.

33 Newton Papers, M 523/288, f. 13.

34 Pinckard, *Notes, op. cit.*, vol. 1, p. 260.

35 Dickson, *Letters, op. cit.*, p. 20.

36 Pinckard, *Notes, op. cit.*, vol. 2., pp. 112-13.

37 Bayley, *Four Years' Residence, op. cit.*, pp. 417-18.

38 Dickson, *Letters, op. cit.*, p. 136.

39 *Ibid.*, p. 93.

40 Major Wyvill, Memoirs of an Old Officer (1815), f. 386, MS. Division, Library of Congress, Washington, D.C.

41 Higman, *Slave Populations, op. cit.*, pp. 334-35.

42 J. Handler, *The Unapporpriated People, op. cit.*, p. 53; Higman, *Slave Populations, op. Cit.*, p. 383; Morrissey, *Slave Women, op. cit.*, p. 67.

9

An Economic Life of Their Own

Enslaved Women as Entrepreneurs

Studies of patterns of property ownership and resource use in Caribbean slave societies have generally focused on the economic conditions within the free, mostly white, communities. Particular attention has been given, for example, to the manner in which economic relations developed between the dominant mercantile and planting communities. Examinations of the economic experiences of free people of colour have reinforced opinions held about the tendencies of the white elite to monopolise the market. The slaves' independent economic behaviour, especially for the English colonies, has received less attention. The neglect of this subject is surprising since female slave hucksters had great influence over the informal commercial sector of most island economies. Comprehending the economic role of slave marketing practices will provide both a more accurate understanding of female slave life and a firmer basis for interpreting the nature of owner-slave relations in the economic sphere of plantation culture.

Much evidence exists to illustrate that slaves, particularly females, like free persons, sought to increase their share of colonial wealth by participating in the market economy as commodity producers and distributors, with and without their owners' permission. Although they were undoubtedly the primary victims of colonial economies, in which they were defined and used as property, generations of slaves managed, nonetheless, to identify and pursue their own material interests.[1] By combining their work as fieldhands, artisans, domestics, or whatever with their own productive and commercial activities, female slaves made economic decisions as 'free' persons.

In nearly all instances, property owning whites, who dominated colonial governments in the Caribbean, objected to market competition from slaves and enacted legislation that gradually proscribed their economic activities.[2] Since slave owners considered the slaves' subordination critical to systems of control, they sought to assert their dominance in all economic relations, no matter how petty. In Barbados, female slaves tenaciously resisted such legislative assaults upon this aspect of their independent economic activities, and made from the outset a determined effort to maintain their market participation. At times, Barbadian slave owners adopted concessionary policies, prompted generally by their desire to secure the wider goals of social stability and high levels of labor productivity. Slaves, in turn, converted the most limited concessions into customary rights and defended them adamantly.

Huckstering, the distributive dimension of small-scale productive domestic activity, was an important part of the socio-economic culture of African women. It was certainly as much part of their gender culture as other more well-known aspects of social life, such as religion and the arts. Its continued attractiveness to women in the Caribbean, however, had much to do with the social and material conditions of their enslavement. Huckstering afforded women the opportunity to improve the quantity and quality of their nutrition in environments where malnutrition was the norm.[3] It allowed them to possess and later own property, which in itself represented an important symbolic offensive mission against the established order. It also enabled them to make profitable use of their leisure time. And it afforded them the chance to travel and normalised their social lives as much as possible under highly restrictive circumstances.

The relations between slaves' independent production and huckstering provides the context in which the development of the internal marketing systems can be understood. In what accounts to a typology of food production, Sidney Mintz and Douglas Hall[4] have shown how the autonomous economic life of female slaves in Barbados, and other smaller sugar monoculture plantation colonies, differed from that of their Jamaican counterparts. Within this analysis, they divided plantation systems into two basic categories: first, those in which slaves were fed by their owners, such as Barbados; and, second, those in which slaves were largely responsible for producing their own subsistence, such as Jamaica.

In Barbados especially, planters allotted 'land to food cultivation only by impinging on areas which, generally, could be more profitably planted in cane'. The planters' policy was to 'restrict the land at the disposal of the slaves to small house plots', import food for the slaves, and include 'some food production in the general estate program'.[5] In Jamaica, owners allotted their slaves large tracts of land unsuited to cane production in the foothill of the mountain ranges and there encouraged slaves to produce their own food. These provision grounds or polinks represented the primary form of food cultivation, and slaves were given managerial authority in this activity. In addition to these provision grounds, which were generally located miles from their homes, Jamaican slaves also cultivated little 'house spots'.

The provision grounds on which Jamaican female slaves became experienced proto-peasants constituted the basis of their entry into, and subsequent domination of, the internal marketing system. White society came to depend heavily upon the slaves' produce. There was, as a result, no persistent legislative attempt to arrest and eradicate the slaves commercial activities and, by the mid-eighteenth century, the slaves' domination of the provisions market was institutionalised.[6]

The experience of slaves in Barbados was somewhat different in scale and character than that of those in Jamaica. Barbadian slaves had no provision grounds. They were fed from the owners' stocks, which were both imported and locally produced. Imported salted meat and plantation grown grain were allocated to slaves by their overseers, sometimes on Friday night, but mostly on Sunday morning. Slaves possessed only little house spots, generally no more than 25 yards square, on which to root their independent production and marketing activity. They could not therefore be defined as anything more than 'petty proto-peasants', and yet the vibrancy of their huckstering activities was no less developed than that in Jamaica where slaves cultivated acres of land.

Several visitors to Barbados paid attention to the relationship between female slaves' receipt of food allowances and their huckstering. Dr George Pinckard was especially perceptive. He noted that slaves received their subsistence on a weekly basis, 'mostly guinea corn, with a small bit of salt meat or salt fish', which served for 'breakfast, dinner and supper'. This diet, he added, was 'for the most part the same throughout the year', though 'rice, maize, yams, eddoes, and sweet potatoes form an occasional change'. But the women, 'in order to obtain some variety of food', were often seen 'offering guinea corn for sale' and using the proceeds obtained to 'buy salt meat or vegetables'. When slaves were asked why they preferred to sell or barter their food allocations, Pinckard declared, they would commonly express themselves: 'Me no like for have guinea corn always! Massa gib me guinea corn too much – guinea corn today – guinea corn tomorrow – guinea corn eb'ry day – me no like him guinea corn – him guinea corn no good for guhyaam.'[7] In his 1808 History of Barbados, John Poyer, a white creole social commentator, agreed with Pinckard that slaves would generally 'barter the crude, unsavory, substantial allowance of the plantations for more palatable and nutritious food'.[8]

Pinckard, however, recognised that women did not rely fully on food rations in creating supplies of marketable goods. Rather, he observed, 'those who are industrious have little additions of their own, either from vegetables grown on the spot of ground allotted to them, or purchased with money obtained for the pig, the goat, or other stock raised about their huts in the negro yard'.[9] He regarded it as 'common for the slaves to plant fruit and vegetables, and to raise stocks'. At one hut on the Spendlove estate Pinckard 'saw a pig, a goat, a young kid, some pigeons, and some chickens, all the property of an individual slave'. He observed the advantages of these activities for both slave and owner, for he thought garden plots and livestock afforded slaves 'occupation and amusement for their leisure moments', and created 'a degree of interest in the spot'.[10]

Bayley's account of the slaves' domestic economy, like that of Pinckard's, emphasized the raising of poultry and animals, as well as the cultivation of roots, vegetables, and fruits. He described as 'pretty well cultivated' the 'small gardens' attatched to slave huts. For him, 'slaves have always time' to cultivate their 'yams, tannias, plantains, bananas, sweet potatoes, okras, pineapples, and Indian corn'. To shade their homes from the 'burning rays and scorching heat of the tropic sun', noted Bayley, slaves planted a 'luxuriant foliage' of trees that bear 'sweet and pleasant fruits', such as the mango, the Java plum, the breadfruit, the soursop, the sabadilla and the pomegranate'. In 'every garden' could be found 'a hen coop' for some 'half dozen of fowls' and, in many, ' a pigsty', and 'goats tied under the shade of some tree'. Bayley also observed that while the animals were 'grazing or taking a nap' a watchful 'old negro woman was stationed near' to ensure that 'they were not kidnapped'.[11]

Retailing was black women's principal means of raising the cash necessary for their purchases, and many produced commodities specifically for sale. Sunday was their main market day (until 1826, when it became Saturday), although it was customary for 'respectable overseers and managers' to grant slaves time off during the week when 'work was not pressing' in order to market 'valuable articles of property'.[12] The established Anglican Church was never happy with Sunday marketing. In 1725 the catechist at Codrington Plantation informed the Bishop of London, under whose See Barbados fell: 'In this Island the Negroes work all week for their masters, and on the Lord's Day they work and merchandise for themselves; in the latter of which they are assisted, not only by the Jews, but many of those who call themselves Christians'.[13] Efforts made by the estates' managers to prevent Sunday trading were unsuccessful, and many insurbordinate slaves went to their beds 'with very sore backsides unmercifully laid on'. The catechist suggested that the 'force of custom' among slaves in this regard would inevitably break' through 'managerial resolve'.[14]

Descriptions of slave huckstering illustrate the extent to which these fettered entrepreneurs made inroads into the colony's internal economy. Dickson reported in the late eighteenth century that black women were seen all over the island on Sundays walking 'several miles to market with a few roots, or fruits, or canes, sometimes a fowl or a kid, or a pig from their little spots of ground which have been dignified with the illusive name of gardens'.[15] J. A. Thome and J. H. Kimball, who witnessed the disintegration of Barbados slavery, had much to say about the role of black women – slave and free – in the internal marketing system. They were impressed by the spectacle of these 'busy marketeers', mostly women, 'pouring into the highways' at the 'crosspaths leading through the estates'. These plantation hucksters were seen 'strung' all along the road 'moving peaceably forward'.

Thome and Kimball described as 'amusing' the 'almost infinite diversity of products' being transported, such as 'sweet potatoes, yams, eddoes, Guinea and Indian corn, various fruits and berries, vegetables, nuts, cakes, bundles of fire wood and bundles of sugar canes'. The women, as elsewhere in the Caribbean, were in the majority. They described one woman with 'a small black pig doubled up under her arm'; two girls, one with 'a brood of chickens, with a nest coop and all, on her head', and another with 'an immense turkey' also elevated on her head. Thome and Kimball were not only impressed with the 'spectacle' of these women marching to the Bridgetown market, but also with their commercial organisation, especially the manner in which their information network conveyed 'news concerning the state of the market'.[16]

Female huckster slaves dominated the sale of food provisions in the Bridgetown market. Numerous urban slaves, however, retailed their cakes, drinks, and a range of imported goods. According to Bayley, many Bridgetown inhabitants gained a livelihood by sending slaves about the town and suburbs with articles of various kinds for sale. These hucksters, mostly women, carried 'on their heads in wooden trays' all sorts of 'eatables, wearables, jewelry and dry goods'. Bayley also commented on the social origins of free persons who dir- ected female huckster slaves. Most, he stated, were less fortunate whites, but it was common for members of the 'higher classes of society' to 'endeavour to turn a penny by sending their slaves on such money-making excursions'.[17] Such slaves retailed exotic items such as 'pickles and preserves, oil, noyau, anisette, eau-de-cologne, toys, ribbons, handkerchiefs, and other little nick-knacks', most of which were imported from the neighbouring French island of Martinque.

Town slaves, who sold on their own account, marketed items such as 'sweets and sugar cakes'. Bayley described these items as 'about the most unwholesome eatables that the West Indies produce'. Female hucksters could be found 'at the corner of almost every street' in Bridgetown, 'sitting on little stools' with their goods neatly displayed on trays. Plantation hucksters, then, posed no competition for their urban counterparts. There was a mutually beneficial relationship in which each provided a market for the others's goods.[18]

From the early eighteenth century, government policies respecting slave hucksters were informed by the planters' beliefs that a significant proportion of the goods sold at the Sunday markets were stolen from their estates. The assumptions that the tiny garden plots cultivated by slaves could not support the quantity of produce marketed and that hucksters were not sufficiently diligent and organised to sustain an honest trade throughout the year underpinned the debates in the Assemblies and Legislative Councils. It was more in the slaves' nature, planters argued, to seek the easier option of appropriating plantation stocks. The charge of theft, therefore, featured prominently in the planter's opinions and policies towards slave hucksters.

The acquisition of plantation stocks by slaves was one likely way to obtain items for the Sunday markets, though such acts of appropriation were difficult to separate from scavenging by malnourished slaves looking to improve their diet. There was little planters could do to eradicate the leakage of stocks into slave villages. In spite of the employment of numerous watchmen and guards to protect their property, they complained constantly about the cunning and deviousness of slaves in this regard.

Contrary to the planters, Pinckard found evidence of a sort of moral economy in which slaves asserted a legitimate right over a satisfactory share of the produce of their labour. Many slaves, he stated, were firm in the opinion that it was not immoral to appropriate plantation stock, but rather it was the master's inhumanity that denied them what was rightfully theirs, an adequate proportion of estate production. Slaves, he said, 'have no remorse in stealing whensoever and wheresoever' and do not accept the notion of 'robbing their masters'. They would commonly respond to the charge of theft, Pinckard added, with the expression: 'me no tief him; me take him from mass'.[19] The slaves' perception of the planter as the guilty party may have fuelled the highly organised system through which they sought redress by the clandestine appropriation of estate goods.

A case illustrative of female slaves' determination to increase their share of estate produce can be extracted from events on the Newton plantation between 1795 and 1797. During this time the manager, Mr Wood, made several references to the confiscation of stocks by slaves and considered it a major problem. Wood's account of the slaves' organised appropriation under the management of his predecessor, Mr Yard, provides a detailed view of extensive contact between plantation theft and huckstering. Dolly, the daughter of Old Doll, the estate's retired housekeeper, was brought into the house by Yard and kept as his mistress. On account of their intimate relations, Dolly obtained access to all stores, and it was believed that she 'pilfered' for the enrichment of her family.

Sir John Alleyne, the estate's attorney, discovered the sexual relation between Yard and Dolly on a surprise visit to the property, and Yard's services were terminated. Dolly was removed from the household, but the flow of goods continued. When Wood conducted his investigation he realised that Billy Thomas, Dolly's cousin, who worked for Yard and was held 'in great confidence' and, trusted with everything', was the culprit. Billy, noted Wood, 'had an opportunity of stealing the key of the box which held the key of the building'. This gave him and his family access to 'the rum, sugar, corn, and everything else which lay at their mercy'. Billy's aunt, Betsy, also a plantation slave, was married to a free black huckster who, 'through these connections', was 'supplied plentifully with everything'. Old Doll also did some huckstering and her home was described by Wood as a 'perfect out-shop for dry goods, rum, sugar, and other commodities'.[20]

A greater problem was posed for planters, however, when their slaves plundered the property of other persons, which was also another way of obtaining articles – especially fresh meat – for sale. Such cases involved more than estate discipline, and at times required criminal litigations. The records of Codrington Estate, for example, show that neighbouring planters commonly sought compensation outside of court when Codrington slaves were presumed guilty of theft. In some instances, however, courts settled such matters. In 1746, for example, Richard Coombs was paid £1 by the estate 'for a hog of his kill'd by the plantation negroes'. The following year James Toppin was paid 3s 9d 'for a turkey stolen from him', and in 1779 the manager paid William Gall £8 when he agreed not to sue at law 'for a bull stolen' from him by a group of field slaves.[21] It was suspected that these stocks found their way onto the market through white intermediaries who worked in league with slaves.

Most contemporaries believed that the typical huckster's income, outside of what was earned from the occasional sale of high priced fresh meats, was meagre.[22] Bayley offered an account of a woman's annual earnings by estimating the values of produce she sold. In normal times, he noted, 'a tray of vegetables, fruits, calabashes, etc.' brought in gross annual receipts of six or seven shillings. The sale of poultry and animals, in addition to 'cane, cloth, and sugar', would increase receipts to about 'ten shillings'.[23] Such an income level, Bayley suggested, could not sustain a slave's life without plantation allowances. Free blacks or poor whites with such an income would have had to resort to the parish for relief.

Bayley, however, considered such modest incomes the result of the slave huckster's lack of the accumulationist spirit. Slavery, he believed, was responsible for the suppression of their acquisitive impulse. He made reference to slaves who had 'the power of earning' but 'frequently neglected it'. He attributed this to 'the cursed spirit of slavery' which 'leaves too many contented with what they deem sufficient for nature, without spurring them to exert themselves to gain an overplus'. Such persons, he added, would 'only cultivate sufficient ground to yield them as much fruit, as many vegetables as they require for their own consumption'. As a result, according to Bayley 'they have none to sell'.[24]

Bayley believed a minority of 'more enterprising' hucksters, who 'strive to make as much as they can', generally do very well. Some even accumulated enough cash to purchase their freedom. Most financially successful slaves in Bayley's opinion, however, lacked the appetite for freedom. 'I have known several negroes', he averred, who had

> accumulated large sums of money, more than enough to purchase their emancipation, but that as they saw no necessity for changing their condition, and were very well contented with a state of slavery, they preferred remaining in that state and allowing their money to increase.[25]

His belief, however, was tempered by the recognition that many slaves realised that free black's material and social life was frequently not an improvement over their own. Consequently, for some slaves it made more sense to seek the amelioration of their condition by the purchase of a 'host of comforts'. The use of cash to facilitate the education of their children was as important as the purchase of a 'few luxuries for their huts', Bayley concluded.[26] Plantation hucksters, who were mostly field slaves, did not live as well as the mechanics, artisans, domestics and drivers or other members of the slave elite. One was more likely to find a driver in a position to offer a visitor 'a glass of wine and a bit of plumcake' than a huckster.[27]

The poor white, living on the margins of plantation society, developed the most noticeable contacts with slave hucksters. From the seventeenth century, many white women labourers, mostly former indentured servants and their descendants, made a living by selling home-grown vegetables and poultry in the urban market. Largely Irish catholics, they were discriminated against in the predominantly English protestant community. They formed their own communities in back country areas of the St Lucy, St John, St Andrew, St Joseph, and St Philip parishes, where they cultivated crops as subsistence peasants on a variety of rocky, wet and sandy, non-sugar lands. Descriptions of their huckstering activity differ little from those of the slaves.

Dickson, who studied the poor whites closely, offered a detailed account of their huckstering culture. Labouring Europeans, mostly women, he stated, 'till the ground without any assistance from negroes', and the 'women often walk many miles loaded with the produce of their little spots, which they exchange in the towns for such European goods as they can afford to purchase'.[28] Their gardens were generally larger than those utilised by slaves, as was the volume of commodities they traded. But in spite of their disadvantage, slaves offered their white counterparts stiff competition especially at the Sunday markets.

The relationship between slave and white hucksters was complex. Both Dickson and Pinckard commented that the marketing patterns and customs of the two showed similarities. White women hucksters were typically seen carrying baskets on their heads and children strapped to the hip in a typical African manner, which suggests some degree of cultural transfer. Dickson stated that some white hucksters owned small stores in the towns and most of these depended upon the exchange of goods with slaves. These hucksters, he said, 'make a practice of buying stolen goods from the negroes, whom they encourage to plunder their owners of everything that is portable'.[29]

Dickson made a strong moral plea for the protection of slave hucksters in their unequal relationship with their white counterparts. Until 1826 slaves had no legal right to own property, and they suffered frequent injustices in their transactions with whites. Many white hucksters, Dickson stated, 'depend for a subsistence on robbing the slaves' by taking their goods 'at their own price' or simply 'by seizing and illegally converting to their own use, articles of greater value', which the 'poor things may be carrying to market'. 'For such usage', he added, 'the injured party has no redress' and so 'a poor field negro, after having travelled eight or ten miles, on Sunday, is frequently robbed by some town plunderer, within a short distance of his or her market, and returns home fatigued by the journey, and chagrined from having lost a precious day's labour'.[30] Slaveowners were not prepared to offer huckster slaves – even those who sold on their account – protection from these white 'plunderers'. Many saw the matter as nothing more than thieves stealing from thieves, from which honest folk should distance themselves.

The detailed descriptions and accounts of slave huckstering offered by visitors to Barbados present a static image which underestimates the social and political tension and conflict that surrounded it. Concealed in these reports was an important social crisis. However common, huckstering was never fully accepted, and slave women struggled to maintain their marketing rights against hostile legislation. From the mid-seventeenth century Barbadian lawmakers designed legislation to prevent slave huckstering by linking it directly to a range of illicit activities. In addition, authorities formulated policies to mobilise the entire white community against the slaves' involvement in marketing by stereotyping slaves as thieves and receivers of stolen goods. Against this background of persistent efforts to criminalise huckstering, slaves attempted to maintain an economic life of their own.

Initially, legislators considered it possible to prevent women slaves going from 'house to house' with their 'goods and wares'. But a difficulty was recognised in that so many whites declared a willingness to accept slave hucksters. Legislators, therefore, had to differentiate this 'deviant' element within the white community and target it for legal consideration. The 1688 Slave Code provided, for instance, that Justices of the Peace were required to identify such whites and warn them against transacting business with slave hucksters.[31] The law also empowered Justices to take legal action against persistent offenders.

In 1694 an assemblyman who considered the 1688 provisions insufficient, introduced two bills designed to remove slaves from the internal market economy. The first bill prohibited 'the sale of goods to negroes' and the second barred 'the employment of negroes in selling'.[32] The debate over this legislation focused on the need to prevent the employment of slaves in activities other than those related to plantations. Some planters, however, expressed concern that a curtailment of slaves' 'leisure' would impair already fragile labour relations on the estates. Slaves had grown accustomed to considerable freedom of movement during non-labouring hours and marketing was a direct consequence of this independent use of leisure time. The implementation of the proposed restrictions would entail closer surveillance of slaves – undoubtedly a major administrative task for local officials and slaveowners alike.

The legislation never became law, but persistent complaints from small-scale white cash-crop producers, urban shopkeepers, and other of the slaves' competitors kept the subject at the forefront of discussion concerning the 'governing' of slaves. In 1708 the first of many eighteenth-century laws was finally passed attempting to undermine the huckstering culture of slave. This 1708 law tackled every aspect of slave huckstering, both as a planter-controlled enterprise and as an independent slave activity. The preamble to the act linked huckstering to slave insubordination and criminality, stating that 'sundry persons do daily send their negroes and other slaves to the several towns in this island to sell and dispose of all sorts of quick stock, corn, fruit, and pulse, and other things', with the result that slaves 'traffick among themselves, and buy, receive and dispose of all sorts of stolen goods'. The 1708 law, therefore, flatly disallowed any white person from sending or employing a slave to sell, barter, or dispose 'of any goods, wares, merchandize, stocks, poultry, corn, fruit, roots, or other effects, or things whatsoever'.[33]

While provisions were made for the punishment of whites – who either transacted with or employed slave hucksters, as well as for the hucksters themselves, the law of 1708 also implicitly recognised the hucksters' existence by stating conditions and terms under which they could legally function. Offending white persons found guilty could be fined £5, while slaves convicted for selling or bartering could receive 'one and 20 stripes on his or her bare back upon proof thereof made by any white person'. Exempted hucksters were allowed to sell 'stocks' to their masters, overseers and managers, and 'milk, horse meat or firewood' to any person. But this concession was also granted on terms that dehumanised the huckster and symbolised criminality, for the huckster had to wear 'a metaled collar' locked about his or her neck or legs. The collar had to display the master's and maker's name and place of residence.[34]

Legislators were concerned specifically with plantation slaves huckstering in Bridgetown, as they had suspected collusion between these slaves, white hucksters and shopkeepers. The 1708 law thus required 'the clerk of the market' to hire annually two able men to apprehend slaves that 'come into the said town to sell' without 'a metal collar' or accompanied by a white person. Magistrates were also empowered to remove all slaves from 'tippling houses, huckstering shops, markets, and all other suspected place' where they might trade with whites.[35]

During the eighteenth century, elements in the white community and their elected representatives remained dissatisfied with the ineffectual nature of the 1708 law. Bridgetown continued to attract large numbers of hucksters from the countryside, who, like the residents in the town, appeared determined to ignore the law. During the 20 years after 1708 reports reaching the government confirmed the continued expansion of huckstering in Bridgetown. In 1733 the island's assembly passed a new law to strengthen and expand the provisions of the 1708 act. This time the law enumerated the foodstuffs and other items that hucksters were allowed to sell. It also enlarged the range of commodities which slaves could not trade, either on their own or their masters' account.[36]

The 1733 law was undoubtedly a response to the growing number of slave hucksters in the years after 1708. It suggests that the planter-controlled government saw hucksters as a threat to efficient slave control and its own economic dominance. The list of commodities that constables and market clerks were empowered to confiscate from slave hucksters now included sugar cane, 'whole or in pieces, syrup, molasses, cotton, ginger, copper, pewter, brass, tin, corn, and grain'. Particular concern was expressed for the welfare of petit white and small planters, whose profits were adversely affected by intense slave competition. In order to protect these persons, the act made it unlawful for slaves to plant crops for the use of anyone but their masters.

Cotton and ginger were singled out; any slave found selling these two crops could be charged for selling 'stolen goods'.[37] In addition, white persons who purchased such items from slave hucksters could be prosecuted for receiving stolen goods. The 1733 Act was amended in 1749, making it illegal for slaves to assemble 'together at Huckster shops' for any reason.[38] Still slaves refused to comply, rendering these provisions ineffective. For example, in 1741 the manager of Codrington plantation, reporting on his slaves' attitudes towards these laws, stated that nothing short of 'locking them up' could keep slaves away from the markets, and such an action would probably result in a riot.[39]

In spite of these laws, then, slave women continued to participate actively in the internal marketing system. In 1773 the legislature came under pressure from Bridgetown merchants who claimed that slave and white hucksters posed unfair competition for their businesses and a public nuisance on account of the noise and litter the slaves' created. The Legislative Assembly responded by appointing a committee to 'settle and bring in a bill for putting a stop to the Traffick of Huckster Negroes'.[40] The committee's bill became law in 1774, proscribing 'free mulattoes and negroes', who hitherto were not singled out for legal discrimination, from the marketplace.[41]

The 1774 act sought to diffuse three decades of accumulated grievances among the island's merchants. This time, however, the Legislature's emphasis was not to attempt the impossible – that is, eradicate huckstering – but to seek its containment. Provisions were made for the punishment of slaves and free people of colour who sold meat to butchers and who operated on 'Sunday, on Christmas Day and Good Friday'. The 1774 law also outlawed slave huckstering 'in or about any of the streets, alleys, passages, or wharfs of any of the towns' and on 'any of the highways, broad-paths and bays'.[42] Slaves found guilty of these offences were to be imprisoned and have their goods confiscated.

The small measure of legitimacy given 'country' hucksters by the 1733 Act was retained in 1774. Such slave hucksters could 'sell firewood and horse meat', items which posed no competition to small white merchants and planters. No mention was made of milk, the sale of which had been allowed under the 1708 act. To those enterprising hucksters, however, who were accused of creating commodity shortages and inflating prices, legislators were particulary hostile. They singled out women hucksters 'who go on board vessels' and who 'go a considerable way out of the respective towns to meet' country hucksters, in order to 'buy and engross' produce with the result that 'the price of stock and provisions are greatly advanced'. Such attempts by slaves to manipulate even corner, the market were outlawed. Offending slave hucksters were liable to receive 21 lashes. Since some offenders were likely to be women, law makers, sensitive to the ameliorative spirit of the time, included a provision that 'the punishment of slaves with child may, in all cases, be respited'.[43]

Established Bridgetown merchants remained dissatisfied with these legal provisions and they lobbied for still tougher measures. In 1779 the 1774 Act, like its predecessors, was amended.[44] The new law aimed to end the 'traffick carried on by slaves' and limit the number of free hucksters – white, coloured, and black. For the first time white hucksters were subject to official regulation, and categorized with free coloureds and free blacks. All free hucksters were now required to obtain a trade licence from the Treasurer at an annual cost of £10, in addition to a processing fee of 25 shillings. This levy, which also served as a revenue measure, sought to eliminate marginal hucksters.

In 1784 an amendment to the 1779 act provided for a penalty of up to three months imprisonment for white persons convicted of buying 'cotton or ginger' from slaves.[45] In November 1784, shortly after the 1779 act was amended, the Barbados Mercury reported that the number of hucksters on the streets of

Bridgetown continued to increase.[46] The Court of Quarter Session subsequently urged the government to adopt a policy towards huckstering which emphasised formal organisation and legitimisation rather than opposition. The government agreed, and hucksters in Bridgetown were instructed to confine themselves to the 'public market place called the Shambles adjoining the Old Church Yard'.[47]

John Poyer, the local historian, opposed the reasoning behind the legislative provisions of 1774, 1779 and 1784, and welcomed, for women's sake, the institutionalisation of the huckster market.[48] Attempts to eradicate slave hucksters and penalise free hucksters, he argued, reflected the monopolistic thinking and tendencies of the commercial élite, which ultimately burdened the majority of the island's inhabitants. Both free and slave hucksters, he insisted, displayed survival skills and energy under adverse circumstance which should be encouraged. White hucksters, he stated, were in great part 'aged and infirm' and women whose capital 'in very few instances' was equal to the 'sum required for a licence'. These persons, he added, could not afford to pay such a levy, and would be forced out of business, resulting in their families becoming 'burdensome to their parish'.[49] As for the slaves, the huckster trade allowed them an income with which they could vary their nutrition. 'Let not the hapless slave', he argued, 'be denied these needful comforts by absurd and unnatural policies.'[50] Poyer led the lobby which in 1794 succeeded in repealing the 1774 and 1779 laws. As a result, huckster markets, such as the Shambles, became accepted in law, and a victory against discriminatory legislation partly won.

During the June 1811 sittings of the Assembly, members were informed that 'Roebuck (a central Bridgetown street) was as much crowded as ever by country negroes selling their goods'.[51] Reportedly, hucksters refused to be confined to the Shambles, which they considered out of the way of pedestrians. From their perspective, Roebuck Street was ideally situated, and it attracted hucksters in spite of stiff penalties attached to street vending. The Assembly also learned that slave hucksters 'do not like to go there [Shambles] because the persons about the market set whatever price upon their commodities and the poor negroes are compelled to take that price'. Hucksters associated the new market with consumer domination, something they were determined to destroy. Freedom of movement, they believed, was the most effective way of gaining some measure of control over prices.

The Shambles became a place of open hostility between female hucksters and constables. Disagreements among hucksters and between hucksters and customers sometimes resulted in affrays. In these instances the clerk of the market would instruct constables to arrest offending hucksters and confine them to the stocks. Stocks were eventually fixed adjoining the market where 'disorderly' hucksters were imprisoned and flogged. In 1811 the Grand

Session was notified that the Shambles had become a public flogging place to the great disgust and annoyance of all who go there and buy and sell.

By the beginning of the nineteenth century the huckster market had become an entrenched institution within the colony, commonly described by visitors as colourful, exciting and attractive. Alongside this formal arrangement, street vending proliferated, and each was an important part of the internal marketing system. In 1826 the 'Sunday and Marriage Act', designed to accelerated the pace of slave Christianisation, finally outlawed Sunday markets and Saturday became the major market day until the present time. After emancipation female hucksters continued to dominate in the marketing of food provisions, although plantations sometimes sold food directly to the public. As in other Caribbean colonies, former slaves took to other types of work, but huckstering remained an attractive occupation.[52] It was an economic niche for women which they had identified and protected during slavery, and which, in freedom, became a cornerstone in the survival strategies for many households.

During slavery the Barbadian internal marketing system revealed the female slaves' struggle to achieve an economic life of their own. Unlike their Jamaican counterparts, Barbadian slaves pursued this objective within the context of persistently hostile legislative interventions from their owners. Evidence confirms the aspect of the Mintz and Hall account which shows that in the sugar monoculture colonies of the English Caribbean slaveowners did not, or could not, make provisions that would enable slaves to produce their own subsistence. A close look at slave huckstering in Barbados, however, requires an important revision of the Mintz and Hall analysis by demonstrating that, in spite of the land handicap suffered by 'small island' slaves, they too were able to establish their own vibrant economic culture based upon the exchange of food allocations, the raising of poultry and stocks, and the intensive cultivation of lands that surrounded their huts.

Endnotes

1 Hilary Beckles, *Natural Rebels, op. cit.*, pp. 72-7; Robert Dirks, *The Black Saturnalia: Conflict and Its Ritual Expression on British West Indian Slave Plantations* (Gainesville, 1987), 69-80; Handler, *The Unappropriated People, op. cit.*, pp. 125-33; Hilary Beckles and Karl Watson, 'Social Protest and Labor Bargaining: The Changing Nature of Slaves' Responses to Plantation Life in 18th Century Barbados', *Slavery and Abolition*, 8 (1987), pp. 272-93; Edward Brathwaite, *Contradictory Omens: Cultural Diversity and Integration in the Caribbean* (Kingston, 1974), 41-3; Sidney W. Mintz and Douglas Hall, *The Origins of the Jamaican Internal Marketing System*, Yale University Publications in Anthropology No. 57 (New Haven, 1960); Sidney W. Mintz, 'Caribbean Market Places and Caribbean History', *Nova Americana* 1, (1980-81), 333-44; John H. Parry, 'Plantation and Provision Ground: An Historical Sketch of the Introduction of Food Crops in Jamaica', *Revista de Historia de America* 39 (1955), 15-18.

2 In 1711, the Jamaican Assembly prohibited slaves from owning livestock, or from selling meat, fish, sugar cane, or any manufactured items without their masters' permission. In 1734 and 1735, the St Lucian Assembly prevented slaves from selling coffee or cotton. Between 1744 and 1765, the French Antillean slave owners passed laws prohibiting slaves from huckstering in towns or trading coffee. In 1767, the St Vincent Assembly forbade slaves to plant or sell any commodities that whites esport from the colony. See Franklin Knight, *The Caribbean: the Genesis of a Fragmented Nationalism* (New York, 1378), p. 92; Beckles, *Black Rebellion, op. cit.*, pp. 71-72; Long, *The History of Jamaica, op. cit.*, vol. 2, pp. 486-87.

3 For an account of slave nutrition, see Kiple, *The Caribbean Slave, op. cit.*, On the impact of malnutrition upon mortality levels, see Richard B. Sheridan, *Doctors and Slaves: A medical and Demographic History of Slavery in the British West Indies, 1680-1834* (Cambridge, 1985): 'The Crisis of Slave Subsistence in the British West Indies during and after the American Revolution', *William and Mary Quarterly*, 3rd series, 23 (1976), 615-43.

4 Mintz and Hall, *Origins, op. cit.*, p. 23.

5 *Ibid.*, 10.

6 Mintz and Hall note that laws in force during the seventeenth century 'make plain that a number of markets were established, formalized, and maintained under government provision . . . ', and that 'formal legal acknowledgment of the slaves' right to market had been in negative form at least, as early as 1711'. Restrictions were applied to the slaves' sale of beef, veal and mutton, but they were allowed to market provisions, fruits, fish, milk, poultry and small stocks. *Ibid.*, 15.

7 Pinckard, *Notes, op. cit.*, vol. 2, p. 116.

8 Poyer, *The History of Barbados, op. cit.*, p. 400.

9 Pinckard, *Notes, op. cit.*, 2: 116-17.

10 *Ibid.*, 1: 368.

11 Bayley, *Four Years Residence, op. cit.*, p. 92.

12 *Report of a Debate in Council on a Dispatch from Lord Bathurst* (Bridgetown, 1822), p. 8.

13 Bennett Jr., *Bondsmen and Bishops, op. cit.*, p. 26

14 *Ibid.*, 24-5.

15 Dickson, *Letters, op. cit.*, p. 11.

16 J. A. Thome and J. H. Kimball, *Emancipation*, p. 66.

17 Bayley, *Four Years Residence, op. cit.*, pp. 60-61.

18 *Ibid.*

19 Pinckard, *Notes, op. cit.*, vol. 2: p. 118.

20 Sampson Wood to Thomas Lane, 1796, M523/288, Newton Papers, Senate House Library, Unitversity of London.

21 Bennett, *Bondsmen and Bishops, op. cit.*, p. 25.

22 In 1822, Mr Hamden, a member of the Legislative Council, reported, 'The goods which they have to take to market are comparatively insignificant; nor are the supplies which they procure from thence less so. The poultry which they raise with the superfluity of their allowance, or the surplus of allowance in kind, which can never be considerable, are the only objects of honest traffic which they have', *Report of a Debate in Council*, 8.

23 Bayley, *Four Years Residence, op. cit.*, p. 422.

24 *Ibid.*, p. 423.

25 *Ibid.*, p. 425.

26 See also Hilary Beckles, 'The Literate Few:An Historical Sketch of the Slavery Origins of Black Elites in the English West Indies', *Caribbean Journal of Education*, 11 (1984), 19-35; Claude Levy, *Emancipation, Sugar, and Federalism: Barbados and the West Indies, 1838-1876* (Gainesville, 1980), 19.

27 Bayley, *Four Years Residence, op. cit.*, p. 425

29 Dickson, *Letters, op. cit.*, p. 41.

29 *Ibid.*, 41-2. In 1741, Abel Alleyne, manager of Codrington Plantation informed the estate owner that the white huckster are 'often worse than the negroes, by receiveing all stolen goods'. Alleyne to the Society for the Propagation of the Gospel in Foreign Parts, 9 Dec. 1741, Letter Book, Vol B8, 51, SPGFP Archives, London. Whites were protected by law from slaves' evidence; also, white hucksters could not be prosecuted if their slave suppliers informed legal authorities. In 1788, Joshua Steele informed Governor Parry that 'under the disqualification of Negro evidence the crime of *receiver of stolen goods* cannot be proven against' white hucksters, and that this acts as an encouragement to them. Reply of Joshua Steele to Governor Parry, 1788, *Parliamentary Papers*, 1789, Vol. 26, 33 (italics in original).

30 Dickson, Letters, *op. cit.*, pp. 41-2.

31 An Act for the Governing of Negroes, 1688, in Richard Hall, *Acts Passed in the Island of Barbados from 1643-1762 inclusive* (London, 1764), 70-71.

32 Journal of the Assembly of Barbados, 17 Oct. 1694, Colonial Entry Book, Vol. 12, 484-6, Public Record Office, London. Also, *Calendar of State Papers, Colonial Series*, 1693-6, 381.

33 An Act to Prohibit the Inhabitants of this island from employing their Negroes and other slaves in selling and Bartering; passed 6 Jan. 1708. See Hall, *Laws, op. cit.*, pp. 185-7.

34 *Ibid.*, pp. 185-6.

35 *Ibid.*, p. 187.

36 An Act for the Better Governing of Negroes, and the more Effectual Preventing the Inhabitants of this Island from Employing their Negroes or Other Slaves in Selling and Bartering, Passed 22 May 1733, Hall, *Laws, op. cit.*, pp. 295-9.

37 *Ibid.*, pp. 298.

38 An Act for Governing Negroes, 1749, in Hall, *Laws, op. cit.*, pp. 355-6.

39 Bennett, *Bondsmen and Bishops, op. cit.*, pp. 24-5.

40 Minutes of the House of Assembly, 6 July 1773, HA 3/15, 1772-4, Barbados Archives.

41 'An Act for the better to Prohibit Goods, Wares, and Merchandize, and other things from being carried from House to House, or about the roads or streets in this Island, to be sold, bartered, or dispose of . . . and to remedy the mischief and inconveniences arising to the Inhabitants of this Island from the Traffic of Huckster Slaves, Free Mulattos, and Negroes', passed 15 March 1774, in Samuel Moore, *The Public Acts in Force, Passed by the Legislature of Barbados, from May 11th, 1762 to April 8th, 1800, inclusive* (London, 1801), 154-71.

42 *Ibid.*, 164.

43 *Ibid.*, 167.

44 *Ibid.*, 212-7.

45 *Ibid.*, 251-5.

46 *Barbados Mercury*, 20 Nov. 1784.

47 *Ibid.*

48 Poyer, *History of Barbados, op. cit.*, pp. 398-419.

49 *Ibid.*, 400-401.

50 *Ibid.*, 400.

51 Minutes of the House of Assembly, 14 June 1811, CO 31/45, PRO.

52 See Handler, *The Unappropriated People, op. cit.*, pp. 125.

10

Taking Liberties

Enslaved Women and Anti-slavery Politics

'My honoured master, I hope you will pardon the liberty your slave has taken in addressing you on a subject which I hope may not give you the least displeasure or offense': thus began a letter dated Barbados 1804 from Jenny Lane, an enslaved creole black woman, addressed to Thomas Lane, her owner. The text of Jenny's letter contains a detailed proposal for the negotiation of her freedom. From Newton Plantation in the southern parish of the island colony, this correspondence, constructed in a language of submission, but bearing the ideology of self-liberation, reached its destination in the City of London through much the same channels as monthly reports from the estate manager concerning the governance of slaves. It was ironical, Thomas Lane thought, that Jenny's letter arrived shortly after a routine correspondence from Mr Wood, his estate Manager, indicating that ill-discipline and turbulence among the slaves necessitated the strict application of laws designed for their suppression.[1]

While such letters are rare, the abundance of evidence that documents women's efforts at negotiating terms of personal freedom stands in contrast to the paucity that details engagement in the bloody warfare that typified the relations between enslaved black and whites in the Caribbean. The archives yield this much about sex, race and anti-slavery politics. Reflecting notions derived from this reading of the evidence, Morrissey asserts: 'women seldom exercised active leadership in Caribbean slave revolts. We have tended lately, therefore, to focus on their participation in indirect forms of protest.'[2] In developing this argument, she concluded:

> Women slaves did not generally fulfill prominent leadership roles in traditionally understood vehicles for revolt, that is, Maroon Communities and rebel movements. They did, however, fill subsidiary

> positions and give many kinds of support to male rebels. Female insurgency may have sometimes been expressed in malingering and in the refusal to conceive and bear children. But evidence of these practices is limited, and their incidence is at odds with other more fully documented tendencies, including physiologically based female subfecundity and high levels of work productivity.[3]

The questions that follow from this statement are many. What is the political significance of an argument which says that physical combat in war should be privileged above broad-based ideological preparation? Why should the male warriors be centred and the non-violent protests of women that harnessed and directed anti-slavery politics be peripheralised? What is the influence of gender representation on anti-slavery historiography?

The search for answers to these questions should begin by recognising that during slavery the right to life and social liberty was denied blacks, not on the basis of gender, but by the race inequities of colonial culture. Differences in life experiences among males and females, however, served to demonstrate how gender constructions assisted in the promotion and maintenance of social and material inequalities. White males, who considered the project of colonialism their conquistadorial creation, believed that the system of slavery devised by them was in part the legitimate outcome of their military conquest of black males in Africa. While the initial labour preference at the frontier was for males, small numbers of black women entered the colonies in the formative stage. It was immediately recognised, however, that under favourable conditions the natural reproduction of slavery was an alternative to slave trading; also, that by securing females on a systematic basis, slave managers could meet the social and sexual demands of favoured male slaves.

At two levels, then, black women were targeted by the socio-economic logic of the plantation enterprise. Their integration into this patriarchal agrarian world – of white and black males – was an entry into a gender-order that represented them as social objects of competing masculinities. On encountering the shared design of hegemonic (white) and marginalised (black) masculinities to secure their subordination within the gender-order, enslaved black women sought to develop autonomous identities by resisting oppressive ideological and institutional sources of power. But as the slave system expanded and matured, the black woman occupied positions at its centre that were of critical social and economic importance. Its survival depended upon her enslavement; as a result her survival struggle assumed more complex dimensions than that of her male counterpart whose gender ideologies she also contested.

Slavery meant enforced labour for life and control over the physical self of the slave during non-labouring periods; it was as much about the slave's total accountability for 'self' as it was about the slaveowner's legal right to demand labour. This, in part, is why Mary Prince, the West Indian ex-slave, wrote that her resistance to slavery had much to do with the denial of a right to time for 'herself'.[4] For many blacks the unacceptability of slavery as a violently enforced system of relations was most acutely felt when 'free' time was rejected and their total time subjected to the authority and interest of enslavers. This is why the role of gender to an understanding of individual's relationship to their 'body' is critical in the study of slavery. With the enslaved woman the matter of 'the body' created a special set of circumstances that centred her sex within the slave owner's gender constructions of slavery. The notion of slavery as the 'using up' of the body – day and night – had clearly differentiated sex and gender implications. The exploration of this issue should speak directly to an analysis of female slavery. It draws attention to the specific ways in which the experiences of enslaved women differed from those of men, and how gender was constructed and reproduced, and ultimately determined the peculiar patterns and forms of anti-slavery responses.

The entire enterprise of slavery, therefore, was organised upon the basis of race and sex, with considerable importance for the (re)production of gender ideologies and social representations. It follows that the integration of the enslaved woman into the systems of socio-economic and ideological production was rather different from that of the enslaved man – and with important far-reaching implications. Enslaved men certainly possessed the distinct privilege of being able to father free-born children. No attempt should be made to minimise the importance of this issue. Rather, it should be recognised that within the context of slave societies the issue of freedom loomed large as the most aggressively pursued, and protected, social prize. But more importantly, the woman was perceived as a flexible and versatile investment with several streams of social, economic and psychological returns.[5]

It follows, furthermore, that enslaved women were structurally positioned and ideologically gendered to have unique experiences. A common survival response from them was to develop and maintain a network of attitudes and actions that countered efforts at the moral and political legitimation of their relationship to the system. The millions of black women who were bought and, despite resistance in Africa and the middle passage, brought to the colonies, as well as those delivered on plantations by 'enchained wombs', had set their minds against slavery. What was left to be done was to identify and determine terms of endurance consistent with survival. There were many ways to negotiate these terms, which accounted for the diverse personality types within slave villages and the overall chronic and endemic instability of the system. For this reason there was nothing peculiar about Jenny's letter or phenomenal about the two slave women in the British Virgin Islands who, in 1793, took a cutlass and severed a hand in protest against enslavement. That this case became famous in Britain speaks more to the consciousness of the imperial community than it does about the nature of women's anti-slavery attitudes.[6]

The severing of the hand that was expected to work and feed the young suggests, therefore, a complex set of relations between resistance to the labour regime and labour reproduction. It makes no sense to negate the anti-slavery importance of refusal in the area of fecundity, fertility and reproduction. Throughout the slavery period evidence indicates that enslaved women had extended their resistance network into bio-social zones associated with maternity. Child-bearing became politicised in ways that tortured enslaved women to a degree that historians may never comprehend. An examination of the changing background to slave owners' natal policy, and the diverse responses of enslaved women, is therefore necessary in order to understand the battle over babies that informed women's anti-slavery.

From the mid-eighteenth century, when slave prices in the British West Indies started a steady upward climb, the matter of slave 'treatment' assumed enlarged proportions among slave owners. Reacting partly to increasingly effective anti-slave trade politics, managerial emphasis shifted slowly from 'buying' to 'breeding' as a labour supply strategy. West Indian societies entered, after the 1770s, a phase of social reform that has been described as the 'age of amelioration'. In economic terms, amelioration was no more than a policy which suggested that marginal benefits could be derived from investing the money that would have been spent on buying new slaves in a maintenance programme for existing slaves. An objective of amelioration was to create for women a pro-natalist environment in order to stimulate procreation. It entailed less work and better nutrition for pregnant and lactating women, as well as the availability of child care facilities. In addition, money was offered to women for delivering healthy children; slave midwives were offered more money than mothers, an indication of slave owners perception of their prime responsibility for high infant mortality rates on estates.[7]

Natural reproduction, rather than importation, suggested the targeting of *Slave Women*'s fertility. The systematic offering of natal incentive to women meant that slave owners considered it possible to influence the socio-sexual behaviour of enslaved women. Throughout the seventeenth century and early eighteenth century, plantation managers reported their inability to explain satisfactorily low birth rates and high infant mortality rates. Most were suspicious that slave women were applying 'unnatural' brakes upon the reproductive process. They did not know how it was done, and they speculated. The widespread belief, however, was that it was part of an anti-slavery strategy that had become endemic. By declaring gynaecological warfare upon slavery, enslaved women were accused of engaging in a most effective form of resistance.

The tragic demographic performance of slave populations up to the end of the eighteenth century in Jamaica, Barbados and the Leeward Islands, cannot be explained without some understanding of these matters. By the 1780s, Barbadian slave owners, taking the lead in an effort to break this resistance, and win the baby war, had put in place the most comprehensive and far-reaching package for the encouragement of pregnant and lactating mothers. In addition to offering financial and material incentives to slave women to produce healthy children, they invested in the promotion of institutional contexts, such as access to family life, christian marriage and labour reduction. By 1800, Barbados, unlike its neighbours, was experiencing sustained natural growth among slaves. Slaveowners got their babies, and boasted in 1807 when slave trading was illegalised, that they feared having too many. slave women also got, finally, part of what they wanted: a social and material environment which seemed less hostile to childbearing, parenting, family and domesticity.[8]

Specific patterns of anti-slavery politics emanated from these changing forms of engagement with the slave system. Undoubtedly, some women appeared broken psychologically by the overwhelming power of slave owners.[9] Such women expressed patterns of behaviour that have been described as psychotic on account of an overt display of seemingly mindless subservience. Referred to a 'Quasheba', the female version of 'Quashee' (or Sambo), this gendered personality type could be transformed suddenly into an agent bearing unexpected social rage. Such cases can be found in abundance throughout plantation documents. In many instances slave owners would make reference to the general kindness shown the female and her positive response, before describing their shock and dismay at the violent action taken.[10] A common conclusion drawn by slave owners in these circumstances was that the loyalty and subservience projected by gender representations of slave women did not conform to social reality, which made for considerable insecurity in everyday life.[11]

Quasheba, who wet-nursed and raised her owner's children, was never fully trusted. She was unpredictable, however, not only in relations with her owners, but also with the black community. We see evidence of this in the judicial records when slaves appear before the criminal (in)justice system. The records of the 1736 Antigua slave plot speak to this issue. Philida, the sister of Tomboy, the alleged leader of the conspiracy, was arrested and charged with being a leading provocateur. She was accused of publicly making 'some virulent expressions . . . upon her brothers's account', an action which ran counter to her owner's perception of her character. It was also Philida, however, who allegedly provided the intelligence to her master that led to the disclosure of the rebel leadership. Her testimony indicates that she was present at the meeting when plans were designed and discussed, and that other women, most notably

Obbah an 'Old Queen', also participated in leadership activity. Obbah, it was intimated, performed traditional Akan ritual functions designed to enhance secrecy and solidarity among the rebels. But it was Philida, the rebel, who was accused of divulging the information leading to the discovery of leaders.[12]

Much has been said about the supportive roles that were assigned to women in the mobilisation of culture as a force in resistance politics. Bush maintains that 'women were in the vanguard of the cultural resistance to slavery which helped individuals survive the slave experience'. For her, it 'was this cultural strength, however, which helped women resist the system in their more "public" lives as workers'. In the case of the 1736 Antigua plot, the evidence indicates that 'Old Queen' may have assumed the role of a traditional Akan queen mother who held tremendous political influence in the slave yard. Certainly, this was the case with the Jamaica conspiracy of 1760 in which rebels declared their intention to appoint Abena, the Akan slave, as 'Queen of Kingston'. The relation between the ritual politics of queen mothers and the more precise roles of magic-religious leaders, the voodoo priestess in particular, is not always clear. But the quest for loyalty, as an enhancer of discipline and secrecy, was often said to be a role assigned to 'spirit mothers' whose claim to direct access to ancestral worlds was recognised and respected within slave communities. Gautier has shown, for example, that their knowledge and practice of 'le Vaudou' fortified slave troops in the successful Saint Dominique revolution.[13]

As shown in the previous chapter, the economic culture retained by Africans in the Caribbean was also used for resistance strategies in which women gained considerable social visibility and provided consistent leadership.[14] In West African societies women were dominant in the small-scale internal marketing of foodstuffs. Despite enslavement in the New World, this culture persisted. Huckstering of foodstuffs on street corners, in markets, and from house to house, engaged the energies of slave women in spite of hostile legislative opposition. Slave hucksters grew crops, bought and sold foodstuffs, appropriated goods from plantation stores for resale, bartered their food allowances for other goods and services, in the promotion of commercial activities.[15] The attempted abolition of the slave huckster's market in Antigua in 1831 sparked riotous behaviour by women slaves. Earlier, the Barbadian slave owners, recognising the folly of police and legislative action in the face of such determination, had resorted to the issuing of licences as the principal method of control and regulation.

Often, this rebellious commercial culture was linked to a complex network of social relationships on the estates.[16] Such issues raise the question of women's invisibility within historical records, a matter that has been considerably overstated. Describing the enslaved woman as essentially a 'submerged mother', Brathwaite locates her 'invisibility' within the 'archival material' and suggests that it is but an 'aspect of that general invisibility which haunts [black history]'.[17] For him, the slave woman, being black and female, suffered a 'double invisibility' which in turn promoted an historiography of neglect. There is, however, a significant conceptual and empirical problem to be tackled with respect to the 'invisibility thesis'. It has to do with the fact that the evidence historians have (over)used as base lines for social history narratives – deeds, wills, manumission lists, diaries, plantation accounts and managers reports – says considerably more about enslaved women than it does about enslaved men.

This characteristic of the evidence has to do with the female-centred nature of the slave system, particularly its concern with their maternity and fertility, the management of white households, and the socio-sexual expression of patriarchal power and ideology. More is recorded about slave mothers than slave fathers; more was said about female slave lovers of white males than about male slave lovers of white women. Certainly, in this last regard, enslaved men have been rendered largely invisible, though partly, it should be said, for their own safety. The general intimacy of slave women with the empowered agents of the colonial world – white male and female – placed them at the top of the documentary queue. In these records women appear in diverse social actions other than those related to labour and crime. On the whole the records yield a relatively greater visibility for enslaved women.

During the 1970s, Lucille Mair, working with Jamaican records, initiated a research project that asked some of these questions about the condition and nature of West Indian historiography and archives. On reflection, it now seems clear that the manner in which she asked these questions was an indication of the issues facing professional historians at that time in the West Indies. The anti-colonial movement had called upon historians to document and interpret the traditions of struggle against colonial domination, particularly with respect to the relatively longer and more determining period of slavery. Male historians had played prominent leadership roles in the anti-colonial labour movement, and as politicians they presented interpretations of their own actions that were rooted conceptually within the traditions of anti-slavery struggles. Newly recreated heroes of anti- colonialism were those who had led slave revolts and organised anti-slavery maroon communities.

A principal task of Lucille Mair's was to add women to the historical narrative, and to locate their anti-slavery contributions firmly within the vanguard of the political project of nation-building. Another was to challenge academics to question disciplinary and gender biases, and to approach archives with greater ideological sensitivity. The first aspect of Mair's concerns produced a body of literature on women's anti-slavery actions that resulted in a political promotion of the notion of the 'rebel woman'.[18] This figure was the quintessential anti-slavery matriarch who organised slave communities and directed their political postures with respect to survival options. Nanny, leader of an early eighteenth-century Jamaican maroon band, took pride of place in this discourse, and now enjoys the constitutional status in Jamaica of a national heroine.

In Barbados, Nanny Grigg, a principal conceptualiser and ideologue of the 1816 slave rebellion, gained historiographical prominence. The records never hid the fact that Grigg was a central figure in the rebellion. They presented her as the person who conveyed news of developments in the Haitian revolution to other slaves, and successfully propagandised a cadre of enslaved males around its ideas and actions. Both Nanny of the Maroons and Nanny Grigg constituted matriarchal leadership within the revolutionary tradition of anti-slavery. They organised men and minds for violent anti-slavery warfare.

Nanny of the Maroons led an army of enslaved men and women against British imperial soldiers and planter militia forces. Robert, a slave giving evidence before the Committee established by the Barbados government to investigate the causes and nature of the rebellion, stated that Nanny Grigg told slaves on the estate that 'they were all damned fools to work, for that she would not, as freedom they were sure to get', and that the way to get it was 'to set fire, as that was the way they did it in St Domingo'.[19] After four days of widespread arson and bloody rebellion the slaves were defeated. Nanny Grigg and 'near a thousand' slaves lost their lives in the military contest and subsequent executions carried out by imperial soldiers and planter militias.

During the 1980s the concept of the 'rebel woman' was placed within a wider context that recognise rebelliousness in different forms and shapes, ranging from collective nonviolent protest to individual negotiation and compromise. In an assessment of the 'organs of discontent' on West Indian slave plantations, Dirks argued that 'when discontent arose, it was usually the female gang members who complained the loudest because everyone knew that they were less likely to be flogged than men. It earned women the reputation for being the instruments of instability and the 'more unmanageable element of the work force.' While the evidence does not come down in favour of women's inequality under the whip, it does indicate a prominence for women in the creation of turmoil and the articulation of protest on plantations. Jacob Belgrave, for example, the mulatto owner of a large Barbados sugar plantation, told the authorities that shortly before the April 1816 slave revolt, he was verbally abused by a gang of slave women who alleged that he was opposed to the British parliament taking steps toward the abolition of slavery. During the revolt his estate was singled out for special treatment. He claimed property destruction of £6,720, the third highest in the island, from a total of 184 damaged estates.[20]

In this regard, Bush's work has done much to extend the parameters of the historiographic framework. In a series of essays, the themes of which occupy the empirical core of a subsequent monograph on enslaved women in the Caribbean, she demonstrated the fluidity in forms of women's struggles, and the diversity of actions and attitudes that constituted anti-slavery. Enslaved women, Bush showed, promoted a culture of intransigence in relation to work, ran away from owners, terrorised white households with chemical concoctions, refused to procreate at levels expected, insisted upon participation in the market economy as hucksters, slept with white men in order to better their material and social condition, and did whatever else was necessary in order to minimise the degree of their unfreedom. Through such 'channels', Bush states, 'women helped to generate and sustain the general spirit of resistance'.[21]

A common reaction to Bush's notion that the diversity of women's reactions to enslavement constitute 'channels' through which a 'spirit of resistance' was fostered, is that her definition of resistance is weakened by excessive elasticity, and has lost sight of what constitutes 'political' action. Much can be said about the question of elasticity in the conception of women's anti-slavery action, especially in reaction to a feminist and post-modern context in which the 'personal' is considered the core of the 'political'.

Slaves daily negotiation for betterment, which often involved both sexual submission and refusal, as well as verbal protest, has had to struggle to find a place within the pantheon of anti-slavery activity traditionally occupied by acts of violent rebellion and marronage. The implications of this process of redefinition for an interpretation of women's social history are obviously important. In a seminal essay published in 1973 on day-to-day resistance, Monica Schuler effectively destabilised traditional definitions and perceptions of resistance. Her intentions were not guided by considerations of writing feminist or gender history, but were narrowly empirical in that she sought to list and legitimise non-violent protest actions, and a wide range of personal refusals, as acts that undermined and weakened the slave system.[22]

Schuler provided a methodological opening for a more sophisticated assessment of the range and specificity of women's reaction to enslavement. It became possible, as a result, for Bush to argue that the slave family was the crucible for resistance. Bush was keen to demonstrate that the slave family was more than a locus of conspiracy, but by virtue of its overwhelming matrifocal nature, constituted a social agency that was propelled and directed by a distinct female consciousness. Families, then, and by extension, communities, expected women to lead as ideologues – whether in the forms of 'spirit mothers', through whom ancestors speak, or queen mothers, as organisers of more secular action. The suppression of fertility by use of abortifacients and infanticide, and the search for freedom by manumission through social and sexual intimacy with whites, all speak to the same point that actions designed to prevent the perpetuation of slavery should be considered as anti-slavery.

The concern remains that such a redefinition is tantamount to an unnecessary kicking open of the barn door. It is assumed that the specifics of women's resistance can be identified without stretching the understanding of anti-slavery to include social behaviours that were not overtly 'political' in terms of direct challenges to power and authority. Morrissey, for example, has called for a 'more critical perspective', but accepts as common sense that slave women's commitment to kith and kin 'in specific ways contributed to tensions and contradictions in slavery' that oftentimes drove women to kill, burn and plunder.[23] The other side of this commitment and contradiction, she acknowledges, drove many women to use sexuality in the pursuit of freedom by manumission.

Among enslaved women, brown-skined black women, and mixed-race (or coloured) women, were more successful in extracting socio-economic benefits – and legal freedom – from propertied white males and females. Some slave women gained legal freedom through the route of the overlapping roles of prostitution and concubinage. In these ways, they earned the necessary money to effect their manumission, or came in contact with clients who were prepared to assist them in doing so. Legal freedom, however, did not always result in a distancing from these roles.[24] Since the mid-eighteenth century, West Indian legislators seemed determined to restrain white males from manumitting their black and coloured 'favorites'. But slave women continued to be freed in significantly larger numbers than men for the rest of the slavery period.[25]

The notion of a 'rebel woman', then, seems to narrow the conceptual possibilities with respect to the understanding of formal political struggles, rather than seeking to disclose insights into the processes through which individual women made social space in order to enjoy and endure the results of the liberties they took. Analytically, it is static and conceals the importance of diverse social experience and personal reactions in the shaping of heterogeneous anti-slavery mentalities. Brathwaite took the first step towards a critique of the concept of the 'rebel woman' as an organising category in anti-slavery discourse when he stated with respect to the multi-layered interface of slave women with the slavery system: 'The whole fact of slavery affected the woman in such ways that she began to conceive of the notion of liberation naturally (liberation for the slave first of all, and secondly, at the same time, liberation of herself).'[26] Brathwaite's argument, furthermore, is that since slavery penetrated, and integrated into production, the 'inner worlds' of the woman – commodifying her maternity and sexuality – she resisted enslavement instinctively or 'naturally'.

Recognising the one dimensionality and framed image derived for the 'rebel woman' concept, this author proceeded to confer on his book on female slavery in Barbados the title, *Natural Rebels*.[27] In this text it is argued that the heterogeneity of women's actions was probably the most outstanding characteristic of their anti-slavery resistance. This position emerged from the general observation that women's vision of survival and protection of a sense of self-worth defined and shaped their resistance to everyday life which was problematised by the demands of slavery upon all spheres of existence – work, sexual relations, leisure activity and family life. The 'natural rebel' may not have been a public heroine or martyr in the way that the 'rebel woman' gained recognition. Like Jenny, who wrote letters pleading for freedom, she could have been protecting her sexuality from a rapist overseer; she could have been Quashebah, the slave at Codrington estate in Barbados, who ran away in August, September and December 1775, August 1776, January 1777, and September 1784, before she was finally confined to the stocks.[28] She could also have been Nanny of the Maroons whose preference for death over slavery impressed followers and foes alike.

The difficulty, however, with the concept of the 'natural rebel' is that perceptions of human behaviour as 'natural' are problematic in so far as they negate the potency of cultural and environmental forces. Women's behaviour is particularly vulnerable to the ideological charge that assertion identified with a well-known representation of women by a hostile patriarchy. The term is used in this context, however, not with any specific reference to the biological determination, but in relation to a cultural proclivity by enslaved women to consciously reject and resist enforced access by slaveowners to the sexuality.

It follows, then, that an important but grossly neglected aspect of women's resistance had to do with their unequal and often unjust relation to slave men within their own communities. This point should be understood and given weight within women's anti-slavery experiences. The white male bought, sold and degraded the black woman. In the process he placed her in a social position to be further degraded and exploited by the black male who frequently targeted her as an object with which to act out a strategy for the restoration of his crippled and dysfunctional masculinity. The 'natural rebel', on occasions, had to resist the tyranny of enslaved black men with the same degree of tenacity and may have experienced the struggle against slavery as an expedition against tyrannical male power. Such struggles were not confined to issues of sexuality, but concerned access to material resources, career opportunities and domestic arrangements.

Male slaves who were assigned privileged occupations within the production system, such as drivers, overseers and artisans, were likely to use their authority against slave women. Stedman gave an example from eighteenth-century Surinam in which a young slave girl was severely punished by a black overseer for resisting his sexual advances. Thomas Thistlewood's diary contains references to spousal abuse by slave men and other acts of male aggression against women. 'Courrier les filles' (girl-hunting) was a past time among male slaves in Saint Dominique, which sometimes resulted in rape and kidnapping of women on neighbouring and distant estates. In addition, the kidnapping of women by maroon men in order to find wives and labourers figured prominently in the social history of all colonies that harboured maroon communities.[29]

Little is known of the life-experiences of slave women who were integrated into the polygynous households of elite male slaves. In maroon communities especially, women, particularly those kidnapped from the estates, performed the arduous agricultural duties.

The internal relations of maroon communities have not been adequately studied for the slavery period, and it remains difficult to speak of the perceptions of these women about their social conditions. It is entirely possible, however, that some maroon women experienced at the hands of black men a continuation of the kinds of occupational and resource discrimination that typified enslavement on the plantations.

It should be emphasised, argues Moitt, 'that the structure of plantation society was sexist and that sexism was reflected in the organisation of labour'. The *Slave Women*'s plight, he suggests, 'resulted largely from patriarchy and the sexist orientation of Caribbean slave plantation society which put them into structural slots that had no bearing on their abilities. This meant', he concludes, 'that women were not permitted to move into roles traditionally ascribed to [black] males.' Slaveowners consistently discriminated against slave women in the allocation of access to skilled professions, and they were never allowed to hold the principal offices of head driver and overseer.[30] Victor Schoelcher, the French anti-slavery campaigner of the early nineteenth century, explained the entrapment of most women slaves in the field gangs of Martinique as follows:

> It is often the case in the field gangs that there are more women than men. This is how it can be explained. A plantation is, in itself, a small village. As it is usually established a considerable distance from major centres, it must provide of all its needs . . . masons and blacksmiths as well as animal watchmen. All the apprentices who are destined to replace them are now in the field gangs (the slave driver included), and this diminishes the male population available for field work.[31]

In the sugar factories women were not trained as boilers and distillers – prestigious, high-technology tasks. Slave women, then, experienced the male slave labour 'aristocracy' as representing another level of male authority not necessarily supportive of their own sense of freedom and betterment.

Another neglected area has been the anti-slavery culture of black women as it relates specifically to slave-owning white females. White women, we now know, may have owned and managed as much as 25 per cent of Caribbean slaves, with a greater concentration of ownership in towns. We know from the slave registration records for the British colonies that during the last decades of slavery white women owned more female than male slaves.[32] It is reasonable, to conceptualise female slavery, particularly as it relates to black women's anti-slavery activities, in relation to a discussion of white women as principal slaveowners. The perception of black women resisting their enslavement by white women poses a number of interesting questions for the discourse on the relations between race, sex, class and gender. It also highlights another set of special and unique aspects to women's resistance that has eluded scholars of anti-slavery.

Brathwaite suggests that we should begin by recognising how and why the attitudes and activities of propertied white women supported the establishment. How else to begin an explanation for their inability or unwillingness to offer a public political critique of slavery. Mair tells us that the white woman was socialised as the 'second sex' with the whole thrust of her upbringing designed to make her 'pretty polly, pretty parrot'. Unlike her British counterpart, she launched no missiles on behalf of anti-slavery as she was conditioned 'to rock the cradle, not the boat'.[33] Slave women, therefore, had no reason to see in their white mistress a source of amelioration or freedom.

The available manumission records for colonies show that white males were by far the most frequent liberators of slaves. Male visitors to the colonies were consistent in reporting what Bayley did in 1833: 'female owners are more cruel than male; their revenge is more durable and their methods of punishment more refined, particularly towards slaves of their own sex'.[34] Turnbull's account of the ideas of a Cuban creole slave mistress supports this stereotyped opinion. With respect to her attitudes to domestic slaves he states:

> The mistress of many a great family in Havana will not scruple to tell you that such is the proneness of her people [domestics] to vice and idleness, she finds it necessary to send one or more of them once a month to the whipping post, not so much on account of any positive delinquency, as because without these periodical advertisements the whole family would become unmanageable, and the master and mistress would lose their authority.[35]

The daily resistance of Elizabeth Fenwick's female slaves to her authority may be indicative of the contest of race, sex, class and gender. They refused to work, lied, stole, ignored instructions and showed contempt for her authority. While she did not report being in fear for her life, her letters indicate the extent to which her female slaves sought to destroy whatever ambition she may have had about being an effective slave manager. They caused her 'endless trouble and vexation', refused to respond to any 'gently and kindly impulses', and undermined any notion she cherished about Barbados as a 'paradise'. Her solution was to sell the females and purchase male slaves.[36]

Jenny's letter, then, when placed within the dominant historiographic tradition, symbolised a rather complex pattern of representations. Some of these were constructed before and during her own lifetime and persist beyond the parameters of the slavery epoch. Concepts of gender are buried but skin-deep within her words which were arranged in patterns of meaning indicative of a particular representation of the feminine experience, though concerning matters that had nothing whatsoever to do with sex or gender. It may seem altogether female, for example, within the dominant system of gender representation, for a slave to enquire about the health and well-being of a master and mistress – and their 'good' children – just to complete the enquiry with a request for freedom from their benevolence. There was no cutlass, musket nor bloodshed; only determination in the second of gentle words that managed, in this case, to throw Mr Lane, her owner, into a rage which he knew, ultimately, was of no value in the stern face of a well-reasoned claim to freedom.

Furthermore, Jenny's history is offered as a window through which to view the diverse experiences of different types of enslaved black women, and it is presented in order to illustrate how gender operated through the specific institutional forms of West Indian slave society. The objective of this approach is to demonstrate that while women's and gender history were divergent methodologically, they share and embrace a common end – how to document and offer historical explanation for the dynamic interactivity between lived experiences and ideological representations at specified moments. How gender worked to construct black and white masculinities, and the experiences of males in slavery are necessary prerequisites for an understanding of the experiences of enslaved women. One does not have to travel very far into the literature to encounter signposts which indicate, with respect to anti-slavery activity, that different vehicles were often used by enslaved men and women.

If female slaves expressed a more complex and contradictory set of responses to their enslavement than men, it had to do with the more diverse and dynamic patterns of female gender representations, and the multi-layered challenges of black women in their private and public lives. If many women acquiesce in the face of slave-owner power, producing the smiling, subservient but unstable, Quasheba personality type, and her male counterparts have been historiographically indicted for the capitulation that produced the stereotyped Quashee, only a merging of gender and women's history can give us the insights needed to write the social history of slavery.

Methodological connectivity can be discerned, it seems, when the slaves are allowed to speak for themselves. Chains apart, the voices of slaves – and ex-slaves – were often made vague by the very writers that committed their thoughts to print. It is necessary, however, even in such difficult circumstances, to 'feel' the texture, and hear the tone, of their indirect or engineered voices. Much can be made, for example, of the autobiographical record of Mary Prince as an instrument of literary representation. She 'cared' for the children of a mistress and valued her own 'womanness' in the process. The force of her self-understanding as a woman, ran contrary to that of her mistress who had her 'horsewhipped' for marrying without permission.

Mary Prince did much to be a loyal and 'good' slave while at the same time confronting her mistress with the idea that 'to be free is very sweet'. White people, she wrote, all had their 'liberty', and 'that's just what we want'. 'Freedom' and 'liberty' are words that appear like monuments on the pages of her text.[37] It is necessary, then, to excavate the foundations of these 'structures' for the full context of social attitudes and behaviour. In the case of enslaved women it is critical to begin the dig at the centre and work outwards. The centre of which I speak deals with the commodification of their 'inner world' and natural resistance to it, a dynamic that is only now coming in clear focus for historians of anti-slavery ideology and action.

Endnotes

1 Jenny Lane to Thomas Lane, 9 August, 1804, Newton Papers M.523/579, Senate House Library, London University. Jenny obtained her freedom, and in 1813 petitioned Thomas Lane for the emancipation of her sons, Robert 26, a joiner, and Henry 24, a tailor; Jenny Lane to Thomas Lane, 4 March, 1813, M.523/690.

2 Morrissey, *Slave Women, op. cit.*, p. 153.

3 *Ibid.*, p. 156.

4 Ferguson (ed.), *The History of Mary Prince, op. cit.*, p. 84.

5 See for a discussion of these themes, Beckles, 'Sex and gender', *op. cit.*, pp. 125-40. Also in this volume, Moitt, 'Women, work and resistance', *op. cit.*, pp. 155-76.

6 Issac Dookhan, *A History of the British Virgin Islands, 1672-1970* (Epping, Caribbean Universities Press, 1975), p. 83; also cited in Morrissey, *Slave Women, op. cit.*, pp. 155-6.

7 For a detailed discussion of ameliorative reforms to the British West Indian Slave System at the end of the eighteenth century, see Ward, *British West Indian Slavery, 1750-1834, op. cit.*; Bennett, *Bondsmen and Bishops, op cit.*; Michael Craton, 'Hobbesian or Panglossian? The two extremes of slave conditions in the British Caribbean, 1783-1834', *William and Mary Quarterly*, 3rd Series, 35 (1978), pp. 324-56; K. F. Kiple, 'Deficiency diseases in the Caribbean', *Journal of Interdisciplinary History*, 11:2 (1980), pp. 197-205; 'The crisis of slave subsistence', *op. cit.*, pp. 615-41.

8 Barry Higman, 'Growth in Afro-Caribbean slave populations', *American Journal of Physical Anthropology*, 2nd Series, 1 (1979), pp. 373-85; 'Slave populations of the British Caribbean: some nineteenth-century variations, in S. Proctor (ed.), *Eighteenth-century Florida and the Caribbean* (Gainesville, Universities Press of Florida, 1976), pp. 60-70; Stanley Engerman and Herbert Klein, 'Fertility differentials between slaves in the United States and the British West Indies: a note on lactation practices and their possible implications', *William and Mary Quarterly*, 3rd Series, 35 (1978), pp. 357-74; Richard Sheridan, 'Slave demography in the Britsish West Indies and the abolition of the Slave trade', in D. Eltis and J. Walvin (eds), *The Abolition of the Atlantic Slave Trade* (University of Wisconsin Press, Madison, 1981), pp. 295-319.

9 See Hilary Beckles, 'Property rights in pleasure: the prostitution of enslaved black women in the West Indies', in Roderick McDonald (ed.) *West Indian Accounts: Essays on the History of the British Caribbean and the Atlantic Economy in honour of Richard Sheridan* (Kingston, The Press: University of the West Indies, 1996).

10 See Brathwaite, 'Caribbean women', *op. cit.*

11 See for a description of the 'Quashee' personality type, Patterson, *The Sociology of Slavery, op. cit.*, pp. 174-81.

12 David Gaspar, 'Deep in the minds of many: Slave women and resistance in Antigua, 1632-1763: a preliminary inquiry', paper presented at the 19th Annual Conference of the Association of Caribbean Historians, Martinique, 1987. See pp. 22-5.

13 Barbara Bush, 'Towards emancipation: Slave women and resistance to coercive labour regimes in the British West Indian Colonies, 1790-1838', in David Richardson (ed.), *Abolition and its Aftermath: The Historical Context, 1790-1916* (London, Frank Cass, 1985), pp. 27-54.

14 See Mary Turner, 'Slave workers, subsistence and labour bargaining: Amity Hall, Jamaica, 1805-1838', and Hilary Beckles, 'An economic life of their own: slaves as commodity producers and distributors in Barbados', in Ira Berlin and Philip Morgan (eds), *The Slaves Economy: Independent Production by Slaves in the Americas* (London, Frank Cass, 1991), pp. 92-107, and 31-48 respectively; see also Sidney Mintz, 'Caribbean market places and Caribbean', *op. cit.*, pp. 333-44; Beckles and Watson, 'Social protest', *op. cit.*, pp. 272-93.

15 Sampson Wood to Thomas Lane, 1796, M. 523-288, Newton Papers.

16 *Ibid.*

17 Brathwaite, 'Caribbean women'. *op. cit.*, pp. 16-17.

18 Mair, *The Rebel Woman, op. cit.;*' The arrival of black woman', *op. cit.*, pp. 1-10; See also Brathwaite, 'Caribbean women'.

19 Beckles, *Black Rebellion, op. cit.*, pp. 86-106; 'The slave drivers' war', *op. cit.*, pp. 85-111.

20 Dirks, *The Black Saturnalia, op. cit.*, pp. 160-1. Beckles, *Black Rebellion, op. cit.*, p. 111.

21 Bush, 'Towards Emancipation', p. 239; 'White "ladies"', *op. cit.*, pp. 253-4; 'The family tree is not cut: women and cultural resistance in slave family life in the British Caribbean', in G. Y. Okihoro (ed.), *In Resistance: Studies in African, Caribbean and Afro-American History* (Amherst, University of Massachusetts Press, 1986).

22 Monica Schuler, 'Day to day resistance to slavery in the Caribbean in the 18th century', Association for the Study of Africa and the West Indies, *Bulletin* 6 (1973).

23 Morrissey, *Slave Women*, p. 98.

24 Parliamentary Paper, Garnette to Beckwith, December, 1811, Vol. 7 (1814-15),p. 3; Joseph Husbands, *An Answer to the Charge of Immorality Against Inhabitants of Barbados* (New York, n.p., 1831), p. 19.

25 Minutes of the Assembly of Barbados, 15 March, 1774, Barbados Department of Archives, Black Rock, Barbados.

26 Brathwaite, 'Caribbean women', *op. cit.*

27 Beckles, *Natural Rebels, op. cit.*; see Graham Hodges, 'Reconstructing black women's history in the Caribbean: Review Essay', *Journal of American Ethnic History*, Fall (1992), pp. 101-7.

28 See Beckles, *Black Rebellion, op. cit.*, p. 76.

29 J. G. Stedman, *Narrative of a Five Years Expedition against the Revolted Negroes of Surinam, 1806* (Amherst, University of Mass. Press, 1971), pp. 177-8; the Jamaica Diaries of Thomas Thistlewood, 1751-1768, Lincolnshire Records Office, England; Leslie Manigat, 'The relationship between marronage and slave revolts and revolution in St Dominique–Haiti', *Annals of the New York Academy of Sciences*, 292 (1977), pp. 420-38.

30 Moitt, 'Women, work and resistance', *op. cit.*, p. 162.

31 Victor Schoelcher, *Des Colonies Francaises: Abolition Immediated de l'Esclavage* (Society d' Histoire de la Guadeloupe, Basse-Terre,1976), pp. 23-4.

32 Beckles, 'White women', *op. cit.*, pp. 66-82.

33 Brathwaite, 'Caribbean women', *op. cit.*, p. 17.

34 See Beckles, 'White women', *op. cit.*, p. 76.

35 *Ibid.*, pp. 76-7.

36 See Fenwick (ed.), *The Fate of the Fenwicks, op. cit.*, pp. 163-75.

37 Ferguson, *The History of Mary Prince, op. cit.*, p. 84.

Part Four

Summation

11

Historicising Slavery in Caribbean Feminism

Historians of the Caribbean have had little difficulty discerning traditions, dating back to the beginning of European colonialism, of womens' public activity. An examination of these traditions allows for the isolation and assessment of women's ideas and perspectives about the changing nature of their identities and interests. Collectively, their public expressions constitute the emergence within colonialism of the infrastructure of a feminist sensibility. While women of all races and classes did not retreat from publicly voicing their experiences, there was no politicisation of their gender identity within the mission of Enlightenment democratisation (e.g. civil equality and social justice). It remains difficult, therefore, to map the evolution within written texts of a coherent feminist genre. The overall result, then, is a historiographical textual representation of women as victims, in diverse ways and to varying degrees, of the masculinist enterprise of colonialism.[1]

Women were socially differentiated within the gender orders of slave-based societies. Indeed, the very notion of 'woman' was consistently challenged by some women, and for them it was a deeply problematic category. Women were principal participants in the contests over the definitions and characteristics of womanhood and femininity. The denial by some women of the 'womanness' of other women became the basis of a conflict that internally exploded the potential of coherent politic of feminine identities and weakened the analytical value of the concept of 'woman'. As a consequence, historians of slavery can now speak about the internal chaos of the concept as it relates to gender and race.

The diversity of women's experiences in West Indian slave societies, undermines formal claims to order in the knowledges conceived by the politically challenged term 'woman', as well as feminism as an advanced, radical conceptual device. Encounters with the historical contexts and meanings of these categories have been divisive to say the least. Responses by female scholars especially have ranged from eclectic extractions for the construction of political projects of mythic glorification (such as the invention of heroism and the propagation of super-survivalist narratives that illuminate women's persistent civil rights struggles for social justices) to the outright denial of the value of 'history' in the organization and promotion of relevant feminist knowledges.[2]

Recent histories of women in slave societies have promoted perceptions of their diverse mentalities and confirmed the extreme historical disunity in notions of feminine identity. Reflecting on this state of affairs, contemporary women activists recognise that future integrative, trans-feminist strategies for solidarity are likely to generate further fragmentations and contests. Histories, as organized knowledge, then, have produced for women's movements and feminist theorists something of a mixed bag. For some, these works constitute an enormous reservoir waiting to burst forth and wash away the debris placed in its path; for others, they represent 'another country' whose inhabitants are long dead, buried, and therefore silenced. Either way, histories of the slavery experience are viewed with considerable ambivalence and scepticism.[3]

It has not helped matters that dominant textural constructs of the slavery regime, the longer part of the colonial period, represent it as the social experience on which rests contemporary ideologies of race, class and gender relations. Slavery is conceived also as the master mould from which are cast the persistent conflicts among women over definitions and ideological ownership of womanhood and femininity. The contested politics of woman hood furthermore, has been accounted for in terms of women's formally differentiated exposure to slaveowning colonial masculinities and institutionalised hegemonic patriarchy. These politics have also been explained in relation to the changing gender orders promoted by slavery and expressed culturally through civic institutions and productive arrangements. An important consequence of this internal political fracture in feminine identity was hardened ethnic and class positions between women that made problematic all projects of post-slavery rapprochement.

Élite white females in slave society sought to exclude, on the basis of race, black and brown females from membership of the ideological institutions of womanhood and femininity – and, by extension, access to socially empowering designations such as 'lady' and 'miss'. The attack upon non-white female identity promoted a gender culture of exclusion that was rationalised and maintained as new gender representations surfaced in distinct ideological and material situations. Texts written by white women with a social familiarity of slavery yield ready evidence of these developments. Carmichael, for example, described black women in her published travelogue as 'masculine', brutish, and lacking feminine sensitivities.

Carmichael's reference was consistent with white men's view about the labouring capacity of female slaves. For her, black women were outside the pale of feminine identity – hence her conclusion that 'to overwork a negro slave [of any sex] is impossible'. Such texts served to consolidate and propagate the general opinions formulated by white male overseers and managers about black women. Plantation records prepared by white men, for example, speak of black women's apparent ease at 'dropping children', capacity for arduous physical labour, and general 'amazonian cast of character'. Collectively, these accounts, written by white women and white men, indicate the varying ways and intensity with which the ideological project of defeminising the black woman was carried out.[4]

The Caribbean experience is consistent with the findings of Elizabeth Fox-Genovese on US southern slavery. Fox-Genovese has argued that rather than exerting a gender politic that softened the 'evil and harshness' of black women's enslavement, élite white women lived, and knew they lived, as privileged members of a ruling class, and were fundamentally racist in outlook. The worlds of white and black women, as a result, despite dramatic experiences of intimacy, were filled with mutual antagonism, cruelty and violence. slave women did not reasonably expect protection and support from white women, and had no line of defence against sexual assault. Patricia Morton asserts that, as a consequence of the damage done by slavery to gender identities, black women confronted the master's power in 'ultimate loneliness' and that in this circumstance 'gender counted for little'.[5]

The power relations of race, class and sex, as the constituent elements of an economic accumulationist strategy, are significant in understanding why women adopted divisive ideological positions. But the politics of gender denial had much to do with white women's perceptions of self-interest in slave societies that virtually guaranteed the social insecurity of property-less persons, and celebrated the cultural crudity resulting from moral deregulation at the frontier. Freedom was scarce, unfree life was cheap, and any social representation that offered privileges was aggressively pursued as a matter of life and death. White women used their caste and class power to support the patriarchal pro-slavery argument that black females were not 'women' in the sense that they were, and certainly not feminine in the way that they wished to be. For the black woman the scars of centuries of denial went deep; with the onset of free society the raw wounds remained, sending tensions down the spine of all recuperative socio-political strategies.

The centering of 'woman' within slavery provided the context within which definitions of womanhood and femininity was contested. The black woman was situated at the (re)productive core of the slave system with a unique legal status. The white woman was locked into constitutional mechanisms that ensured her progeny's alienation from slavery and her association with the reproduction of freedom. Slavery and freedom, as an Enlightenment paradigm in action, situated black and white women in bi-polar relations that promoted the interests of patriarchy, and, more importantly, produced among women contradictory perceptions of identity and self-interests. The importance to the black woman of the fact that neither the white woman, nor her progeny, could be enslaved should not be minimised. Across imperial lines and through time the slave woman was legally constructed in one consistent way; she was the principal barrier to freedom since all children at birth took the status of mothers and not fathers. The very small minority of mixed-race children with white mothers were born free; their enslaved or free black fathers more often than not paid dearly, mostly with their lives. These provisions were established in slave codes that organised race and gender relations in all colonial jurisdictions.[6]

Free black women were not targeted in this way by colonial legislatures. White society merely assumed that all black and mixed race women were slaves, imposing on them the onus to prove otherwise. Their freedom, then, was compromised by its vulnerability to constant scrutiny and violation. Since the concept of a free black woman seemed contradictory, most free black women found themselves constantly challenging attempts to reinstate them; many were unable to prove and enforce their freedom, often times because they were kidnapped and removed to unfamiliar jurisdictions. Their offspring, nonetheless, were entitled to freedom at birth, irrespective of the status of fathers, which in the theory placed them on an equal footing before the law with white women. As members of the community of free women, however, their lives were shaped by fundamentally different experiences, the result of their race and gender locations with the slave system (Sio 1987, pp. 166-82; Heuman 1991; Campbell 1976).

The first radical opposition and movement of Caribbean women, however, emerged within the politics of the bloody wars the autochthons launched against colonialism and slavery, Kalinago (Carib), Taino (Arawak) and Ciboney women, in the Lesser and Greater Antilles, are referred to in texts written by European conquistadors as militant and generally hostile to the imperial enterprise. Though there are no detailed accounts of women who emerged as heroic leaders in these battles, scattered references document aspects of their daily social and military offensive against Europeans. The memoirs of Michel de Cunes, for instance, in which details of Columbus' second voyage are outlined, tell us about the armed resistance of native women to the Spanish landing at St Croix and Guadeloupe. He described them as 'armed to the teeth' with bows and arrows, and even when subdued and captured resisted demands upon their labour and sexuality. He tells us, furthermore, about Columbus' refusal to adopt a less sanguine response to these women warriors. They were fired upon by his soldiers in the normal manner of war – captured and taken prisoners.[7]

It was the norm in most parts of the Caribbean to enslave indigenous women taken as prisoners. As such, they did not expect to live in ways dissimilar to enslaved African women. They certainly worked on the plantations and in the mines of Spanish hacendados alongside African women. In the English and French colonies, however, it was not uncommon to find some of them treated in ways more 'free' than 'slave'. Many were also recruited on the mainland and indentured in the islands as domestics and artisans. Reference to their cultural resistance under circumstances of domestic slavery also require careful examination. Tragically, their political voice within anti-colonial and anti-slavery movement has not been invoked by feminist historians in ways that offer historical depth, ideological tone and texture to the radical tradition.

The stereotyped perception of free, mixed-race women as 'divided to the vein', in terms of their political and ideological positions within the race and gender orders of slave society, has proven useful in critical analyses of Caribbean social history. It should be emphasised that, as far as the sugar colonies are concerned the majority of mixed-race women remained enslaved, worked in field-gangs and were not differentiated from African women in terms of life experiences. Few escaped slavery, and most remained consigned to labour gangs alongside their black mothers. They lived in the plantation villages created by their African family and shared their experiences.

That some African women were also 'brown' in complexion complicated the idea that miscegenation assured social privilege. As a result, it was common for most mixed-race women to be socially absorbed into the dominant African mainstream, thereby negating the impact of the colour coding system that characterised the hierarchical order of colonial society. Miscegenation, however, did open doors for a few black women and the rush to enter liberated spaces was a feature of everyday life.

Mixed-race women who attained legal freedom established in conjunction with their male counterparts a distinct sociopolitical identity. Some, however, were forced by circumstances of birth to retain social connections with their enslaved kith and kin. For sure they did not wish to return to slavery, but sought to enhance the civil rights options of their offspring by adopting strategic political positions. One such strategy was to opt for procreation with propertied white men. Another was to enter intimate social friendships with élite white women whose need for friendship and companionship reflected the considerable restrictions placed on their lives within the patriarchal system. Examples of the success of these strategies are well known. Nugent, for example, encouraged into her inner circle a cadre of 'coloured ladies' whose support she counted on, and who were set apart from the creole white women she could hardly tolerate. Nugent's 'coloured ladies' represented her chamber in waiting, and were considered by her more suited to this role than the 'uneducated' white creole woman she encountered.

The black females of the Governors's household were also excluded from the inner circle. These women Nugent described as her 'blackies', and in her opinion were childlike, lazy, dirty, and morally undeveloped. While she held considerable class antipathy for Jamaican creole white women, and racist attitudes to black women, the coloured ladies of property she found to be of a high civic quality, though victims of what she considered the disgraceful sexual adventurism of undisciplined élite white males. She supported her husband's colonial enterprise in much the same way that the coloured ladies supported hers. As 'in-betweeners', Nugent and her coloured ladies formed a social alliance. She offered these co-opted women a considerable measure of social respectability and psychological comfort, though these benefits carried little prospect for expanded civil rights.[8]

At the same moment in Barbadian society Elizabeth Newton, owner of Newton and Seawell plantations, had cultivated a special friendship with Old Doll, her housekeeper. Doll subsequently claimed that she was assured freedom for herself and three daughters on her mistress's return to England. Elizabeth did return to England, but made no legal arrangements for their manumission. Doll and her daughter continued to work on the estate as housekeepers under successive managers and pressed their claims for treatment as privileged, if not free, persons. The success of their mission was striking, but most impressive were the multiple levels on which the strategy was carried out. Doll's daughters were skillful advocates of their own interests; Jenny had a child with a white man; Betsy 'ran away' to England and became free; and Dolly lived as the 'wife' of the white manager. Over time a section of the family 'whitened' through miscegenation, acquired artisan skills, literacy, freedom, and considerable property – including slaves.[9]

It is instructive to note, however, that while Doll and her daughters initially benefitted from the special relationship with a white woman, most mixed-race women were linked to white males and acquired their advancement as part of a negotiated package that included sexual arrangements. It was the common charge during the eighteenth century, by persons opposed to this avenue to freedom, that the overwhelming majority of manumitted coloured and black women were mistresses and prostitutes to white men of property. It was also generally asserted that these women bore the scorn and endured the envy of the sexually repressed white wives of such men. The image that emerges from these records is of intense sexual contest between white, and coloured and black women for the loyalty and favours of élite males who considered the matter settled by the offer of marriage and title to the former and sex and freedom to the latter. Beyond this point of reference, images of the mixed race free woman disintegrate into archival fragments awaiting social reconstruction.

The fact should not be ignored that while slaves were constitutionally prohibited from owning property they were allowed by custom to possess and 'freely' use properties, including other slaves. What set apart Doll's family on Newton's estate was not only their 'semi-free' status, derived from a special relationship with their owner, quasi-ownership of slaves acquired through family links with a white male. Mary Ann, Doll's half-sister and a free mulatto, owned slaves who were placed at the disposal of her enslaved black sister and nieces. Slave owning and usage protected Doll's daughters from various forms of hard labour and enabled them to develop attitudes towards manual work that corresponded with those held by white women.

All free women, then, were socialised culturally within the colonial project to function in ways supportive of the slaveowning system of accumulation. It is also in their roles as rural slaveowners and estate managers that white women are seen clearly, and in larger numbers, as autonomous participants. Nugent, for example, spoke very highly of Lady Temple, owner/ manager of Hope sugar plantation in Jamaica. Her skills as an entrepreneur and slave manager are described in a manner that indicated her enormous success in a 'man's world. Mrs Simpson, owner/manager of Money Musk plantation, also received commendation from Nugent for her shrewd estate management, as well as her determined effort to resist male suitors in pursuit of her property and subsequent reduction to 'wife' and housekeeper.[10]

Mary Butler's analysis of planter women, furthermore, shows the extent to which they were important players in the capital markets of Jamaica and Barbados. While Butler does not suggest their centrality in terms of shaping colonial policy or wielding political power, she does indicate that no section of society saw them in these roles as unusual or unacceptable. It was normal, for example, to see a white woman as rational business agent examining the genitals of male slaves on the auction block before making purchases, or to see them in solicitors' offices negotiating the purchase, sale or mortgage of significant urban and rural properties. Such images reflected the commonplace nature of business activity within white households.[11]

Slave holding records for towns in most English colonies show that urban white women generally owned more female than male slaves. 'Female on female slavery', then, was the principal model of urban slavery. The interpretation of slaveowning data has influenced the writing of both woman's history and gender history, and has enabled historians to propose complex theoretical readings of slavery traditions. The analytical methodologies they have used present social radicalism as endemic to slave relations, and suggest that it resulted from the ways in which anti-slavery consciousness and politics developed around modernist ideals such as individual liberty and social justice.

Blacks, it seems, had taken responsibility for the popularisation of the idea that as colonial subjects they had a stake in the Enlightenment project of human progress. Slave society, then, could produce only one kind of organised radicalism that is recognisable within modern political thought – anti-slavery struggle. Slaveowners' anti-colonial activities, tied largely to issues such as imperial taxation and constitutional autonomy, would not qualify since the politics of these ideas were not radical from a subaltern perspective in so far that it lacked liberationist values in terms of the race class and gender order of colonial society.[12]

White female slaveholders did not adopt publicly an anti-slavery stance. Rather, despite their own marginalised social position within dominant patriarchy, with its repressive socio-sexual culture, they were known for their private and public support of the pro-slavery enterprise. While their pro-establishment politics can be understood, the privileged positions they occupied perhaps placed them in a position to have presented colonial society with an alternative social vision. Their pro-slavery positions stand in stark contrast to those of their ethnic sister in the US slave colonies and metropolitan Europe, whose struggles in the vanguard of anti-slavery movements may have won the day for abolitionists by winning the popular support for legislation on emancipation.

White women, then, offered the faint heart-beat of a feminist opposition to supportive 'texts' during the long slavery period, though it may be suggested by way of mitigation that their private miscegenation with black men, and their occasional private grumbles about the 'horrid nature of slavery, should be taken into account as part of a discreet, subjective oppositional politics. Nugent's decision to dance with a black man during a ball at the Governor's residence sent an enormous shock through the sensitivities of upper-class female Jamaican society. It was understood, and stated, that only a Governor's wife could possibly have survived the disdain and derision that followed. The aggression shown by the same female élite society towards Elizabeth Manning who, as a prominent member, was accused by her husband of extensive sexual relations with enslaved black men on the estate, helps to discredit the claim that there was perhaps a silent, submerged anti-slavery conscience among sections of white female upper-class society.[13]

The suggestion that manumission rates are the crucial element in understanding slavery in particular jurisdictions, constitutes an interesting test of the extent to which different categories of slaveowners sought to promote freedom for their own slaves. The evidence available to us indicates two important trends; one, that freed non-whites were more likely to free their slaves than whites; second, that white women figured very low in their responses to slave freedom through this mechanism. Higman has shown, for example, that though white women constituted the majority social category of urban slaveholders in Bridgetown, they were the least significant in terms of manumitting slaves. The period 1817-20, for which reliable figures are available, show that some 10.4 per cent of the slaves owned by free black men were manumitted, followed by those belonging to free coloured men (3.0 per cent), free black women (2.7 per cent) free mulatto women (1.6 per cent), and white women (1.5 per cent). White men, whose slaveowning was concentrated largely in the rural economy accounted for 0.6 per cent White women, then, compared to free black or coloured women, were less willing to free their mostly female slaves.[14] Women's groups such as the 'Ladies Society for the Promotion and Encouragement of Arts and Manufactures', which was established in Barbados in 1781 as the woman's wing of a planter élite organisation by the same name, was concerned with the alienation of white males and female labourers and artisans within the plantation economy. They lamented the way in which slavery had undermined the chances of social advancement for white workers by enabling blacks to monopolise skilled occupations. As an organisation it was dedicated to promoting the welfare of propertyless whites and functioned as a pressure group within the context of pro-slavery political economy. At no stage did its members oppose the logic and specific natures of slavery as oppressive relations of race, class, sex and gender. It constituted more of a precursor for subsequent public alms institutions than an oppositional force within the slave system.[15]

Considering the view that free-coloured women experienced contradictory relations to slave society, it should not be surprising to find that some of them publicly opposed slavery and appeared in the vanguard of the anti-slavery movement. For such women the need to protect their kin, and make sense of their own experiences, informed the public postures that constituted their anti-slavery politics. Some of them, in addition, developed sophisticated philosophical critiques of the slave system as representing a moral contradiction of humanist and Christian values. Sarah Ann Gill of Barbados, for example, comes forcefully to mind. Described in the 1820s as a 'Christian heroine of Barbados', Gill used her platform in the Methodist Church to campaign in a way that no one else did on the principle that slavery and Christian morality were incompatible, and that a good Christian could not be a slaveholder.

By urging Christian whites to free their slaves and take a general anti-slavery posture, Gill incurred the public political wrath of Barbadian slave-owning white society. Following the infamous destruction of the Methodist chapel in Barbados in 1823 by a mob of irate Anglican whites, Gill used her home as the meeting place for her political campaign. In 1824, whites who wished to commemorate the anniversary of the destruction of the chapel threatened to destroy her home. Her tenacity and persistence won the admiration of slaves in Barbados as well as the support of metropolitan leaders in the Methodist ministry – including abolitionist advocates such as Thomas Buxton who secured a debate in the House of Commons of the circumstances surrounding the destruction of the chapel. No free woman in the West Indies positioned herself in the deep end of public anti-slavery politics in the way that Gill did. When the Methodist Church removed her from the Barbados context and assigned her to South Africa, she continued her work in the anti-slavery campaign, and established a reputation on both sides of the Atlantic within the movement.[16]

Less effective, but more intellectually radical, were the Hart sisters of Antigua whose contributions to Caribbean anti-slavery politics and letters mark them as formidable figures of their time. Anne and Elizabeth Hart were free-coloureds who came to prominence as young poets, pamphleteers and polemicists. Like Gill, they were associated with radical Methodists within the religious opposition to slavery. Their critique and rejection of slavery in Antigua during the era of amelioration was highly provocative and their literary work rated among the best in the region. The Hart sisters were pioneers within the ranks of free Caribbean women of their time in terms of the ideas about women's rights, gender issues, and the wider question of social justice.

Elizabeth, in particular, was publicly abused by slaveowners during the 1820s on account of her radical demands for public education for slaves, and the protection of slave women from the sexual tyranny of white males. She maintained, however, a reputation as an aggressive anti-slavery thinker and writer until her death in 1833. The focus of her politics was the impact of slavery on the black family, the moral erosion of community life by slavery, and the call for the educational tutoring of all women and children. She spoke about the devastation of slavery on the intellectual capabilities of black children, as well as its assault upon the feminine identity of black women. Her multi-layered critique of slavery shattered the coherence of pro-slavery arguments in Antigua. Moira Fergusson has suggested that the work of both sisters constitutes a reply 'to all those who cast aspersions on the intellect of African Caribbeans'. They drew to public attention the oppressiveness of the gender order of slave society by speaking and writing about the sexual vulnerability of young black women, and described sexually exploitative white males as 'predators' who subjugated enslaved women for perverse pleasure.

The Harts' campaign for the protection of young slave women from sexual abuse was linked to their aggressive literary polemic against female prostitution in the colony. On these issues they were also organizational activists. Their role in the establishment of a support network within Methodist evangelicalism for young black women can be seen in the extensive fund-raising efforts carried out during the 1820s on behalf of the 'Ladies Negro Education Society' They were not only literary advocates of women's self-help strategies, but committed organizers and institution builders. For them, then, feminist radicalism entailed two levels of public engagement: first, a vocal intellectual opposition to the gender and racial order, and second, an activism within organizations that brought them into close contact with the pro-slavery forces of society.[17]

Enslaved black women, however, presented slave society with its principal feminist opposition. Oppressed by the gender orders of black and white communities, and with little room to manoeuver to acquire the respectability necessary to secure a platform for public advocacy, slave women were undoubtedly the most exploited group. The inescapable tyranny of white and black masculinity created several levels on which gender oppression was experienced and resisted. Their problematisation of everyday life was a response to their core function as the conduit through which slavery was naturally reproduced, and their vulnerability to legally sanctioned sexual exploitation. They developed integrated systems of thought and actions that countered efforts to morally and politically legitimise their enslavement. Resistance began in West Africa and continued during the middle passage. Anti-slavery mentalities, therefore, preceded the plantation. It connected African women to their creole progeny delivered on the plantations by enchained wombs; collectively, these women set their hearts and minds against slavery.

In an assessment of the 'organs of discontent' on West Indian slave plantations, Dirks argued that when conflict arose it was usually the 'female gang members who complained the loudest because everyone knew that they were less likely to be flogged than men'. It earned women the reputation, he noted, for being the instruments of instability and the more unmanageble element of the work force. The evidence, furthermore, comes down in favour of *Slave Women*'s equality under the whip, and indicates their prominence in the creation of social turmoil and the articulation of protests. Jacob Belgrave, for example, the free-coloured owner of a large Barbados sugar plantation, told the authorities that, shortly before the April 1816 slave revolt, he was verbally abused by a gang of slave women who alleged that he was one of the fellows opposed to England's abolition of slavery.[18]

In this regard, Bush's work has done much to extend the conceptual parameters of the analysis. In a series of essays, the themes of which constitute the empirical core of a subsequent monograph on enslaved women in the Caribbean, she demonstrated the fluidity and range in forms or women's struggles, and the diversity of their anti-slavery actions and attitudes. Enslaved women, she showed, promoted a culture of intransigence in relation to work; they ran away from owners, terrorised white households with chemical concoctions, refused to procreate at levels expected by their owners, insisted upon participation in the market economy as independent hucksters, slept with white men as part of a strategy to better their material and social condition, and did whatever else was necessary in order to minimise the degree of their unfreedom. Through such 'channels', Bush states, 'women helped to generate and sustain the general spirit of resistance'. The Black women's anti-slavery continuum, then, acted as a political infrastructure that destabilised the terms of everyday life within the race, gender, and class order.[19]

The tale of the two Nannys is particularly instructive of the way in which historians of the Caribbean have constructed an heroic feminism within the radical tradition. The reference here is to Nanny of the Maroons, Jamaica's sole official national heroine, and Nanny Grigg who has more recently been similarly honoured for her role in the 1816 Barbados slave rebellion as a revolutionary ideologue. Both Nannys are described as militant women who led, physically and conceptually, their menfolk into violent confrontation with slave owners and the imperial troops who defended them. Nanny of the Maroons was a guerrilla commander whose successes against pro-slavery forces in Jamaica are now legendary. The Barbados Assembly's official report into the 1816 rebellion describes Nanny Grigg as a literate, knowlegeable woman who believed and propagated the view that in order to secure freedom it was necessary to replicate the Haitian Revolution. The report stated that she held considerable political authority among her male peers and swayed them in favour of the armed solution to the slavery question.[20]

Slave women like Mary Prince, on the other hand, who neither led troops into battle, nor mobilised any community for such action succeeded, nevertheless, in making a considerable contribution to the radical tradition through the writing of memoirs. As a freed woman in England she presented an effective critique of pro-slavery ideology and interest. Her 'voice' in metropolitan anti-slavery circles constituted an important 'literary' force from the West Indian women's anti-slavery vanguard. Prince left no room for an ambivalent interpretation of slavery; black women wanted freedom from slavery, she argued, and did all that was possible to this end. In her acclaimed narrated autobiography, Prince speaks of the 'sweetness' of personal freedom, and the collective desire for liberty that kept the black community in endemic opposition to the colonial order. She 'wrote back' in ways similar to the Hart sisters, and echoed the voices of all black women who could not be heard.

The details of Princes's life story illuminate the experiences of black women within the gender order of slavery. With respect to Mrs Wood, her mistress, she was particularly consistent. Prince brands Mrs Wood as a racist, a sadist, and lacking in feminine sensitivity. Prince recalls cases of brutality she and other women suffered at Mrs Wood's hands. She documents Mrs Wood's contempt for the marriages of slavewomen, and the malice directed towards their husbands. Critically, she tells of Mrs Wood's description of her as a 'black devil', and the punishments she received for thinking and speaking about freedom. Prince's expression of compassion for suffering slave women linked her in solidarity to the politics of the Hart sisters; like them she held the belief that black women suffered to a more degrading degree the inhumanity of slavery.[21]

Texts produced by enslaved women constitute the most reliable site from which feminist scholars can depart in the development of a critique of plantation culture, particularly its masculinist social ideology and practice. The reading of these texts as presentations of knowledge in the radical tradition, however, has contributed to two discernible ideological positions within feminist thinking, the first of which ironically has militated against its development and maturity. The first position concerns the manner in which the stereotyped armed and deadly 'rebel woman' was singled out and promoted as a heroine within the struggle against slavery and patriarchy. The process of selection for this status resulted in the exclusion of other types of less well-documented rebellious women whose oppositional politics remains textually suppressed.

The deification of the militant 'rebel woman' demanded in turn the promotion of mythic narratives that represented them as persons larger than life, and alienated them from the 'common' woman who laboured in the trenches of everyday resistance. The second position has to do with the less developed concept of the 'natural rebel' as a discursive instrument. It has been argued that the adoption of this concept would revolutionise the theory of anti-slavery by moving it away from the limited parameters of armed struggle to embrace popular culture, religion, and economics – indeed the areas of social encounter where oppositional social consciousness was expressed and registered.

Reading the theoretical significance of this conceptual diversity is important in developing explanations for the strategic positions adopted by feminists in recent times. The reason why institutional political projects, such as independence', took hegemonic precedence over women's liberation has not been rigorously debated by theoreticians of the women's movement. The continued political containment of women's resistance to patriarchy became an important sub-project of post colonial discourse. Feminist radicalism that could not be accommodated within the official parameters of the emergent nation-states was deemed subversive, anti-social and unpatriotic. Feminists, then, had a difficult time locating and practising a nationalism that did not betray the core tendencies of their radical traditions. The effective 'nationalisation' of the radical women's movement, and in turn the ascendancy of liberal feminists, can therefore be read, in part, as a history of ideological acquiescence. The state offered many benefits, and these were attractive and considerable. Some women fell in line, and radical feminism was put aside as articulations of extremists within the 'lunatic fringe'.

The construction of the nation-state as the final victory for anti-colonial forces carried within its very conception and design several layers of enforced agreement that quickly emerged as the new and revised oppressive hegemony. Emphasis upon national unity as the ultimate social condition meant that political contests over inequitable ownership and control of productive resources, women's objection to masculinist domination of public institutions, resistance to racism against people of African descent in everyday life, and the critique of socio-cultural privileges attained by representatives of white supremacy ideologies, were oftentimes presented as hostile to the national interest. Newly politically empowered men, described as 'founding fathers' of nation-states, who in fact were essentially leaders of political parties and corporate institutions, defined and declared what was the national interest and how it should be protected. They alone determined finally who were the supporters and enemies of the nation, and which discourses wee nation-building and which were subversive.

There was no autonomous, privileged place for feminist movements within the hegemonised masculinist politics of nation-building. Tokenism and paternalism, however, ran rampant within the formative years of post-colonialism. Radical feminists were prominent occupants of a discredited community that included Rastafarians, religious fundamentalists, communists, black power chanters, and other advocates of allegedly 'untenable' causes. Black men especially considered themselves politically enfranchised, if not liberated, by their social 'ownership' and management of state power. They possessed the public institutions of governance, stamped their personalities on them, and cultivated political cultures that were patently hostile to female participation.

Nation-states, as hegemonic civic enterprises, functioned essentially as 'boys only clubs' – the odd woman was admitted but on terms set out by her 'brethren'. It became fashionable to have one woman in each high office – the cabinet, judiciary, diplomatic corp, permanent secretariat, and so on. In cases where women's radical tradition was strong, as in Jamaica, it was strategically contained by calling upon women to form their own wing within the political party. These fora in turn became places where radical feminists were isolated and critiqued, and despite the enormous display intellectual and organisational energy on the part of many, official leadership tended to fall into the lap of their liberal pro-establishment sisters.

The set back to radical feminism, therefore, took place at two levels; one, conceptual self-subjection to invented notion of nationhood as a cul-de-sac of the historic struggles against imperialism and male domination; two, acceptance of the nationalist paradigm in which development discourse fixed 'Independence' as a seminal moment for women within the evolution of feminist identity. A political effect of these strategic positions was that women, formerly enslaved and colonised, but now 'free' and empowered with citizenship, scaled down and subordinated their struggle against male political power and economic domination; conceptually it meant the acceptance by some women that their histories and identities would in future be decisively determined by forces opposed to their conflict with patriarchy.

The break with Empire, it seemed, became a critical movement in women's liberation, and the beginning of a reformulation of political identity. The accepted idea that colonialism was a principal driving force in shaping women's experiences and consciousness allowed nationalism to function for them as a splintering ideology. While it was recognised, by socialist theoreticians especially, that the constitutional design and ideological make-up of the nationalist state was politically reactionary, feminists did not politicise the implication of this argument for women's movements. While they may have been distracted by the popular realisation that socialists themselves did not break with liberal democrats on issues of sex and gender, questions about their greater responsibility for the objectives of women's movements remain unanswered.

There were many lessons that West Indian feminists could have learnt from studies of the rise of the Haitian nation-state between 1804 and 1826. Despite the abundance of evidence which shows the active involvement of women in the revolutionary process; the independent nation of Haiti was constructed, in both its constitutional and administrative scaffolds, as an expression and representation of masculinist authority that systematically sidelined and repressed women into second-class citizenship. Indeed, successive constitutions, within the first two decades of independence, denied women rights that men took for granted as expressions of their citizenship. Restrictions on employment, access to public office, the setting of terms on the exercise of the franchise, alienation from land ownership rights, and control over marital relations, were imposed throughout regional jurisdictions. In order to ensure that 'foreign' [white] men could not own land in Haiti, women who married such men were deprived of citizenship in order to prevent white inheritance by marriage. The same penalties did not apply to Haitian men who married white women.

Haitian women, then, the first females in the Caribbean to achieve citizenship within a modernising nation, were constitutionally reduced to inferior status through a virulent masculinist ideological praxis that designed and promoted the state as an instrument of the military élite whose socio-economic status was rooted in landownership. President Dessalines' Independence Constitution of 1805 provided in article 9 that 'no one is worthy of being a Haitian if he is not a good father, a good son, a good husband, and above all a good soldier'. Lands appropriated by the state following the defeat of the slaveocracy were distributed among soldiers according to rank, and to male public servants in lieu of wages. Women received no land under either policy. With respect to adult suffrage, says Leyburn, President Petion's constitution of 1816 targeted women punitively when the right to vote was denied 'women, crimminals, idiots, and menials'.[22] Since women were alienated from landownership and denied access to the military their powerlessness and honourlessness within the emergent nation was assured. Freedom from slavery and the destruction of colonialism were objectives for which women had fought and died, and nationalism did not secure them an equal return.

The refusal of feminists to draw upon and theorise such historical encounters within their radical tradition has to do with the selective, eclectic approaches adopted with respect to reading history. The Haitian Revolution occupied a central place in the knowledges organised by recent femininist leaders and writers. The pantheons of national heroes established in most West Indian post-colonial societies connect directly to an understanding of history in which Haitian revolutionaries are idealised. Toussaint L'Ouverture emerges as the 'Abraham' – the father of fathers – in the redemption of the black race. He was not associated, however, with statements and policies supportive of the political empowerment of females who fought in the war of liberation. Neither did Jean-Jacques Dessalines, the first President, target women for equal recognition.

Feminists selected aspects of this revolutionary process that strengthened their analysis and agendas, but ignored those features that spoke more concretely to their gendered condition as women. The same can be said of their readings of maroon history and societies. While maroon societies represented movements of heroic resistance, careful and balanced research should also show how enslaved women on the estates were kidnapped by maroon men, pressed into oppressive social relations, and otherwise kept in bondage.

Recently, Eudine Barriteau-Foster, Caribbean feminist social scientist, lamented the fact that the considerable research done under the auspices of the 'Women in the Caribbean Project' (WICP), academically administered and conceived by 'liberal feminists', furthered the crisis of radical feminism and problematised the advance of postmodern feminist theory-building. The limitations of the liberal feminist research agendas, she asserts, resided in its deliberate submission to Enlightenment political discourses that could not subvert or destabilise the hegemonic gender power relations of patriarchy. The social and ideological effect of this academic politics, she concludes, was that liberal feminists continued into post-colonialism to 'emphasize the homogeneity of women and call for their integration into public life, which they saw as gender neutral and therefore potentially benefitting to women', Recognising, however, that West Indian women were excluded from the centre spaces of modernising nation-building projects, WICP leaders resisted the critique of 'epistemologies and methodologies that maintained that exclusion in the first place'. As a consequence, Barriteau-Foster calls, for historical research that would promote the task of producing a locally grounded postmodern feminist theory.[23]

What is not clear, however, is how a postmodern approach will perform both tasks; explain the historical circumstances that produced systems of knowledge and social organization that disaggregated and excluded women, and at the same time provided them with liberationist epistemologies and a working agenda for collective strategic action. The idea that postmodernism generates intellectual positions rather than political strategies that de-energise the subaltern by emphasising the endless incoherence of social action and the imprisonment of social agency within language and texts would require a systematic response from Barriteau-Foster. Her ultimate challenge, then, would be to redefine and relocate Caribbean women's movements within the ideological space provided by postmodern feminism in order to create and promote social activism that reflects a coherent feminist opposition and vanguard.

Postcolonial social relations, framed as national society, continue to express and promote enormous diversity in the mentalities and experiences of women. To account for these gender interactions in terms of encounters with, and reactions to, representations of masculinity, and its patriarchal structures, is to deny, in great measure, that there is a historically created feminine cosmology that cannot be conceptually domesticated in this way. Patriarchy does not define and texture all spaces of lived experiences, particularly those that are newly excavated or created specifically by women in action. Practices such as the 'higglerisation' (of women's lives and national society) constitute a case in point. Working-class women, the evidence suggests, have historically popularised, before the colonial encounter, the economic institution of commodity trading. During slavery and after they protected this economic culture in many ways, but used it strategically in circumstances of economic decline and material crisis. Everywhere, black women were found buying and selling (confronting the licencing authority of the state) a range of goods and services – some procured from distant countries – and creating in the process what formal economists now call the informal sector.

Postcolonialism, then, cannot claim credit for the intense social activism found among women. National society did offer an environment more conducive to its proliferation in so far as it facilitated and offered liberating forms of personal freedom in areas such as professionalism and petty entrepreneurship. Working-class women have struggled to find survivalist activities which, within the context of national economies dominated by men, are always considered stabilising and subversive. Such activities, however, offer areas of analysis that speak of social empowerment, contestations with hegemonic economic spheres, and political recognition for women as autonomous accumlators. Middle-class and professional women have found space within the proliferating Non-Government Organizations movement that sought to perform development services on behalf of communities considered not capable of helping themselves.

Higglerization and NGO's, therefore, stand as a dichotomy within the struggle of a radicalised and conceptually fragmented West Indian women's movement challenging the issue of scarce resources and its relation to poverty and women's liberation. These mentalities and experiences are considered oftentimes as poles apart in terms of development discourse. Encounters by the women reveal that they do not always see each other as working towards the same end. Indeed, there is considerable mutual suspicion and empathy. Postmodern feminist theorisations should ideally recognise and accept these radically different strategic approaches by women to decision making, and reflect the extent to which specific searches for autonomy and empowerment transcend the notion of an all embracing woman's identity.[24]

In conclusion, then, it seems that it will not be possible to generate – from the extreme diversity of women's experiences with slavery and colonialism and postcolonialism – a viable or attractive theory of women's oppression and liberation in the Caribbean. What existing theory has done, particularly with regard to slavery's legacies in postcolonialism, is to reveal the poverty and dangers of theory in general, and calls into question the very project of feminist theorising. Attempts to deal with contemporary social relations in terms of cohesive sex and gender categories will certainly open more analytical doors than any one house can possibly have, hence the futility of seeking to conceptualise a unified structure that can account for a flow of traffic from all directions. Conceptual openness, methodological plurality, vigorous social history, and less historical eclecticism, may better serve the task of understanding and changing the oppressive power systems of the gender order. A major task of conceptual deconstruction is therefore required.

Historical paradigms derived from slave society, such as 'white women consumed, black women laboured and coloured women served', need to be destabilised by sound detailed historical research that views these diverse experiences of women in terms of multiple encounters with complex systems of wealth and status accumulation rather than as direct expressions of hegemonic patriarchy. The visibility of those many white, coloured, and black women who traded in slaves in West Africa and the New World, owned plantations or urban properties, and therefore, subscribed to the principles of colonial accumulation within the Atlantic, should be carefully researched as a way of understanding the importance of gender to colonial discourse. Likewise, ongoing projects of nation-state building that promote allegedly gender free notions of nationalist cohesion should be contested and unmasked as skillful projections of modernising masculine political power.

Endnotes

1 Hilary Beckles, 'Sex and gender', *op. cit.* pp. 125-40; Moitt, 'Women, Work and Resistance', *op. cit.*, p. 155-76; Graham Hodges, 'Restructuring Black Women's History in the Caribbean : Review Essay', *Journal of American Ethnic History*, 1992, Fall, pp. 101-07.
2 Silvestrini, 'Women and Resistance' *op. cit.*; Reddock, '*Women and Slavery*', *op. cit.*, pp. 63-80; Gautier, 'Les esclaves femme', *op. cit.*, pp. 409-35.
3 Morrissey, 'Women's Work', *op. cit.* pp. 339-69; Brereton, 'Text, Testimony and Gender', *op. cit.*, pp. 63-93.
4 Bush, 'White "Ladies"', *op. cit.*; pp. 245-62; Gregg, 'The Caribbean (as a certain kind of) woman:', *op. cit.*; Carmichael, *Domestic Manners*, *op. cit.*, pp. 12, 96; Eric Williams, *Capitalism and Slavery* (London: André Deutsch, 1990 edit.), p. 198.
5 Elizabeth Fox-Genovese, *Within the Plantation Household: Black and White Women of the Old South* (Chapel Hill: University of North Carolina Press, 1988) pp. 33, 47-48, 326-27, 333; Patricia Morton (ed), *Discovering the Woman in Slavery: Emancipating Perspectives on the American Past* (Athens: University of Georgia Press, 1996), p. 9.
6 Arnold Sio, 'Marginality and Free Coloured Identity in Caribbean Slave Society', *Slavery and Abolition*, vol. 8, No. 2, 1987, pp. 166-82; Gad Heuman, *Between Black and White: Race, Politics, and the Free Coloured in Jamaica, 1792-1865* (Greenwood Press: Westport, 1981); Mavis Campbell, *The Dynamics of Change in a Slave Society* (Rutherford: N.J., 1976).
7 J. M.Cohen (ed), *The Four Voyages of Christopher Columbus* (London: Century Hutchinson, 1988), pp. 136, 196; Virginia Kerns, *Women and their Ancestors: Black Carib Kinship and Ritual* (Chicago: University of Illinois Press, 1983).
8 Nugent, *Lady Nugent's Journal*, *op. cit.*, pp. 47, 66, 76, 125.
9 Beckles, *Natural Rebels*, *op. cit.*, pp. 65-68, 127-28, 159-62.
10 Nugent, *Lady Nugent's Journal*, *op. cit.*, pp. 28, 58-59.
11 Butler, *The Economics of Emancipation*, *op. cit.*, pp. 92-109.
12 Beckles, 'White Women', *op. cit.*; Burnard, 'Family Continuity', *op. cit.*
13 Brathwaite, "Caribbean Woman", *op. cit.*; Nugent, *Lady Nugent's Journal*, *op. cit.*, p. 156.
14 Higman, *Slave Populations*, *op. cit.*, p. 385-86; Jerome Handler and John Pohlmann, 'Slave Manumissions and Freedmen in 17th Century Barbados', *William and Mary Quarterly*, vol. XLI, 1984, pp. 390-408.
15 Handler, *The Unappropriated People*, *op. cit.* p. 124.

16 *Ibid.*, pp. 157-58.

17 Moira Ferguson (ed), *The Hart Sisters: Early African Caribbean Writers, Evangelicals, and Radicals* (London: University of Nebraska Press, 1993).

18 Beckles, *Natural Rebels, op. cit.*, p. 171; Robert Dirks, *Black Saturnalia: Conflict and Its Ritual Expressions on British West Indian Plantations* (Gainesville: University presses of Florida, 1987), pp. 160-61.

19 Bush, "Towards Emancipation", *op. cit.*, p.239.

20 Mair, *The Rebel Woman, op. cit.*; Beckles, *Black Rebellion, op. cit.*

21 Moira Ferguson (ed), *The History of Mary Prince: A West Indian Slave, Related by Herself* (London: Pandora, 1987).

22 Mimi Shelter, 'Engendering citizenship: nationhood, brotherhood, and manhood in the Republic of Haiti in the 19th Century', paper presented at the Caribbean Studies Association Conference, North London University, July, 1996; James Leyburn, *The Haitian People* (New Haven: Yale University Press, 1980), p. 243.

23 Eudine Barriteau-Foster, 'Postmodernist feminist theorising and development policy and practice in the Anglophone Caribbean: the case of Barbados', in Marianne H. Marchand and Jane L. Parpart (eds), *Feminism/Postmodernism Development* (London: Routledge, 1995) pp. 142-59.

24 Elsa Leo-Rhynie et al. (eds), *Gender: A Caribbean Multi-Disciplinary Perspective* (Kingston: IRP, 1997).

Select Bibliography

Abénon, L (1987) *La Guadeloupe de 1671 à 1759*, 2 vols. (Paris, L'Harmattan).

Aidoo, Agnes (1980) 'Asante Queen Mothers in Government and Politics in the 19th Century' in Steady, F. (ed), *The Blackwoman Cross-culturally* (Cambridge, Schenkman).

Alexander, Adele (1991) *Ambiguous Lives: Free Women of Color in Rural Georgia, 1789-1879* (Fayetteville: Univ. of Arkansas Press).

Alonzo, Andrea (1989) 'A Study of Two Women's Slave Narratives', *Women Studies Quarterly*, 17, Nos. 3, 4.

Amos, V. and Parmar, P. (1984) 'Challenging Imperial Feminism', *Feminist Review*, 17.

Anon. (1743) *Memoirs of the First Settlement of the Island of Barbados . . .* (London).

Anon. (1823) *The West Indian Agricultural Distress* (London).

Aptherker, Bettina (1982) *Woman's Legacy: Essays on Race, Sex, and Class in American History* (Amherst: University of Mass. Press).

Arhin, Kwame (1983) 'The Politial and Military Roles of Akan Women', in C. Oppong (ed), *Females and Males in West Africa* (London: Allen and Unwin).

Azize-Vargas, Yamila (1989) 'The Roots of Puerto Rican Feminism', *Radical Review*, vol.32, No.1.

Bascom, W., Herskovits, M. (eds) (1950) *Continuity and Change in African Culture* (Chicago, University of Chicago Press).

Barker-Benfield, G.J. and Clinton, C. (eds) (1991), *Portraits of American Women: From Settlement to Present* (N.Y.: St Martin's Press).

Bariteau, Eudine (1998) 'Liberal Ideology and Contradictions in Caribbean Gender Systems', in C. Barrow (ed) *Caribbean Portraits*.

_____ (1992) 'The Construct of a Postmodern Feminist Theory For Caribbean Social Science Research', *Social and Economic Studies* (41: 2).

_____ (1996) 'Postmodernist Feminist Theorising and Development Policy and Practice in the Anglophone Caribbean' in M. Marchand, et al. (eds) (N.Y., Routledge).

Bayley, F.W. (1833) *Four Years' Residence in the West Indies* (William Kidd: London).

Bean, Richard (1975) *The British Trans-Atlantic Slave Trade, 1650-1775* (New York, Arno Press).

Barrow, Christine, (ed) (1998) *Caribbean Portraits: Essays on Gender Ideology and Identities* (Kingston, Ian Randle Publishers).

Beal, Francis (1975) 'Slave of a Slave No More: Black Women in Struggle', *Black Scholar*, 6, No. 6.

Beckles, Hilary McD. (1991) 'An Economic Life of their Own: Slaves as Community Producers and Distributors in Barbados', in Ira Berlin and Philip Morgan (eds), *The Slaves' Economy: Independent Production by Slaves in the Americas* (London, Frank Cass).

_____ and Watson, Karl (1987) 'Social Protest and Labour Bargaining: the Changing Nature of Slaves' Responses to Plantation Life in 18th Century Barbados', *Slavery and Abolition*, 8, pp. 272-93.

_____ (1982b) 'The 200 Years War: Slave Resistance in the British West Indies: An Overview of the Historiography', *Jamaica Historical Review*, vol. 13.

_____ (1984a) 'The Literate Few: An Historical Sketch of the Slavery Origins of Black Elites in the English West Indies', *Caribbean Journal of Education*, vol. 11, no.1.

_____ (1984b) 'On the Backs of Blacks: the Barbados Free-Coloureds' Pursuit of Civil Rights and the 1816 Rebellion', Immigrants and Minorities, vol.3, no.2.

_____ (1984) Black Rebellion in Barbados: The Struggle Against Slavery, 1627-1938.

_____ (1985) 'The Slave Drivers' War: Bussa and the 1816 Barbados Slave Uprising', Boletín de Estudios Latinamericanos y del Caribe, no.39, Dec.

_____ (1986) ' "Black Men in White Skins": the Formation of a White Proletariat in West Indian Slave Society', *The Journal of Imperial and Commonwealth History*, vol. XV, no.1.

_____ and Andrew Downes (1987) 'The Economics of Transition to the Black Labor System in Barbados, 1630-1680', *Journal of Interdisciplinary History*, vol. xviii, no. 2.

_____ (1989) *Natural Rebels: A Social History of Enslaved Black Women in Barbados* (London: Rutgers Univ. Press Zed Press).

_____ (1993) 'White Women and Slavery in the Caribbean', *History Workshop Journal*, issue 36.

_____ (1989) *White Servitude and Black Slavery in Barbados, 1627-1715* (Knoxville Tennessee Univ. Press).

_____ (1995) 'Sex and Gender in the Historiography of Caribbean Slavery', in Verene Shepherd et al. (eds), *Engendering History: Caribbean Women in Historical Perspective* (Kingston: Ian Randle Publishers).

_____ (1996) 'Property Rights in Pleasure: The Prostitution of Enslaved Black Women in the West Indies', in Roderick McDonald (ed), *West Indian Accounts: Essays on the History of the British Caribbean and the Atlantic Economy in Honour of Richard Sheridan* (Kingston: The Press: University of the West Indies).

Bennett, J. Harry (1951) 'The Problem of Slave Labour Supply on the Codrington Plantations', *Journal of Negro History*, vol.36.

_____ (1958) *Bondsmen and Bishops: Slavery and Apprenticeship on the Codrington Plantations of Barbados, 1710-1838* (University of California Press: Los Angeles).

Berlin, Ira, et at. (1988) 'Afro-American Families in the Transition from Slavery to Freedom', *Radical History Review*, 42, Fall.

Bernhard, Virginia, et al. (1991) (eds), *Southern Women: Histories and Identities* (Knoxville: Univ. of Tennessee Press).

Bhabha, Homi, (1983) 'Difference, Discrimination, and the Discourse of Colonialism', in Francis Barker (ed) *The Politics of Theory* (Colchester, Univ. of Essex Press).

Blackburn, George, and Sherman, Ricardo (1981) 'The Mother-Headed Family among Free Negroes in Charleston, South Carolina, 1850-1860', *Phylon*, 42, No. 1.

Bleser, Carol, (ed) (1991) *In Joy and in Sorrow: Women, Family, and Marriage in the Victorian South, 1830-1900* (N.Y.: Oxford Univ. Press).

Bohanan, P. and Dalton, G. (eds) (1969) *Markets in Africa* (Northwestern University Press, Evanston).

Bowen, E. (1747) *A Complete System of Geography*, 2 Vols. (London).

Brathwaite, Edward (1971) *The Development of Creole Society in Jamaica*, 1770-1820 (Oxford: Oxford University Press).

_____ (1975) 'Submerged Mothers', *Jamaica Journal*, 9, nos.2/3.

_____ (1984) 'Caribbean Woman during the Period of Slavery', Elsa Goveia Memorial Lecture, Cave Hill Campus, Barbados.

Brereton, Bridget (1993) 'Text, Testimony and Gender: An Examination of some Texts by

Women on the English-Speaking Caribbean, 1770s to 1920s', a paper presented at the Symposium – Engendering History: Current Directions in the Study of Women and Gender in Caribbean History', U.W.I., Mona. Also in Shepherd, et. al. *Engendering History.*

Brodber, Erna (1988) *Myal* (London: New Beacon).

_____ (1994) *Louisiana* (London: New Beacon).

_____ (1980) *Jane and Louisa Will Soon Come Home* (London: New Beacon).

_____ (1982) *Perceptions of Caribbean Women: Towards a Documentation of Stereotypes* (ISER, UWI, Barbados).

Brown, Ira (1983) '"Am I not a Woman and Sister?' The Anti-Slavery Convention of American Women, 1837-1839"', *Pennsylvania History*, No. 50.

Burgess, Norma (1994) 'Gender Roles Revisited: The Development of the 'Woman's Place' among African American Women in the U.S.' *Journal of Black Studies*, 24.

Burnard, Trevor (1992) 'Family Continuity and Female Independence in Jamaica, 1665-1734'. *Continuity and Change*, 7, (2).

_____ (1997) 'Inheritance and Independence: Women's Status in early colonial Jamaica', *William and Mary Quarterly*, vol. xxxiv.

Burton, A. (1984) Burdens of History: British Feminists, Indian Women, and Imperial Culture, 1865-1915 (Chapel Hill: University of North Carolina Press).

_____ (1992) 'The White Woman's Burden: British Feminists and "the Indian Woman", 1865-1915', in N. Chaudhuri and M. Strobel, Western Women and Imperialism: Complicity and Resistance (Bloomington: Indiana University Press).

Bush, Barbara (1982) 'Defiance and Submission: The Role of the Slave Woman in Slave Resistance in the British Caribbean', *Immigrants and Minorities*, vol.1.

_____ (1986) 'Towards Emancipation: slave women and Resistance to Coercive Labour Regimes in the British West Indian Colonies,.1790-1838', in David Richardson (ed.) Abolition and its Aftermath: The Historical Context, 1790-1916 (London: Frank Cass).

_____ (1990) *Slave Women in Caribbean Society, 1650-1838* (London: James Currey).

_____ (1991) 'White "Ladies", Coloured "Favourites" and Black "Wenches": Some considerations on Sex, Race and Class Factors in Social Relations in white Creole Society in the British Caribbean' (*Slavery and Abolition*, 2).

Bush-Slimani, B, (1993) 'Hard Labor: Women, Childbirth, and Resistance in the British Caribbean Slave Societies', *History Workshop*, No. 36.

Butler, K. Mary (1982) 'Mortality and Labour on the Codrington Estates, Barbados'. Paper presented at the 14th Annual Conference of Caribbean Historians, Puerto Rico.

_____ (1995) *The Economics of Emancipation : Jamaica and Barbados 1823-1843* (Chapel Hill: Univ. of North Carolina Press).

Bynum, Victoria (1992) *Unruly Women: The Politics of Social and Sexual Control in the Old South, 1830-1900* (N.Y.: Oxford Univ. Press).

Campbell, John (1984) Women, Pregnancy and Infant Mortality among Southern Slaves, *Journal of Interdisciplinary History*, vol. 14, No. 4.

Carby, Hazel (1985) '"On the Threshold of Women's Era"': Lynching, Sexuality and Empire in Black Feminist Theory" *Critical Inquiry*, 12, No. 1.

Carmichael, A.C. (1969) *Domestic Manners and Social Condition of the White, Coloured, and Negro Population of the West Indies*, 2 vols: 1833 (New York: Negro Universities Press edition).

Cashin, Joan (1991) *A Family Venture: Men and Women on the Southern Frontier* (N.Y.: Oxford Univ. Press).

Chandler, Michael (1965) *A Guide to the Records in Barbados* (Oxford: Basil Blackwell).

Clarke, H., and Gaspar, Barry (1997) (eds) *More Than Chattels: Black Women and Slavery in the Americas* (Bloomington: Indiana, Univ. Press).

Clarke, Roberta (1986) 'Women's Organisations, Women's Interests', *Social and Economic Studies*, 35, No.3.

Clinton, Catherine (1982) *The Plantation Mistress: Woman's World in the Old South* (N.Y.: Pantheon).

_____ (1987) 'Fanny Kemble's Journal: A Woman Confronts Slavery on a Georgia Plantation', *Frontiers*, 9.

Cole, Johnetta (1978) 'Militant Black Women in Early U.S. History', *Black Scholar*, 9, No. 7.

Coleridge, Henry (1825) *Six Months in the West Indies* (John Murray: London).

Connell, Neville (1978) 'Hotel Keepers and Hotel in Barbados', *Journal of the Barbados Museum and Historical Society*, vol. 33, no. 4.

Cracknell, Everil (ed) (1934) *The Barbadian Diary of General Robert Haynes, 1787-1836* (Hampshire: Medstead).

Crahan, Margaret E. and Knight, Franklin (eds) (1979) *Africa and the Caribbean: The Legacies of a Link* (Baltimore: Johns Hopkins University Press).

Craton, Michael (1974) *Sinews of Empire: A Short History of British Slavery* (London: Doubleday).

_____ (1978) *Searching for the Invisible Man: Slaves and Plantation Life in Jamaica* (Mass.: Cambridge University Press).

_____ (1978) 'Hobbesian or Panglossian? The Two Extremes of Slave Conditions in the British Caribbean, 1783-1834', *William and Mary Quarterly*, vol. 35.

_____ (1979a) 'Changing Patterns of Slave Families in the British West Indies', *Journal of Interdisciplinary History*, vol. X.

_____ (1979b) 'Proto-Peasant Revolts? The Late Slave Rebellion in the British West Indies, 1816-1832', *Past and Present*, vol. 85.

_____ (1980) 'The Passion to Exist: Slave Rebellions to the British West Indies 1650-1832', *Journal of Caribbean History*, vol. 13.

_____ (1982) 'Slave Culture, Resistance and the Achievement of Emancipation in the British West Indies, 1738-1828', in James Walvin, (ed), *Slavery and British Abolition, 1776-1848* (London: Macmillan).

_____ (1982) *Testing the Chains: Resistance to Slavery in the British West Indies* (Ithaca: Illinois University Press).

_____ (1985) 'A Cresting Wave? Recent Trends in the Historiography of Slavery, with special reference to the British Caribbean', *Caribbean Societies*, vol. 2, no. 34. Collected seminar papers of the Institute of Commonwealth Studies, University of London.

Cunningham, Constance (1987) 'The Sins of Omission: Black Women in 19th Century American History', *Journal of Social and Behavioural Sciences*, 33, No. 1.

Curtin, Philip D. (1969) *The Atlantic Slave Trade: A Census* (Wisconsin Univ. Press, Madison).

_____ (1975) *Economic Change in Pre-Colonial Africa: Senegambia in the Era of the Slave Trade* (Madison: Wisconsin University Press).

Dadzie, Stella, (1990) 'Searching for the Invisible Woman: Slavery and Resistance in Jamaica', *Race and Class*, 32, No. 2.

Davies, K.G. (1957) *The Royal African Company* (London: Longman).

Davis, Angela (1981) *Women, Race and Class* (N.Y., Random House).

Davis, Ralph (1962) *The Rise of the English Shipping Industry in the Seventeenth and Eighteenth Centuries* (London: Macmillan).

Debien, Gabriel (1974) *Les Esclaves aux Antilles Françaises, XVIIe-XVIIIe siécle* (Basse-Terre: Société d'histoire de la Guadeloupe).

Deerr, N. (1940-50) *A History of Sugar*, 2 vols. (London: Chapman and Hull).

de Groot, Silvia (1986), Maroon Women as Ancestors, Priests, and Mediums in Surinam", *Slavery and Abolition*, 7, No. 2.

Dickson, William (1789) *Letters on Slavery* (Westport, 1970, Negro University Press Reprint).
_____ (1815) *The Mitigation of Slavery* (Westport, 1970, Negro University Press Reprint).
Dill, Bonnie (1979), 'The Dialectics of Black Womanhood', *Signs*, 4.
Dillman, Caroline (1988) (ed) *Southern Women* (N.Y.: Hemisphere).
Diner, Hasia (1985), 'Black Women in Families: From Field to Factory', *Reviews in American History*, 13, No. 4.
Dirks, Robert (1987) *The Black Saturnalia: Conflict and its Ritual Expression on British West Indian Slave Plantations* (Gainesville: University Presses of Florida).
Donnan, Elizabeth (ed.) (1930-35) *Documents Illustrative of the History of the Slave Trade to America*, 4 Vols. (Washington D.C.: Carnegie Institute).
Du Tertre Jean-Baptiste (Père) (1671) *Histoire générale des Antilles habitées par les Français*, 4 vols., (Fort-de-France: Editions des horizons Caraibe, 1973 edition).
Dunn, Richard S. (1969) 'The Barbados Census of 1860: Profile of the Richest Colony in English America', *William and Mary Quarterly*, vol. 26.
_____ (1973) *Sugar and Slaves: The Rise of the Planter Class in the English West Indies, 1624-1713* (New York: W.W. Norton).
_____ (1977) 'A Tale of Two Plantations: Slave Life at Mesopotamia in Jamaica and at Mount Airy in Virginia, 1799-1828', *William and Mary Quarterly*, vol.34.
_____ (1987) 'Dreadful Idlers in the Cane Fields: The Slave Labor pattern on a Jamaican Sugar Estate, 1762-1831', *Journal of Interdisciplinary History*, vol. XVII, no. 4, Spring.
Edwards, Bryan (1793) *The History, Civil and Commercial, of the British Colonies in the West Indies* (London).
Edwards, Paul (ed) (1789) *Equiano's Travels: His Autobiography: The Interesting Life of Olaudah Equiano or Gustavus Vassa the African* (London: Frank Cass reprint, 1967).
Ellison, Mary (1983), 'Resistance to Oppression: Black Women's Response to Slavery in the U.S.', *Slavery and Abolition*, 4, No. 1.
Engerman, Stanley and Genovese, Eugene (1973) *Race and Slavery in the Western Hemisphere: Quantitative Studies* (Princeton: Princeton University Press).
_____ (1976) 'Some Economic and Demographic Comparisons of Slavery in the United States and the British West Indies', *Economic History Review*, 29.
Evans, Sara (1989) *Born for Liberty: A History of Women in America* (N.Y., Free Press).
Faust, Drew (1992), '"Trying to Do a Man's Business': Slavery, violence and Gender in the American Civil War"', *Gender and History*, 4, summer.
Fenwick, A.F. (ed.) (1927) *The Fate of the Fenwicks: Letters to Mary Hays, 1798-1828* (London: Methuen).
Ferguson, Moira (ed) (1831) *The History of Mary Prince: A West Indian Slave Narrated by Herself* (London: Pandora, 1987 edition).
_____ (1992) *Subject to Others: British Women Writers and Colonial Slavery, 1670-1834* (New York: Routledge).
_____ (1993) (ed) *The Hart Sisters: Early African-Caribbean Writers, Evangelicals and Radicals* (Lincoln and London: University of Nebraska Press).
Finkelman, Paul (ed) (1989) *Women and the Family in a Slave Society* (N.Y.: Garland).
Firth, C.H. (ed) (1900) *The Narrative of General Venables, With an Appendix of Papers Relating to the Expedition to the West Indies and the Conquest of Jamaica, 1654-1655* (London).
Foster, Francis (1981), '"In Respect of Females . . ."': Differences in the Portrayals of Women by male and Female Narrators, *Black American Literature Forum*, 15, No. 2.
Foucault, M. (1980), *The History of Sexuality: An Introduction* (N.Y., Vintage).
Fox-Genovese, Elizabeth (1982) 'Placing Women's History in History', *New Left Review*, no. 133, May-June.

_____ (1978), 'Ultimate Victims: Black Women in Slave Narratives', *Journal of American Culture*, 1, No. 4.

_____ (1983), 'Ante-bellum Southern Households: A New Perspective on a Familiar Question', *Review*, 7, No. 2.

_____ (1986), 'Strategies and Norms of Resistance: Focus on slave women in the U.S.', in G. Okihiro (ed) *In Resistance: Studies in African, Caribbean, and Afro-American History*, (Amherst, University of Mass. Press).

_____ (1988) 'Within the Plantation Household: Black and White Women of the Old South' (Chapel Hill: Univ. of North Carolina Press).

Galenson, David E. (1978) ' "Middling People" or "Common Sort": The Social Origins of Some Early Americans Re-examined', *William and Mary Quarterly*, vol. 35.

_____ (1986) *Traders, Planters and Slaves: Market Behaviour in Early English America* (Cambridge: Cambridge University Press).

Gaspar, Barry (1984) *Bondsmen and Rebels: A Study of Master-Slave Relations in Antigua; With Implications for Colonial British America* (Baltimore: Johns Hopkins University Press).

_____ (1987) '"Deep in the Minds of Many": slave women and Resistance in Antigua, 1632-1763: a preliminary inquiry', paper presented at the 19th Annual Conference of the Association of Caribbean Historians, Martinique.

Gaston-Martin (1948) *Histoire de l'esclavage Dans les Colonies Françaises* (Paris: Presses Universitaires de France).

Gautier, Arlette (1983) 'Les Esclaves femmes aux Antilles Francaises, 1635-1848'. *Reflexions Historiques*, 10:3, Fall.

_____ (1985) *Les Soeurs de Solitude: La condition feminine dans l'esclavage aux Antilles du XVIIe as XIX e siecle* (Paris: Editions Caribbeennes).

Gay, P. (1969) *The Enlightenment: An Interpretation. The Science of Freedom* (New York: W.W. Norton, 1977 edition).

Gemery, Henry and Jan Hogendorn (eds) (1979) *The Uncommon Market: Essays in the Economic History of the Atlantic Slave Trade* (New York: Academic Press).

Genovese, Eugene (1979) *From Rebellion to Revolution: Afro-American Slave Revolts in the Making of the Modern World* (Baton Rouge: Louisiana University Press).

_____ (1991), '"Our Family, White and Black': Family and Household in the Southern Slaveholders' World View"', in Blexer (ed), *In Joy, op. cit.*

Giddings, Paula (1984) *When and Where I Enter: The Impact of Black Women on Race and Sex in America* (N.Y.: William Morrow).

Gordan, Linda (1986) 'What's New in Women's History', in Teresa de Lauretis (ed) *Feminist Studies/Critical Studies*, (Bloomington: Indiana Univ. Press).

_____ (1991) 'Rewriting Women's History' in S. Gunew (ed) *A Reader in Feminist Knowledge* (London, Routledge).

Goveia, Elsa (1965) *Slave Society in the British Leeward Islands at the End of the 18th Century* (New Haven: Yale University Press).

_____ (1970) *The West Indian Slave Laws of the 18th Century* (Bridgetown: Caribbean Universities Press).

Green-Pederson, S. (1971) 'The Scope and Structure of the Danish Negro Slave Trade', *Scandinavian Economic History Review*, vol. 19.

Greenfield, Sidney (1966) *English Rustics in a Black Skin* (Yale University Press, New Haven).

Gregg, Veronica (1993) 'The Caribbean (as a certain kind of) Woman'; paper presented at conference – Engendering History.

Groneman, Carol (1994), 'Nymphomenia: The Historical Construction of Female Sexuality', *Signs*, 19, Winter.

Gundersen, Joan, (1986), 'The Double Bonds of Race and Sex: Black and White Women in a

Colonial Virginia parish', *Journal of Southern History*, vol. 52, No. 3.

Gutman, Herbert G. (1976) *The Black Family in Slavery and Freedom, 1750-1925* (New York: Pantheon).

Gwin, Minrose (1985) *Black and White Women of the Old South: The Peculiar Sisterhood in American Literature* (Knoxville: Univ. of Tennessee Press).

Hall, Catherine (1992) 'Feminism and Feminist Theory' in (ed) *White, Male and Middle Class: Explorations in Feminism and History* (Cambridge, Polity).

_____ (1993) 'White Visions, Black Lives: The Free Villages of Jamaica', *Journal of Negro History*, vol. 36.

Hall, Richard (1764) *Acts Passed in the Island of Barbados from 1643-1762 Inclusive* (London).

Handler, Jerome (1972) 'An Archaeological Investigation of the Domestic Life of Plantation Slaves in Barbados', *Journal of the Barbados Museum and Historical Society*, vol.34, no.2.

_____ (1974) *The Unappropriated People: Freedmen in the Slave Society of Barbados* (Baltimore: Johns Hopkins University Press)

_____ and Frisbie C. (1976) 'Aspects of Slave Life in Barbados: Music and its Cultural Context', *Caribbean Studies*, vol. 11, no. 4.

_____ and Lange, Frederick (1978) *Plantation Slavery in Barbados: An Archaeological and Historical Investigation* (Cambridge, Mass.: Harvard University Press).

_____ (1981) 'Joseph Rachell and Rachael Pringle-Polgreen: Petty Entrepreneurs', in D. Sweet and G. Nash, (eds), *Struggle and Survival in Colonial America* (Los Angeles: University of California Press).

_____ (1982) 'Slave Revolts and Conspiracies in 17th Century Barbados', *New West Indian Guide*, vol. 56.

_____ and Robert Corruccini (1979) 'Weaning among West Indian Slaves: Historical and Bioanthropological Evidence from Barbados', *William and Mary Quarterly*, vol. 43, no. 1, Jan.

Harper, C. W. (1985), 'Black Aristocrats: Domestic Servants on the Ante-bellum Plantation', *Phylon*, 46.

Harris, J. (1992) (ed) *Society and Culture in the Slave South* (N.Y.: Routledge).

Hart, Keith (ed) (1989), *Women and the Social Division of Labour in the Caribbean* (Kingston, UWI).

Hart, Richard (1973/4) 'The Formation of a Caribbean Working Class', *The Black Liberator*, vol. 2, no. 2.

_____ (1989) *Rise and Organise: Rise of the Workers and Nationalist Movements in Jamaica 1936-39* (London: Karia).

Hawks, Joanne, and Skemp, Sheila (eds) (1983) *Sex, Race and the Role of Women in the South* (Jackson: Univ. of Mississippi Press).

Heuman, Gad (ed) (1986) *Out of the House of Bondage: Runaways, Resistance, and Maroonage in Africa and the New World* (London: Frank Cass).

Hersch, B. G. (1978) *The Slavery of Sex: Feminist-Abolitionists in America* (Urbana: University of Illinois Press).

Higginbotham, Evelyn (1989), 'Beyond the Sound of Silence: Afro-American Women's History', *Gender and History*, 1, Spring.

Higman, Barry W. (1973) 'Household Structures and Fertility on Jamaican Slave Plantations: A Nineteenth Century Example', *Population Studies*, vol. 27.

_____ (1975) 'The Slave Family and Household in the British West Indies, 1800-1834', *Journal of Interdisciplinary History*, vol. VI.

_____ (1976) 'The Slave Population of the British Caribbean: Some Nineteenth Century Variations', in Samuel R. Proctor, ed., *Eighteenth Century Florida and the Caribbean* (Gainsville: University of Florida Press).

_____ (1976) *Slave Population and Economy in Jamaica, 1807-1834* (Cambridge, UK: Cambridge University).

_____ (1979a) 'African and Creole Slave Families in Trinidad', in Margaret E. Crahan and Franklin W. Knight, eds. *Africa and the Caribbean: Legacies of a Link* (Baltimore: Johns Hopkins University Press).

_____ (1979b) 'Growth in Afro-Caribbean Slave Populations', *American Journal of Physical Anthropology*, 1.

_____ (1984) *Slave Populations of the British Caribbean, 1807-1834* (Baltimore: Johns Hopkins University Press).

_____ (1987) 'Theory, Method and Technique in Caribbean Social History', in *Journal of Caribbean History*, vol. 20, no.1.

_____ (1976) 'Household Structures and Fertility on Jamaican Slave Plantations: A 19th Century Example', *Population Studies*, vol. 27, 1993; and 'The Slave Family and Household in the British West Indies, 1800-1848', *Journal of Interdisciplinary History*, vol. 6.

_____ (1979) 'Growth in Afro-Caribbean Slave Populations', *American Journal of Physical Anthropology*, 2nd Series, 1.

Hine, Darlene (1979), 'Female Slave Resistance: The Economics of Sex', *Western Journal of Black Studies*, 3, No. 2.

_____ (1989), 'Rape and the Inner Lives of Black Women in the Middle West', *Signs*, 14, Summer.

_____ (1990), (ed) *Black Women in American History: From Colonial Times through the 19th Century*, 4 vols. (N.Y.: Carlson).

Hobsbawm, Eric (1984) *Worlds of Labour: Further Studies in the History of Labour* (London: Weidenfeld and Nicholson).

_____ (1985) 'History from Below: Some Reflections', in Frederick Krantz, ed, *History from Below: Studies in Popular Protest and Popular Ideology* (Quebec: Concordia Univ. Press).

Hoetink, H. (1971) *Caribbean Race Relations: A Study of Two Variants* (London: Oxford University).

Holder, H.E. (1788) *A Short Essay on the Subject of Negro Slavery* (London).

Holt, T. (1992) *The Problem of Freedom: Race, Labor, and Politics in Jamaica and Britain, 1832-1938* (Baltimore: Johns Hopkins University Press).

Hooks, Bell (1982) *Ain't I a Woman: Black Women and Feminism* (London: Pluto).

_____ (1986) 'Sisterhood: Political Solidarity Between Women' *Feminist Review*, 23.

Hughes, Ronald (1982) 'Jacob Hinds (?-1832): White Father of a Coloured Clan'. Seminar Paper No. 2, 1982-83 Session. Department of History, UWI, Barbados.

Hull, Gloria and Scott, Patricia (eds) (1982) *All the Women are White, All the Blacks are Men, But some of us are Brave: Black Women's Studies* (N.Y.: Feminist Press).

Husbands, Joseph (1831) *An Answer to the Charge of Immorality Against Inhabitants of Barbados* (New York).

Innis, F.C. (1970) 'The Pre-Sugar Era of European Settlement in Barbados', *Journal of Caribbean History*, vol. 1.

Inscoe, John (1989) *Mountain Masters, Slavery and the Sectional Crisis in Western North Carolina* (Knoxville: Univ. of Tennessee Press).

Jacobs, Harriet A. (1987) *Incidents in the Life of a Slave Girl, Written by Herself* (edited by Jean F. Yellin, (Cambridge, MA: Harvard University Press, Harvard).

Jernegan, M. (1931) *Labouring and Dependent Classes in Colonial America, 1607-1783* (Chicago: Chicago University Press).

Johnson, Michael (1981), 'Smothered Slave Infants: Were Slave Mothers at Fault?', *Journal of Southern History*, 47, No. 4.

Jones, Jacqueline (1985) *Labour of Love, Labour of Sorrow: Black Women, Work, and the Family: From Slavery to Present* (New York).

Jordan, Winthrop (1968) *White Over Black: American Attitudes Towards the Negro, 1550-1812* (Chapel Hill: North Carolina University Press)

_____ and Skemp, Sheila (eds) (1987) *Race and Family in the Colonial South* (Jackson: Univ. of Mississippi Press).

Just, Roger (1985), 'Freedom, Slavery, and the Female Psyche', *History of Political Thought*, 6, Nos. 1, 2.

Kelly-Gadol, J. (1976) 'The Social Relations of the Sexes: Methodological Implications of Women's History', *Signs* (vol. 1., No.4).

Kerber, Linda (1988), 'Separate Spheres, Female Worlds, Woman's Place: The Rhetoric of Women's History', *Journal of American History*, 75, No. 1

Kiple, Kenneth (1984) *The Caribbean Slave: A Biological History* (Cambridge: Cambridge University Press).

_____ (1980) 'Deficiency Diseases in the Caribbean', *Journal of Interdisciplinary History*, 11:2.

Klein, Herbert S. (1978) *The Middle Passage: Comparative Studies of the Atlantic Slave Trade* (Princeton: Princeton University Press).

_____ and Engerman E. (1978) 'Fertility Differentials between Slaves in the United States and the British West Indies: A Note on Lactation Practices and their Possible Implications', *William and Mary Quarterly*, vol. 35.

_____ (1983) 'African Women in the Atlantic Slave Trade' in Claire C. Robertson and Martin A. Klein (eds) *Women and Slavery in Africa* (Madison: Wisconsin Univ. Press).

Kossek, Brigitte (1993), 'Racist and Patriarchal Aspects of Plantation Slavery in Grenada, White Ladies, Black women Slaves, and Rebels', in W. Binder (ed) *Slavery in the Americas* (Wurzburg, Konigshausen and Newmann).

Krantz, Frederick (ed.) (1985) *History from Below: Studies in Popular Protest and Popular Ideology in Honour of George Rudé* (Quebec: Concordia University Press).

Kruse, Darryn (1985) 'Gender as a Historical Determinant: An Exploration', *Melbourne Historical Journal*, vol. 17.

Lascelles, Edwin, et al. (1786) *The Following Instructions are offered for the Consideration of Proprietors and Managers of a Plantation in Barbados and for the Treatment of Negroes* (London).

Lanaghan, Frances (1967) *Antigua and the Antiguans*, 2 vols (London: Spottiswoode).

Lebsock, Suzanne (1984) *The Free Woman of Petersburg: Status and Culture in a Southern Town, 1784-1860* (N.Y.: W.W. Norton).

Lerner, Gerdda (1990), 'Reconceptualising Differences among women', *Journal of Women's History*, 1, No. 3.

_____ (1983), 'Women and Slavery', *Slavery and Abolition*, 4, No. 3.

_____ (1972) (ed), *Black Women in White America* (N.Pantheon).

Levy, Claude (1980) *Emancipation, Sugar and Federalism: Barbados and the West Indies, 1833-1876* (Gainsville: Florida University Press).

Lewis, Gordon K. (1983) *Main Currents in Caribbean Thought* (Baltimore: The Johns Hopkins University Press).

Ligon, Richard (1657) *A True and Exact History of the Island of Barbados . . .* (London, 1976: Frank Cass edition).

Lovejoy, Paul E. (1983) *Transformations in Slavery: A History of Slavery in Africa* (Cambridge: Cambridge University Press).

_____ (1988), 'Concubinage and the Status of Women Slaves in Early Colonial Northern Nigeria', *Journal of African History*, 29, No. 2.

Lowenthal, David (1976) 'The Population of Barbados', *Social and Economic Studies*, vol. 6, no. 4.

Mair, Lucille (1989) 'Women Field Workers in Jamaica During Slavery', Dept. of History, U.W.I., Mona.

_____ (1974) 'An Historical Study of Women in Jamaica from 1655 to 1844, (Ph.D., U.W.I., Mona, Jamaica).
_____ (1977) 'Reluctant Matriarchs', *Savacou*, vol.13.
_____ (1975) *The Rebel Women in the British West Indies during Slavery* (Kingston).
_____ (1975) 'The Arrival of Black Woman', *Jamaica Journal*, 9.
Malone, Ann (1992) *Sweet Chariot: Slave Family and Household Structure in 19th C. Louisana* (Chapel Hill: Univ. of North Carolina Press).
Manigat, Leslie (1977) 'The Relationship between Marronage and Slave Revolts and Revolution in St Dominique – Haiti', *Annals of the New York Academy of Sciences*, 292.
Mannix, Daniel and Cowley, Malcolm (1962) *Black Cargoes: A History of the Atlantic Slave Trade* (New York: Viking Press).
Marable, Manning (1983), 'Groundings with my Sisters: Patriarchy and the Exploitation of Black Women', *Journal of Ethnic Studies*, 11, Summer.
Marshall, Bernard (1976) 'Maroonage in Slave Plantation Societies: A Case Study of Dominica, 1875-1815', *Caribbean Quarterly*, vol. 22.
Martin, B. and Spurrell, M. (eds) (1962) *The Journal of a Slave Trader: John Newton, 1750-1754* (London).
Martinez-Alier Verena (1974), *Marriage, Class and Colour in Nineteenth Century Cuba: A Study of Racial Attitudes and Sexual Values in Slave Society* (Cambridge: U.K).
McLaurin, Melton (1991) *Celia, a Slave* (Athens: Univ. of Georgia Press).
Meillassoux, Claude (1983) 'Female Slavery' in Robertson and Klein (eds.) *Women and Slavery in Africa*, (Wisconsin University Press, Madison).
Midgley, Clare (1998) (ed) *Gender and Imperialism* (M.U.P. London).
_____ (1992) *Women Against Slavery: The British Campaigns, 1780-1870* (London: Routledge).
_____ (1993) 'Anti-slavery and Feminism in Nineteenth-Century Britain', *Gender and History*, 3:3.
Miers, S. and Kopytoff, I. (eds) (1977) *Slavery in Africa: Historical and Anthropological Perspectives* (Madison: Wisconsin University Press).
Miller, Joseph (1981) 'Mortality in the Atlantic Slave Trade: Statistical Evidence on Causality', *Journal of Interdisciplinary History*, vol. XI, no. 3.
Mintz, Sidney (1980) 'Caribbean Market Places and Caribbean History', *Nova Americana*, 1.
_____ and Douglas Hall (1960) 'The Origins of the Jamaican Internal Marketing System', *Yale University Publications in Anthropology*, no. 57.
_____ (1981) 'Economic Roles and Cultural Traditions', in Filomena Steady, (ed) *The Black Woman Cross-Culturally* (Cambridge, Mass.: Schenkman Publishing Co.).
Mirkin, Harris (1984), 'The Passive Female: The Theory of Patriarchy', *American Studies*, 25, Fall.
Mohammed, Patricia, et al. (eds) (1988) *Gender in Caribbean Development* (Mona: UWI).
_____ (1994) 'Nuancing the Feminist Discourse in the Caribbean', *Social and Economic Studies* (vol. 43, No.3).
Mohanty, C.T. (1991) 'Under Western Eyes: Feminist Scholarship and Colonial Discourse', in C.T. Mohanty, A. Russo and L. Torres (eds), *Third World Women and the Politics of Feminism* (Bloomington: Indiana University Press).
Moitt, Bernard (1993) 'Women, Work and Resistance in the French Caribbean during Slavery, 1700-1848', in Shepherd et al. (ed) *Engendering History*.
_____ (1989) 'Behind the Sugar Fortunes: Women, Labour, and the Development of Caribbean Plantations during Slavery', in S. Chilungu and S. Niang (eds) *African Continuities* (Toronto: Teribi Publication).
Moore, Samuel (1801) *The Public Acts in Force: Passed by the Legislature of Barbados from May 11, 1762 to April 8, 1800* (London).

Moreau de Saint Méry (1797), *Description Topographique Physique, Civile, Politique et Historique de la Partie Francaise de l'isle Saint Domingue* (Paris, 1958 reprint) p.10.

Morton, Patricia (1991) *Disfigured Images: The Historical Assault on Afro-American Women* (West Port: Greenwood Press).

_____ (1996) (ed) *Discovering the Woman in Slavery* (Athens: Univ. of Georgia Press).

Moreton, J.B. (1970) *Manners and Customs of the West India Islands* (London).

Morrissey, M. (1990) *Slave Women in the New World* (Lawrence: University Press of Kansas).

_____ (1986) 'Women's Work, Family Formation and Reproduction among Caribbean Slaves', *Review* 9.

Mullin, Michael (1980) 'Maroon Women'. Paper presented at the 12th Annual Conference of Caribbean Historians, Trinidad.

_____ (1985), 'Women and the Comparative Study of American Negro Slavery', *Slavery and Abolition*, 6, No. 1.

Munroe, Trevor (1978) *The Marxist Left in Jamaica, 1940-50* (ISER, Mona, UWI).

Newman, Louise M. (1991) 'Critical Theory and the History of Women: What's at Stake in Deconstructing Women's History', *Journal of Women's History*, vol.2, no. 3.

Norton, Mary (1980), *Liberty's Daughters: The Revolutionary Experience of American Women, 1750-1800* (Boston: Little, Brown).

Nugent, Maria (1966) *Lady Nugent's Journal of her Residence in Jamaica from 1801 to 1805*, edited by P. Wright (Kingston: Institute of Jamaica).

Oldmixon, John (1708) *The British Empire in America*, 2 Vols. (1741 edition, London).

Oliver, Vere (ed) (1919-11) *Caribbeana: Miscellaneous Papers Relating to the History, Genealogy, Topography and Antiquities in the British West Indies* (London).

Orderson, J.W. (1800) *Directions to Young Planters for their Care and Management of a Sugar Plantation in Barbados* (London).

Ortiz, Fernando (1975) *Los Negros Exclavos* (Havana: Social Science Publishing House).

Ottenburg, P. (1959) 'The Changing Economic Position of Women among Afikpo Ibo', in Bascom and Herskovits, *Continuity and Change in African Culture* (Chicago: University of Chicago Press).

Patterson, Orlando (1967) *The Sociology of Slavery: An Analysis of the Origins, Development and Structure of Negro Slave Society in Jamaica* (London: London University Press).

_____ (1993), 'Slavery, Alienation, and the Female Discovery of Personal Freedom', in A. Mack (ed), *Home: A Place in the World* (N.Y.: New York Univ. Press).

Pease, J. and W. (1990) *Ladies, Women, and Wenches* (Chapel Hill: University of North Carolina Press).

Petraud, Lucien (1897) *L'Esclavage aux Antilles Françaises Avant 1789* (Paris: Hachette).

Pinckard, George (1806) *Notes on the West Indies*, 3 Vols (London: Longman).

Poovey, Mary (1988) "Feminism and Deconstruction', *Feminist Studies*, vol. 14.

Poyer, John (1808) *The History of Barbados from the First Discovery of the Island in the year 1605 till the Accession of Lord Seaforth 1801* (London: Frank Cass 1971 edition).

Price, Richard (1973) *Maroon Societies: Rebel Slave Communities in America* (Baltimore: Johns Hopkins University Press).

Price, Rose (1970) 'Pledges on colonial Slavery, to Candidates for Seats in Parliament, Rightly Considered', cited in M. Craton and J. Walvin, *A Jamaican Parliament: The History of Worthy Park* (Toronto: University of Toronto Press).

Prince, Mary (1831) *The History of Mary Prince, a West Indian Slave Related by Herself*, edited by Moira Ferguson (London: Pandora, 1987 edition).

Proctor, Samuel R. (ed) (1976) *Eighteenth Century Florida and the Caribbean* (Gainsville: Florida University Press).

Puckrein, Gary (ed) (1984) *Little England: Plantation Society and Anglo-Barbadian Politics,*

1627-1700 (New York: New York University Press).

Rabble, George (1989) *Civil Wars: Women and the Crisis of Southern Nationalism* (Urbana: Univ. of Illinois Press).

Reddock, Rhoda (1985) 'Women and Slavery in the Caribbean: A Feminist Perspective', *Latin American Perspectives*, Issues 40, 12:1.

(1993) 'Primacy of Gender in Race and Class' in J. Greene (ed) *Race, Class and Gender in the Future of the Caribbean* (ISER, UWI).

Richardson, David (ed) (1985) *Abolition and Its Aftermath: The Historical Context* (London: Frank Cass).

Robertson, Claire (1987), 'Changing perspectives in Studies of African Women, 1976-1985', *Feminist Studies*, 13, No. 1

Robertson, Claire and Klein, Martin (eds) (1983) *Women and Slavery in Africa* (Madison: Wisconsin University Press).

Rodgers-Rose, La Frances (ed) (1980) *The Black Woman* (Beverly Hills, Sage).

Rose, W.L. (ed.) (1976) A Documentary History of Slavery in North America (Oxford: Oxford University Press).

Rousseau, G. S. and Porter R. (1990) (eds), *Exoticism in the Enlightenment* (Manchester: Manchester University Press).

Rowbotham, Sheila (1992) *Women in Movement: Feminism and Social Action* (London: Routledge).

Said, E. W. (1978) *Orientalism* (Harmonsworth, Penguin, edition 1985).

Schaw, Janet, *Journal of a Lady of Quality; being the narrative of a journey from Scotland to the West Indies, North Carolina, and Portugal, in the years 1774 to 1776*, edited by E.W. Andrews and C.M. Andrews (New Haven: Yale University Press).

Schoelcher, Victor (1976) *Des colonies françaises: abolition immédiate de l'esclavage* (Société d'Histoire de la Guadeloupe, Basse-Terre, 1976 edition).

Schomburgk, Robert (1848) *The History of Barbados* (Frank Cass edition, 1983, London).

Schuler, Monica (1973) 'Day to Day Resistance to Slavery in the Caribbean in the 18th Century', Association for the Study of Africa and the West Indies, *Bulletin*, 6.

Schweninger, Loren (1975), 'A Slave Family in the Ante-bellum South', *Journal of Negro History*, 60, No. 1

Scott, Anne (1991) (ed) *Unheard Voices: The First Historians of Southern Women* (Charlottesville: Univ. Press of Virginia).

_____ (1986), 'Women in Plantation Culture: Or What I Wish I Knew about Southern Women', *South Atlantic Urban Studies*, 2.

Scott, Joan Wallach (1988) *Gender and the Politics of History* (New York, Columbia, Univ. Press).

_____ (1986), 'Gender: A Useful Category of Historical Analysis', *American Historical Review*, 91, Dec.

_____ (1992) 'The Problem of Invisibility' in S. Jay Kleinberg (ed) *Retrieving Women's History* (UNESCO, Berg).

Seacole, M. (1984) *Wonderful Adventures of Mrs. Seacole in Many Lands*, edited by Z. Alexander and A. Dewjee (Bristol, Falling Wall Press).

Shepherd, Verene, et al (eds) (1995) *Engendering History: Caribbean Women in Historical Perspective* (Kingston: Ian Randle Publishers).

Shammas, Carole (1985), 'Black Women's Work and the Evolution of Plantation Society in Virginia', *Labor History*, 26, No. 1.

Shepherd, Verene (1991) 'Trade and Exchange in Jamaican in the Period of Slavery', in H. Beckles and V. Shepherd, (eds) *Caribbean Slave Society and Economy* (Kingston: Ian Randle Publishers).

_____ (1987) 'Problems in the Supply of Livestock to Sugar Estates in the Period of Slavery', UWI, Mona.

_____ (1988) Pens and Penkeepers in a Plantation Society, Ph.D., Cambridge.

_____ (1999) *Women in the Caribbean* (Kingston: Ian Randle Publishers).

Sheridan, Richard B. (1970) *The Development of the Plantations to 1750* (Bridgetown: Caribbean Universities Press).

_____ (1972) 'Africa and the Caribbean in the Atlantic Slave Trade', *American Historical Review*, 77, February.

_____ (1973) 'Mortality and the Medical Treatment of Slaves in the British West Indies', in Stanley Engerman and Eugene Genovese, *Race and Slavery in the Western Hemisphere: Quantitative Studies* (Princeton: Princeton University Press).

_____ (1976) 'The Crisis of Slave Subsistence in the British West Indies during and after the American Revolution', *William and Mary Quarterly*, 3rd Series, 33.

_____ (1985) *Doctors and Slaves: A Medical and Demographic History of Slavery in the British West Indies, 1690-1834* (Cambridge UK: University Press).

Sides, Sudie (1970), 'Southern *Women and Slavery*', *History Today*, 20, Jan.

Silvestrini, Blanca (1989) *Women and Resistance: Her Story in Contemporary Caribbean History* (Dept. of History, U.W.I Mona).

Simmonds, Lorna (1987), 'Slave Higglering in Jamaica, 1780-1834', *Jamaica Journal*, 20, No. 1.

Smith, Abbot (1974) *Colonists in Bondage: White Servitude and Convict Labour in America, 1607-1776* (Chapel Hill: North Carolina University Press).

Smith, Raymond T. (1957) *The Negro Family in British Guiana* (New York: Humanities Press, 1971 edition).

Souden, David (1978) 'Rogues, Whores and Vagabonds: Indentured Servant Emigrants to North America and the Case of Mid-Seventeenth Century Bristol', *Social History*, vol. 3, no.1.

Spivak, Gayatri (1988) 'Can the Subaltern Speaks?' in Cary Nelson, et al. (ed) *Marxism and the Interpretation of Culture* (London: Macmillan).

Spruill, Julia (1938), *Women's Life and Work in the Southern Colonies* (Chapel Hill, University of North Carolina Press).

Staples, Robert (1970), 'The Myth of Black Matriarchy', *Black Scholar*, 2, No. 1.

Steady, F. (ed) (1981) *The Black Woman Cross-Culturally* (Cambridge Mass.: Schenkman Publishing Co.).

Stedman, J.G. (1806) *Narrative of a Five Years' Expedition against the Revolted Negroes of Surinam* (Amherst, University of Mass. Press, edition 1971).

Sterling, Dorothy (ed) (1984) *We are Your Sisters: Black Women in the 19th C.* (N.Y.: W.W. Norton).

Sturge, Joseph and Harvey, T. (1837) *The West Indies in 1837* (London).

Sweet, D. and Nash, G. (eds) (1981) *Struggle and Survival in Colonial America* (Los Angeles: University of California Press).

Taylor Mill, H. (1851) 'The Enfranchisement of Women' [*Westminster Review*]. (1970) *Essays on Sex Equality*, ed. A. S. Rossi (Chicago: University of Chicago Press).

Terborg-Penn, Rosalyn et. al. (eds) (1987) *Women in Africa and the African Diaspora* (Washington D.C., Howard and Univ. Press).

Thome, J.A. and Kimball, J.H. (1838) *Emancipation in the West Indies: A Six Months' Tour in Antigua, Barbados and Jamaica in the year 1837* (New York).

Thompson, William (1825) *An Appeal on Behalf of One Half of the Human Race, Women, Against the Pretensions of the Other Half, Men, to Retain Them in Civil and Domestic Slavery* (London).

Thornton, John (1983) 'Sexual Demography: The Impact of the Slave Trade on the Family Structure', in Robertson and Klein (eds) *Women and Slavery in Africa*.

Tilly, Louise, "Gender, Women's History, and Social History", Social Science History, 13, Winter.

Towne, Richard (1726) *A Treatise of the Diseases most Frequent in the West Indies . . .* (London).

Uya, Okon E. (1976) 'Slave Revolts in the Middle Passage: A Neglected Theme', *The Calibar Historical Journal*, vol. 1, no.1.

Vassel, Linette (ed) (1993) *Voices of Women in Jamaica* (Jamaica: UWI).

_____ (1993) Voluntary Women's Associations in Jamaica: The Jamaican Federation of Women, 1944-1962, M.Phil. Thesis, UWI, Mona, Jamaica.

Venet, Wendy (1991) *Neither Ballots nor Bullets: Women Abolitionists and the Civil War* (Charlottesville: Univ. Press of Virginia).

Wallace, Michele (1980) *Black Macho and the Myth of the Superwoman* (N.Y.: Warner).

Waller, John (1820) *A Voyage in the West Indies . . .* (Richard Phillips, London).

Ward, J.R. (1988) *British West Indian Slavery, 1750-1834: The Process of Amelioration* (Oxford: Clarendon Press).

Ware, V. (1992) *Beyond the Pale: White Women, Racism and History* (London: Verso).

Walvin, James (ed) (1982) *Slavery and British Abolition 1776-1848* (London: Macmillan).

Watson, Karl (1979) *The Civilised Island: Barbados, a Social History* (Bridgetown).

_____ (1984) 'Escaping Bondage: The Odyssey of a Barbadian Slave Family'. Paper presented at the 16th Annual Conference of Caribbean Historians, UWI, Barbados.

Weiner, Marli (1991) *Plantation Women: South Carolina Mistresses and Slaves, 1830-1880* (Urbana: Univ. of Illinois Press).

White, Deborah G. (1985) *Ar'n't I a Woman? Female Slaves in the Plantation South* (New York: W.W. Norton).

_____ (1983), 'Female Slaves, Sex Roles, and Status in the Ante-bellum Plantation South', *Journal of Family History*, 8, No. 3.

_____ (1984), 'The Lives of Slave Women', *Southern Exposure*, 12, No. 6.

Williams, G. (1897) *History of the Liverpool Privateers and Letters of Marque with an Account of the Liverpool Slave Trade* (London).

Wilson, S. (1984) 'The Myth of Motherhood: The Historical View of European Child-rearing', *Social History*, May.

Wollstonecraft, M. (1792) *A Vindication of the Rights of Woman*, edited by C. H. Poston (New York, W. W. Norton, [2nd edition] 1975).

Wood, Betty (1987), 'Some Aspects of Female Slave Resistance in Low Country Georgia, 1763-1815', *Historical Journal*, 30, No. 3.

_____ (1992), 'White Women, Black Slaves and the Law in Early National Georgia – The Sunbury Petition of 1791', *Historical Hournal*, 35, No. 3.

Wrightson, K. (1982) 'In Fanticide in European History', *Criminal Justice History*, vol. 3.

Wyatt-Brown, Bertram (1982) *Southern Honor: Ethics and Behaviour in the Old South* (N.Y.: Oxford Univ. Press).

Yee, Shirley (1992) *Black Women Abolitionists: A Study in Activism, 1828-1880* (Knoxville: Univ. of Tennessee Press).

Yellin, Jean (1989) *Women and Sisters: The Antislavery Feminists in American Culture* (New Haven: Yale Univ. Press).

Young, K. (1988) *Towards a Theory of the Social Relations of Gender* (London: Womankind).

Index

GOSHEN COLLEGE - GOOD LIBRARY
3 9310 01030863 1